Four Tubas, a Guitar, and a Gallery of Cheerleaders

Transition in the Life of a Black Ph.D.

To Mr. & Mrs Carlton,

Mrs. Carlton, taught me how to Read! Mr. Carlton taught me how to play the Tuba!! I appreciate the love and care you have given and will my title.

Four Tubas, a Guitar, and a Gallery of Cheerleaders

Transition in the Life of a Black Ph.D.

A First Person Narrative

Part I.

Sederick C. Rice

AuthorHouse™
1663 Liberty Drive
Bloomington, IN 47403
www.authorhouse.com
Phone: 1-800-839-8640

© *2010 Sederick C. Rice. All rights reserved.*

No part of this book may be reproduced, stored in a retrieval system, or transmitted by any means without the written permission of the author.

First published by AuthorHouse 10/7/2010

ISBN: 978-1-4520-5984-6 (e)
ISBN: 978-1-4520-5982-2 (sc)
ISBN: 978-1-4520-5983-9 (hc)

Library of Congress Control Number: 2010910891

Printed in the United States of America

This book is printed on acid-free paper.

Because of the dynamic nature of the Internet, any Web addresses or links contained in this book may have changed since publication and may no longer be valid. The views expressed in this work are solely those of the author and do not necessarily reflect the views of the publisher, and the publisher hereby disclaims any responsibility for them.

Dedication

This work is dedicated to the people in my life, who have influenced me most. As a Christian man, I am taught to love God, Family and Friends. This book is for them. There have been so many people in my life that made this project possible that I couldn't possibly name all of them, but I will just say thank you to those who are closest to my heart and to those not mentioned.

Thank you God for your Word!

Thank you, Momma for being my Strength and Heart. I miss you but know that God loved you more and knew what was best.

Thank you, Daddy, for being my Wisdom and Morality.

Thank you, Granddaddy Victor, for teaching me how to be a man and exposing me to great role models. I will never forget your words of wisdom. "Keep your mind off them girls, and on them books!"

Thank you, Paw Paw (Joseph Spears, Sr.) for teaching me that "God is bigger than my conscience, and the only way to please God is to have faith!"

Thank you, Mr. Lott, Mr. Carlton, Mrs. Carlton, Mr. Fred Lowe, and Mr. Jimmy Singleton for believing in me as a youth, and encouraging my steps in life. All of you changed my views on things I knew to be true, and then carefully taught me how to approach life the right way.

Thank you, Mrs. Glover and Mr. Woods, for being great role models and people I could talk to when things got rough. I understand what you mean now Mr. Woods, about life, decisions, and learning! I use the phrase "knowledge box," when talking to my students all the time.

Thank you, Mrs. Jewell C. Whatley, for teaching me to be the best at what I do in science and in life. It was your suggestion for me to take AP Biology and go to UAPB instead of USC. Your words of wisdom changed my life. I know now that "Chance really favors the prepared mind!"

Thank you, Dr. Clifton Orr, for giving me an opportunity when I was young to work and learn about cancer research and seeing past my bold ambitions and immaturity. You were a great role model and mentor. I will never forget your influence on my life.

Thank you, Dr. William Willingham, for opening up doors for me, when I really needed help. I believe it was you who contacted Dr. Reed and words cannot describe my heartfelt appreciation.

Thank you, Wash for improving my skills on the Tuba and allowing me to live, learn, and grow under your guidance. Music can sometimes be a reflection of life and I still remember how your openness and heart was responsible for my success.

Thank you, Dr. H. Reed, for being a father figure, who never let me believe I couldn't get a Ph.D., or make excuses for situations I know I could change. Our travels on the highway helped me grow and mature as a man and I model my professional life, after the lessons you taught me. I respect you like my own father and can always count on your words of wisdom and advice.

Thank you, Dr. Mossman, for being patient, kind, and offering tutoring to help me be successful in Biochemistry. I am so grateful for your assistance and your heart. I now operate my life with the goal to be as understanding, thoughtful, and supportive to others as you were to me.

Thank you, Barry, for being Barry, and allowing me to grow in your laboratory, while supporting my extracurricular activities. I never planned to be in Vermont for seven years, but glad you were patient to help see the tough times through. I feel like one of your children and respect you as "Papa!"

Thank you, Cleo, for being a great friend when I needed one and making sure I held on to my dreams. It was tough going to school in Vermont, but your presence made it a little easier. When I needed help you were there and I hope to return the favor one day.

Thank you, Harold, for supporting me when I was in a new place and far away from home. I was so "green" in Chicago that so many things could have happened, but you were there to help me.

Thank you, Dr. Isaac Greggs, for helping, teaching, and mentoring so many musicians throughout the years. Your impact has instilled pride, loyalty, and respect for Southern University and their alumni.

Thank you, Mr. Randolph Johnson (Mr. J.) for giving me an opportunity to learn from you musically and march with the Approach Storm as a graduate student.

Thank you, Josie for being the big sister I never had, and the confidant that listened to my problems without judging me. Your presence in Vermont helped me cope with loneliness, depression, low self-esteem, and being African-American in a predominantly white environment. Your spirit is alive with me and I use the lessons we learned together on a day to day basis. You will always be a motivator, friend, and role model.

Thank you, Indiana Street Baptist Church and Pastor L.K. Solomon, for preparing me to live a Christian life and being a church where *"Everybody is Somebody in Christ!"*

Thank you, Uncle C., Hornbuckle, Mr. Barton, O-tiss, Ike, John, G-Money, Sr., and Mrs. Carmichael for taking over where others left off, in my growth and development. Your influences have created more stories to tell in the transition and life of a Black Ph.D.

Thank you to the Mr. Henri Linton, Sr., Stephanie Sims, Adora Curry and the UAPB Museum and Cultural Center for being home to *Keepers of the Spirit* and sharing your historical and archival knowledge with me as I wrote this book.

Thank you, to all the people God placed in my life along the way to teach, guide, and demonstrate his Goodness and Grace.

To God Be The Glory!

**In Memory of Victor, My Grandfather
February 14, 1920- April 12, 2006.**

*Celebration of the Life
of*

Victor Charles Rice

*Wednesday, April 19, 2006
11:00 a.m.*

Pine Hill Missionary Baptist Church
2101 Reeker Street
Pine Bluff, Arkansas 71601

Reverend Glenn Barnes, Sr., Officiating

VCR

A Grandson's Dedication

Victor Charles Rice was a man of character, vision and respect. He taught me how to work hard and be a man. Before his assignment on this earth was complete, he specifically asked to speak with me, and told me in his own special way, "Be a Man!" He told me "If I fail, fail on my own, and if I succeed, succeed on my own." His words were stressed, but I understood what he meant. He also told me not to take any "wooden nickels." This was his prophetic way of helping me remember the rules of "Manhood," which were to work hard, and use common sense, which in his opinion, wasn't so common. His favorite phrase and lesson for me was "Keep your mind off those girls, and on those books!" He renamed me "Lil' Charles," in my youth, and provided an environment where I could grow up in the shadow of adults and learn how to be a man. I always wanted to make my grandfather proud and am blessed and thankful that I got a chance to tell him that he gave me the same tools he gave my father to be a man. He instilled a work ethic in my father, who passed it on to me. I will miss my grandfather, but will establish and extend his legacy for many generations to come through words and experiences.

Epigraph

The end of education is to know God and the laws and purposes of His universe, and to reconcile one's life with these laws. The first aim of a good college is not to teach books, but the meaning and purpose of life. Hard study and the learning of books are only a means to this end. We develop power and courage and determination and we go out to achieve Truth, Wisdom, and Justice. If we do not come to this, the cost of our schooling is wasted"

John Brown Watson
First President
Arkansas Agricultural Mechanical &
Normal (AM&N) College

What Shall I Call Thee?
God

Alpha and Omega
Elohim
El Shaddai
Jehovah
Redeemer
Jehovah-Jireh
Father
Allah
Jehovah-Shalom
Everlasting
Advocate
I AM THAT I AM
Holy One
Master Architect
Counselor
Light of the World
The Word
Almighty
Jesus
The Author and Finisher of Life

Table of Contents

Chapter 1. *Seed Planted*   3
    Mr. Carl Lott, Jr.
    Mr. Elmer M. Carlton
    Mrs. Carlton
    Mrs. Jewell C. Whatley

Chapter 2. *Band, Books, and Frat!*   20
    Mr. Fred Lowe
    "Wash"
    Mrs. Mattie Glover
    Dr. Shelton Fitzpatrick
    Dr. Clifton Orr
    Mr. Ray Woods

Chapter 3. *Chicago, Illinois*   84
    Harold
    Dr. William Willingham

Chapter 4. *$20.00 Bill*   97
    Dr. H. Reed

Chapter 5. *Dover, Delaware*   108
    Mr. Randolph Johnson

Chapter 6. *Burlington, Vermont*   180
    Dr. Brooke Mossman
    Barry
    "Cleo"
    "Josie"

Chapter 7. *Must Be The Music*   314
    Shirley Ann Rice

> Listen to advice and accept instruction, and in the end you will be wise. Many are the plans in a man's heart, but it is the Lord's purpose that prevails."
>
> **Proverbs 19:20-21 (KJV)**

Foreword

By Charles Marcus Buntin, Ph.D.

Often times when I see and meet people, I wonder who a person really is, what is their life story, why is that person who they are? Life is a gift from God and each life matters. I believe that God has a master plan for the human race. All throughout the Bible you see the hand of God working. His master plan to mature us as individuals and as a race of people dedicated to Him for a higher eternal purpose. Those of us who are living in this present world really don't have a clear understanding of God's glorious purpose for us, but there will come a day when we come to a full understanding of the plan of God for His human family.

> *1 Corinthians 13:11-12 KJVR (11) When I was a child, I spake as a child, I understood as a child, I thought as a child: but when I became a man, I put away childish things. (12) For now we see through a glass, darkly; but then face to face: now I know in part; but then shall I know even as also I am known.*

In God's dealings with mankind, you see a common thread as to how He matures us to walk into the "destiny of greatest" that He has in store for us. That common thread is legacy. The definition of legacy is "a gift or will left to another or something transmitted by or received from an ancestor or predecessor or from the past". Legacy is seen throughout the bible. The pattern is the same; one generation teaches the next generation the wisdom they learned from God. As a result of this transference of legacy, the latter generation increases in blessing beyond the former generation. Legacy not only comes from our family ancestors but can be received from those who are our mentors (a trusted counselor or guide) as well as other friends and associations.

Everybody needs mentors in their life to fulfill their destiny.

God designed the system of life that way because one person cannot learn and know everything. In the Bible, Elisha had Elijah as his mentor, Joshua had Moses, Moses had his father-in-law, Jethro, Isaac had Abraham,

Ruth had Naomi, Solomon had David and the list goes on and on. Legacy also comes as a result of learning about the lives of other people you may not be especially close to or you may not know them at all. We learn from their successes and their mistakes. It is so important that we take the time to build relationships with people, because their lives are connected to ours. The legacy that we receive from other people may be the key to fulfilling our God ordained destiny. As a note of encouragement, if you don't have mentors in your life because of your present circumstances, I want you to know that you are not alone. God Himself will be your mentor if you let Him.

This book, written by Dr. Sederick Rice, is an extraordinary account of his pursuit of a life of excellence including a doctorate degree in the sciences. When "Sederick" asked me to write a forward for his book I was happy to do so and at that same time apprehensive because of my busy schedule. I also knew that there are times that people will write things about themselves that are not particularly interesting or relevant and poorly written. My desire was to read the entire book and express my thoughts from the heart. I have found this book to be absolutely fascinating, instructive and encouraging! As I began to read it, I could not put it down. As an African-American who also pursued and achieved my doctorate degree in engineering, I can identify with much of what Sederick has written in this book. But beyond that, I can see how all of his mentors, family, friends and associations have contributed to this man's extraordinary life.

This book is like watching a suspense-filled movie where it leaves you wondering what will happen next. It is a well-documented autobiography of one man's pursuit of his dreams. I recommend every young person who has a big dream to read this book so that they can see the importance of relationships in order to receive the gift of legacy that others have to offer. I also recommend this book to adults; both young and old, so that you, too, can understand the importance of legacy for your own life and passing legacy to others. I want to thank Dr. Rice and all of his mentors and associations for sharing their experiences with me through this book. You have added to my life and destiny. For those of you who will take the time to read this book, I believe that it will add to your life and destiny, too.

Proverbs 15:22 KJVR *Without counsel purposes are disappointed: but in the multitude of counselors they are established.*

Preface

> For we know in part, and we prophesy in part. But when that which is perfect is come, then that which is in part shall be done away. When I was a child, I spake as a child, I understood as a child, I thought as a child: but when I became a man, I put away childish things.
>
> **I Corinthians 13:9-11 (KJV)**

Men and Conversations

3 a.m. Pine Bluff, Arkansas July 1994

Father: "Good morning, Dr. Reed. How are you?" (Shakes hand)
Dr. Reed: "FINE, and you?"
Father: "Good, good, Sederick, do you have all of your stuff?"
Sederick: "I do!" -Loading bags and clothes in a Blue 2-door Ford pickup truck
Dr. Reed: "Are you ready to ride?"
Sederick: "Ready to go!" Dr. Reed and my father shake hands briskly
Father: "How long is the ride to Delaware?"
Dr. Reed: "About 17 hours, give or take."
Father: "Are you stopping to spend the night?"
Dr. Reed: "We only stop for gas, and will try to get as much highway done as possible before dark."
Father: "Have a safe trip and be careful."
Father: Anxious and nervous about son leaving home for good. Minimal emotion-
Dr. Reed: "Alright!"
Father: He's **"Kinda Green!"**
Dr. Reed: I Understand!

> **"Green"**- youthful and vigorous, not ripened or matured: immature, fresh, new, not fully processed or treated, not aged, unseasoned, not in condition for a particular use, deficient in training, knowledge, or experience, deficient in sophistication and savoir faire, naïve, and not fully qualified for or experienced in a particular function[1].

---

[1] Green- Excerpt and definition used with permission from the American Heritage Dictionary™, as accessed from www.dictionary.com.

I was born on the eight day in the eight month in 1972. My birth certificate read "Sederick Charles Rice," after great debate between my mother and father, as well as intuitive contribution from my Aunt Loretta. My birth home is the great state of Arkansas, known famously throughout history for being a major contributor to the cotton industry. People also think of Arkansas as the *Natural State*, where agriculture is a mainstay of local and rural economies. There is nothing more rewarding for an Arkansas farmer than planting seeds, watching them grow, and then harvesting the crops.

During the planting, growing, and harvesting seasons, Arkansas farmers decide when to plant and pick their crops based on product size and yield, color, and maturity. What is interesting about this semi-annual ritual is that most farmers don't rely on their own wits and intuition for planting and picking crops, they use *The Old Farmer's Almanac* [2] as a guide. The Farmer's Almanac helps them choose the best season, harvesting time, and calculate for factors after seeds are planted, that may affect growth; including lack or abundance of rain or water, more or less sunshine, and the fertility of the ground. The plant-harvest ritual often means that farmers adjust their picking schedules, because the weather and environment can be unpredictable.

To plant anything and have it grow successfully takes skill, but also a measure of faith which is an important concept I want to stress in this book about my life. I am a growing plant; developed from seeds planted by my parents, fed and nurtured by caring mentors, and cultivated to maturity by the influence, will, and guidance of Almighty God. I have grown socially, financially, mentally, but more importantly spiritually, because of my relationship with God.

When seeds are planted, developmental events occur out of the control of the farmers who planted them. Only when the new bud sprouts out of the ground can farmers be more proactive in their crop's growth and development. It takes the right circumstances and seasons to make the endeavor worthwhile. Most of us have experienced seasons of life, which progressed faster or slower based on the makeup of those who planted us, what we were fed, and how we were cultivated. What is certain and inevitable is that attention, care, and patience are needed for any good crop

---

[2] Old Farmer's Almanac- is an annual guide first printed in 1792 and used by farmers to understand weather patterns of past planting seasons to predict when and what crops should be planted that year. It is released on the second Tuesday in September prior to the year of its use and includes planting charts and recipes.

to flourish. I learned later in life that being labeled *Kinda Green* wasn't an indictment on my future successes or failures. My father and Dr. Reed understood that I needed to learn new things, slowly develop over time, and accept the nurturing and care from others to be successful.

This book is about my maturity and transition through life, and the people, places, and things that influenced my development. I will present my life's journey in an autobiographical format with historical contexts. I decided to write this book in the first person participle voice, so that I owned my experiences. Readers will get a glimpse of my sojourn as a person and an inside look at the importance of good mentor relationships in the development of a young African-American man, with a desire to earn a Ph.D. My broader goal is to inspire others to look more closely at their own lives and take time to honor those, who have nurtured their growing crop and share similar stories.

I will introduce my mentors to the reading audience, in the order we met, and discuss how they joined my journey, describe their influence, and explain why they are unique. I am really grateful as an older adult for the influences of my mentors earlier in my life. This book is written as a way to say thanks and serves to connect my life through their impact. As my mentors read about my journey, I hope they learn more about others like them, who also influenced me, and took charge and responsibility when their season in my life was complete. The backdrop of my journey will be lessons learned and how my successes were encouraged, while my limitations were addressed with constructive criticism, kindness, and unconditional love.

I chose *Four Tubas a Guitar and a Gallery of Cheerleaders*, as part of the principal title, to signify my musical background and its impact on my life. Because of music, I have met and learned from so many people, including those highlighted in this book. *Four Tubas, and a Guitar* symbolizes my personal growth, while I lived with and learned from musicians. Their influence was invaluable in my life, because of our common bond. They loved and lived for music, as a career and past-time, which gave me connection. These men and women also had valuable life experiences to share, which helped me tremendously. One of the primary bonds for several of my mentors was that we all studied and played the same instrument, the tuba or sousaphone, which in my opinion is the greatest instrument in the world.

The second part of the principal title, *A Gallery of Cheerleaders,* symbolizes the encouragement I received over the years from my biggest fans and support network. My cheerleaders consisted of people from all walks of life and experiences. This part of the title also describes how their energy helped me overcome many obstacles in my personal and professional life. These cheerleaders were always there to give me encouragement and a boost to help me tackle and overcome any situation or obstacle, and there were many. The subtitle *Transition in the Life of a Black Ph.D.* is self-explanatory, as is my usual writing style, but describes my experiences as an African-American man in pursuit of higher education and my share of the American Dream.

Four Tubas, a Guitar, and a Gallery of Cheerleaders is about my growth, maturity, and life journeys that interconnected me with people who encouraged, motivated, and criticized my steps with love, compassion, and care. The cross roads I later approached during my life would not only support the fact that I am *Kinda Green,* but also be a testimony to how far I have truly come with the help of people closest to me. All terms used to define what it means to be "green" described me then and even now; but being green is not always bad, because it means that I will always have room to grow and mature.

I thank God for wisdom and help beyond my realm and must acknowledge and embrace my greenness. I needed to mature and several people in my life helped me do just that. The coming years of my life would be a testament to that statement Kinda Green, which in one context describes how a person relates to the maturity of a particular agricultural crop. In that same context, green for me represents impressionable states in my life, which were influenced directly by my environment. I acknowledge the greatest farmer, God and reference and cite biblical scriptures, as an indication of life lessons when reflecting on my biggest defeats and greatest accomplishments. I haven't always been mindful of the *Power of God* and how his words and will influenced my life.

As I got older, I read the Bible with more contemplation to get a better grasp of my life's struggles and triumphs. I hope that every time readers open this book, they will first see the powerful words of Almighty God as translated in the King James Version of the Holy Bible. Then, recognize how scriptures are pertinent and relevant to my recognition and transition to a more spiritual approach to life. Bible scriptures helped me embrace perseverance to continue in the midst of adversity, forgiveness to be able to forgive others, so I could be forgiven, and kindness, which was necessary for my transition and growth. I have also learned to be patient in many aspects of my life, which is not my best attribute. Faith has taught me that sometimes when we asked God for things, he can have three specific responses. The first response could be "No, you are not ready!" The second response could be "Not yet, we still have more work to do!" and the third response could be "Yes!" I used the Word to learn patience, which helped me understand that everything comes in due seasons. Understanding the drawbacks of extreme pride humbled me to be able to learn from others. When I was finally ready to be still and listen, that's when my life began to change. Understanding and wisdom were necessary for me to accept the views of my mentors and a desire for knowledge allowed me to put these components together to tell a story of my life.

Throughout the three volumes of this book (Part I, II and III), I will transition from being apprehensive, scared, intimidated, discouraged, idealistic, and disciplined, to demanding, narcissistic, arrogant, and unrealistic, before being humbled by God like the potter's clay. Life's experiences have made me more faithful, aware, appreciative, patient, forgiving, spiritual, wise, understanding, and resolved. It's taken me years to finally realize that my physical strength could only take me so far. It was my spiritual strength and re-connection with God that helped me overcome my greatest obstacles. By the middle of a long journey, I was physically spent and glad that spiritual training as a youth helped me seek divine intervention from God. I hoped God would bless me and change my life, not because of who I was, but in spite of who I was.

> Let the words of my mouth, and the meditation of my heart, be acceptable in thy sight, O LORD, my strength, and my redeemer.
>
> **Psalm 19:14 (KJV)**

Four Tubas, a Guitar and a Gallery of Cheerleaders

Transition in the Life of a Black Ph.D.

A First Person Narrative

Part I.

Kinda Green!

> For if a man think himself to be something, when he is nothing, he deceiveth himself. But let every man prove his own work, and then shall he have rejoicing in himself alone, and not in another. For every man shall bear his own burden. Let him that is taught in the word communicate unto him that teacheth in all good things. Be not deceived; God is not mocked: for whatsoever a man soweth, that shall he also reap. For he that soweth to his flesh shall of the flesh reap corruption; but he that soweth to the Spirit shall of the Spirit reap life everlasting. And let us not be weary in well doing: for in due season we shall reap, if we faint not. As we have therefore opportunity, let us do good unto all men, especially unto them who are of the household of faith.
>
> **Galatians 6:3-10 (KJV)**

Chapter 1.
Seed Planted

> To every thing there is a season, and a time to every purpose under the heaven: A time to be born, and a time to die; a time to plant, and a time to pluck up that which is planted; A time to kill, and a time to heal; a time to break down, and a time to build up; A time to weep, and a time to laugh; a time to mourn, and a time to dance; A time to cast away stones, and a time to gather stones together; a time to embrace, and a time to refrain from embracing; A time to get, and a time to lose; a time to keep, and a time to cast away; A time to rend, and a time to sew; a time to keep silence, and a time to speak; A time to love, and a time to hate; a time of war, and a time of peace.
>
> **Ecclesiastes 3:1-8 (KJV)**

I started my life in a central Arkansas town called Pine Bluff or the Bluff for people familiar with the area. Pine Bluff was aptly named because of the overabundance of rolling bluffs and pine trees that decorated the horizon throughout the city. I don't know the complete history of how my ancestors migrated there from Texas and Louisiana, but growing up in the Bluff was a unique experience. Pine Bluff is located in the mid-south region of Arkansas, in Jefferson County, with a population around 57,000 people. Cotton, soybeans, rice, cattle, poultry, timber, and catfish are its major products, produced abundantly in the rich Arkansas River basin[3].

Growing up was special because of the people and southern atmosphere. Pine Bluff represented people with country values and big city dreams and ambitions. I felt that Pine Bluff, in relationship to the rest of the state and more rural areas, was a metropolis. But, 57,000 people couldn't be described as a metropolis in Arkansas, since the population of Little Rock, the state capitol, was over 150,000. It was fun to believe that our city set the economic, social, and cultural trends for the state, which is why our motto became *Positively Pine Bluff.*

Life in the Bluff was interesting, during my early youth. I saw the city's theme as a constant journey to *"achieve degrees and leave with speed"* as many of my friends expressed it. We were all challenged as children to excel and do better than our parents. Nothing was more competitive than our education. We welcomed any opportunity to be a shining example of successful parenting in the community. I developed a competitive spirit early on to "fit in" and desired to be the best in everything I did. I also wanted be the "center of attention" and very demanding as a child, often feeling entitled and becoming upset when things didn't progress the way I thought they should. These traits didn't change very much as a got older, and actually became more evident as I subconsciously acted on core beliefs and values I thought I grew out of. I was blessed with the will, drive, and strength of my mother and the compassion, logic, and heart of my father.

Most of my early youth was a blur, until I reached high school, when my goals, ambitions, and dreams grew. I do remember the times I played after school and how my transition from *Sam Taylor Elementary* to *Greenville Elementary* was hard. Desires to lead; be smart, popular, and attractive were on the top of my young things to do and be list. But as a typical adolescent, most of my dreams outweighed real life situations. It

---

[3] Arkansas River Basin- covers 195,000 miles and is a part of the Mississippi and Missouri river system.

helped that the Bluff was a place where strong beliefs could compensate for one's deficiencies. Positive thinking was necessary for me to believe that I could achieve. My goals and passions were grand. I loved science and always wanted to be smart and shape the world view.

When people talked about me, I wanted to be remembered as the gifted student, with embossed pocket protectors, colored pens, and bookworm glasses. This was my vision of intelligence. Whatever I could do to feel smarter, I did, including trying to match a perception of intelligence. My other passion was music, which began for me in the third grade, in Music Appreciation classes at Sam Taylor Elementary. I remember the first song I heard and recognized growing up was *You'll Never Find Another Love Like Mine* by Lou Rawls. Every time I heard that song on television or on the radio, I felt nostalgic. Still today, that song is the only one I recognize from the extensive Lou Rawls' greatest hits albums.

Music was very important to me, and when I got to Southeast Junior High School, I played the Baritone horn in my first marching band. I will never forget the first day of band class, when the roll was called, and we were asked to choose the instrument we wanted to play. Most people chose the flute, trumpet, or drums. I was going to do the same, but didn't realize those instruments had to be purchased to use during the year. When I found out otherwise, I chose the baritone horn because it was one of the instruments provided by the school.

My goal was to be the best instrumental player in the band. I wanted to practice every day, which meant taking the instrument home on the bus. There was no peak music season in junior high except during Thanksgiving and Christmas, when the city organized nightly parades. Between fall and winter and into summer before school closed, I carried my loaned baritone home every day. Each morning, I slowly trekked to the bus stop, which was about five blocks from my house and is now the site of *Old St. James Baptist Church*. There, I stood in line nervously, for fear of finding a seat on the bus. The problem was that my instrument would always take up twice as much room, on an already crowded bus.

The first couple of weeks of each school year were rough, because the case and horn were heavy and I wasn't used to carrying it long distances. Eventually, I developed more strength to hold the instrument steady and it didn't seem so big and awkward for me or others. I practiced every day in the kitchen after school, while my mother watched television. Soon,

I developed a strong armature[4], which helped me create a pretty decent sound. The baritone is a cool instrument because of its range and ability to produce bold low tones and crisp high tones.

Mr. Carl Lott, Jr., was my mentor and band director in the seventh grade, and then became my high school band director years later. Mr. Lott gave me an opportunity to learn music and he taught me patiently, but recommended I take additional music lessons from a more seasoned band instructor, Mr. Elmer M. Carlton. Mr. Lott was a new band director out of college and relied on Mr. Carlton to help his amateur musicians improve. His philosophy was that the more we practiced on our own, the better we performed.

---

4   Armature- is used in this context to mean a level of consistent control of my jaw and lips, which supports a uniform stream of air into the instrument and a clear sound.

Mr. Carl Lott, Jr.

Mr. Carlton was also one of my musical mentors. Both he and Mr. Lott treated me with care and compassion, but Mr. Carlton treated me like one of his children. He is responsible for developing my early musical talent on the baritone and eventually teaching me how to play the tuba. I stayed at *Southeast Junior High School* for only one year and then attended *Belair Junior High School* on the opposite side of town, as an eighth grader. There, my musical talents on the baritone improved.

Mr. Carlton practiced with me daily and encouraged my musical growth, while caring for all of his students. He would take extra time to shuttle students home after each practice and shared his family time with us. This was one of the great things about growing up in the south. Older people would mentor youngsters into adulthood, by serving as positive role models, which they called the *southern way* of doing things.

Growing up in the Bluff gave me a strong sense of community. It truly was a small world as I think back, because Mr. Carlton's wife was my second grade teacher. I vaguely remember him visiting our class from time to time to bring her lunch. Mrs. Carlton was a great teacher, who taught me the fundamentals of reading. I don't recall all of my experiences at Belair, because the junior high schools in the city were combined into one larger school that year, creating Pine Bluff Junior High, which was later dedicated as *Jack Robey Junior High School*.

I will never forget the day Mr. Carlton approached me about playing the tuba. I looked at the large white instrument, that sat in a special stand resembling a chair and asked him "What is that?" Mr. Carlton told me he needed me to change my instrument because the band needed more bass, and the tuba was for designed to produce bass. I gazed at the white dry plastered horn with thick tubing like plumbing pipes, with awe and anticipation. It was so much bigger than the baritone. I was nervous because I felt there was no way to fill something that big with air from my lungs. Mr. Carlton was adamant about his request and taught me to use the same techniques I learned to play the baritone, on the tuba, just use more air. His philosophy was that this was the best way to create the same controlled sound effect in a larger instrument.

The first time I tried to play the tuba, it took my breath away, but I eventually got used to it. The scary part was realizing that taking this bigger instrument on the bus would really be a new challenge. I was relieved, but somewhat disappointed to learn that I couldn't take it home every day like I did the baritone, but had to rest it on a stand in the band room after each practice. Months of winded practices and aching back muscles helped me learn to switch back and forth and play the baritone and tuba for different styles of music. My tone on the tuba was clear and crisp because I maintained the same armature used for mid-range tones on the baritone, while working to duplicate each chord structure. The baritone was still my favorite instrument, but more and more, I practiced with the tuba. One of the most memorable but embarrassing moments, during my tenure with the tuba, happened during the yearly state band festival.

Mr. Elmer M. Carlton

Four Tubas, a Guitar, and a Gallery of Cheerleaders

During this competition, students from all over the state would try out and compete to be part of a musical ensemble and give a concert to the organizers. The goal each year was to place and be selected as a *first chair* musician. The competition in the brass groups was tough, but not as tough as the tryouts for woodwinds, because no one wanted to play second or third parts. The tubas really didn't have multiple parts, so to place only meant a difference between seats. This year, I was pumped and ready to compete on the tuba. Mr. Carlton practiced with me to the point that I made a decision to make the tuba my primary instrument. It was big and bold, which made me feel powerful playing it.

In order to compete, we had to travel to Sheridan, Arkansas. I met people from all walks of life, who were doing their best to be apart of the regional concert band. Mr. Carlton talked to me about the competition and we decided to use a concert tuba[5] for the tryout. I was nervous about the concert tuba because it wasn't familiar to me. The case and instrument was also much bigger than I was used to carrying. The first day of competition I was responsible for taking the instrument to the practice area, before I had to play musical scales and site reading exercises. I got off the bus and saw that to get to the practice facility I had to go up a steep hill. My mood changed because I really didn't want to lug that big horn that far from the bus, because I knew I would have to bring it back once the competition was over.

I gathered my strength and took the horn up the hill. The journey up the hill was a real struggle and it seemed like I was the only one moving such a big piece of equipment. I asked Mr. Carlton about leaving the case and just taking the horn. He told me the instrument was brand new, so I had to leave it in the case everywhere it went. When I finished my tryout, I had to make the journey back downhill to the bus and made a decision that changed my relationship with Mr. Carlton.

Instead of carrying the case, with the instrument inside, I decided to drag the case and instrument down the hill to save my strength. The sound that was made as the rocks and concrete scratched up against the bottom of the case made everyone at the competition stop and look. I didn't realize how much noise I was making. All I cared about was getting the case and instrument back to the bus. It sounded like someone was using a metal object to scratch a chalkboard repetitively and before I knew it, I saw Mr. Carlton running up the hill to meet me. I thought he was

---

5   Concert Tuba- often referred to as the Euphonium or tenor tuba, is pitched in B-flat and one octave higher than the BB-flat Contrabass.

coming to help with the tuba case, but he reprimanded me because I was dragging the case down the hill. He asked me why I was dragging a brand new case with a brand new instrument inside of it. I told him because it was heavy. Mr. Carlton looked at me and paused and in a terse voice asked "*Why didn't you ask someone for help?*" I didn't have an answer for his question and he walked away looking disappointed.

When he spoke to me again, he explained that I probably damaged the case beyond repair, and he was responsible as the band director. The rest of our conversation was based on the same issue and by the time I got the instrument back to the bus, we examined the case and the damage was major. Mr. Carlton was disappointed and I was disappointed in my actions, but thought I was taking the most logical approach to the circumstances.

I had never seen Mr. Carlton that angry and just knew I would have to pay for a new case. His final statement to me was "*How can I explain this to the school board?*" I will never forget that day because my judgment was scrutinized and it made me more conscious about everything I did. Mr. Carlton never talked about that incidence or required me to pay for the case. Thankfully, I scored high enough to be selected to participate in the concert and represented Pine Bluff Junior High School in the regional concert band. I loved playing music, but was never inclined to study the tuba beyond basic aptitude for regular sheet music, until I got into high school and studied under Mr. Carl Lott, Jr.

Mrs. Carlton

The High School Years

*"ZEB - RAS, ZEBRAS,
ZEBRAS ARE THE BEST!"*

Four Tubas, a Guitar, and a Gallery of Cheerleaders

Now a freshman in high school, during the late 1980s, I was quite out of my element in the social scene. Students with our status were constantly called "*Slop Dogs*" as a right of passage by upperclassmen. We counted the days until we could exert the same level of ridicule on underclassmen, so it was cool. I joined the zebra marching band, which gave me a core group to be with that had similar goals and talents, all revolving around music. Band practice wasn't always about music. There were many times, when we learned real life lessons from Mr. Lott. We were a close musical group eager to learn about the world outside of high school. Mr. Lott was willing to let us know what was waiting for us, on the other side of the band room door. His favorite phrase was "*Close That Door!*" When we heard that, we knew he would drop his baton and begin to preach, philosophize, speculate, educate, and teach us beyond what our young minds could process at the time. He was our musical leader, sponsor, and mentor and one of the most important high school teachers we had.

Most parents didn't realize we spent more time with him, that with anyone else in high school. Mr. Lott was a great teacher and one of those unique people who touched lives like no one else could. It was funny, because Mr. Lott and I shared similar physical characteristics including facial hair, and disposition, often prompting people to think that I was his son. No other teacher on the campus, besides the football coach, held more closed-door sessions than Mr. Lott. He discussed everything from politics to the future and how every step we take as a band and in life can have consequences. This style of teaching is what makes band directors special. Their ability to teach students how to make melodious music often went well beyond their job description and salary.

Mr. Lott motivated me to become more serious about music, by appointing me tuba section leader. I wanted to lead musically and have others look to me for guidance, but was also interested in science. I joined the science club, and took upper-level courses such as General Science, Biology, Geometry, and Trigonometry. My interests in science were encouraged by Mrs. Jewell C. Whatley, who was one of the most accomplished instructors at Pine Bluff High School. She was also my first science mentor. She was tough, but fair and demanded excellence from me in all of her classes. I wasn't the best student, but she offered me an opportunity to learn Advanced Placement (AP) Biology. I appreciated the offer, for no other reason than it seemed different from what other students could take.

The goal of the class was to learn advanced biology, and take and score on the nationally recognized AP exam. If my scores were high enough, they could help my entrance into competitive colleges and universities across the country. Soon after joining the class, I focused more on biology, but my first love was still music. When the time came to take the AP exam, I didn't score very high, which was disappointing, but I still had music to fall back on. From that point, I thought I might want to be a band director, like my mentors, but opportunities in science were still very important to me.

Following my sophomore and junior years in high school, I became more involved in the zebra marching band. My other interest became writing, so I volunteered as a columnist for the high school newspaper. There were some contentious articles written during the late 1980s, because the Dr. Martin Luther King, Jr. Holiday wasn't adopted by all U.S. states. One of my biggest goals was to get a Black History course added to the high school curriculum. I wrote like I spoke and developed a very chaotic style of prose. I eventually learned to adjust my writing style to use established rules of grammar and diction. Music influenced my writing and I literally fell in love with my pocket radio. I listened to Happy Rap artists such as the *Fat Boys, Kool Moe Dee, Whodini, Queen Latifah*, and *DJ Jazzy Jeff and the Fresh Prince*. I eventually embraced Rap artists such as *Ice-T, Ice Cube, KRS-One, Public Enemy, NWA*, and *Run DMC*. Writing never got in the way of my passion for music, because it was a new hobby, and not my best talent.

My high school years were smooth because of band music and science, which gave me clear direction and goals to push for. By the time I became a senior; I was more focused on science and used band music to balance my life. I did have other interests before band, such as playing football. I had the body type and drive to do so, but by the time my senior year rolled around, I had already missed too many years of *Football 101* and knew I would never see the gridiron in pads and a helmet. I still want to play just one down, during a big game, and hit an opposing player from the middle linebacker position. On the flip side, the great thing about being in the band was that I always had a seat at the football games and got in the stadium early and free of charge. The band's job was to entertain and keep the spirit of our football team high, as we spurred our zebras to victory. We also wanted to break the spirit of rival visiting teams and their bands.

During my senior year of high school, I tried to make the most of it by preparing for college life. I was popular in the band and voted president,

Four Tubas, a Guitar, and a Gallery of Cheerleaders

which meant I was in charge of the committee to decide what gifts to give the band staff, at the end of the year. This was a big deal for each class even though the position held no additional power. Music was my life, but thoughts toward what would really give me a good future, continued to bother me. I wanted to play the tuba, but didn't want that passion to interfere with my goal to be one of the best scientists in the world. I wasn't familiar with the theory of multiple intelligences, so I based my goals on an "all or none" approach. This meant that I believed there was one thing I could be good at and then do that for the rest of my life.

About midway through my senior year, I began thinking about where I wanted to go to school. My ultimate desire was to go to the University of Southern California (USC). Mrs. Whatley was always supportive of my efforts, but she also loved me enough to be honest with me. She let me know that now wasn't the time to *"stray far away from the nest"* and move to California. I trusted her judgment and believed that she wanted the best for me.

I talked with Mr. Lott about the University of Arkansas at Pine Bluff (UAPB), a local school and his alma mater. He agreed with Mrs. Whatley's assessment that I needed to be more grounded before leaving Arkansas, and happily wrote me a letter of recommendation for UAPB. This opened the door to my career at a university located five blocks from my father's house. UAPB was too convenient to pass up. I have always been a *"bird in hand"* person and made sure to embrace all opportunities in front of me. I left Pine Bluff High School, a changed adolescent with the same dreams and hopes, with the goal to realize and experience the world from a greater perspective at UAPB.

I needed band music more now than ever, because it gave me a community of peers with similar interests, which is a big factor for success, during the first couple of years in higher education. The thought of working for more than three years to try to "fit-in" in high school worried me, because I felt I would have to go through the same process at UAPB. My other dilemma was how I would balance academics with a grueling practice schedule and my desire to have personal interests. Somehow, I found a way to balance my life and I began the most amazing journey in self-reflection and growth, at the University of Arkansas at Pine Bluff.

Mrs. Jewell C. Whatley
"Chance Favors the Prepared Mind!"

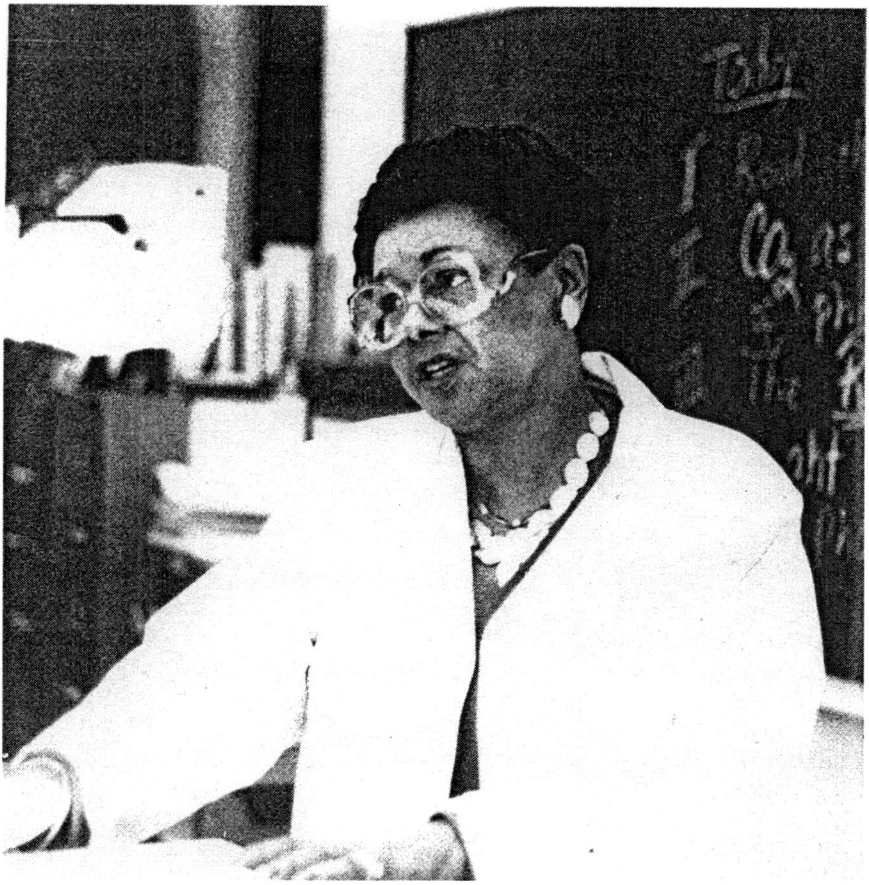

Chapter 2.
Band, Books, and Frat!

> My son, despise not the chastening of the LORD; neither be weary of his correction: For whom the LORD loveth he correcteth; even as a father the son in whom he delighteth. Happy is the man that findeth wisdom, and the man that getteth understanding. For the merchandise of it is better than the merchandise of silver and the gain thereof than fine gold. She is more precious than rubies: and all the things thou canst desire are not to be compared unto her.
>
> **Proverbs 3:11-15 (KJV)**

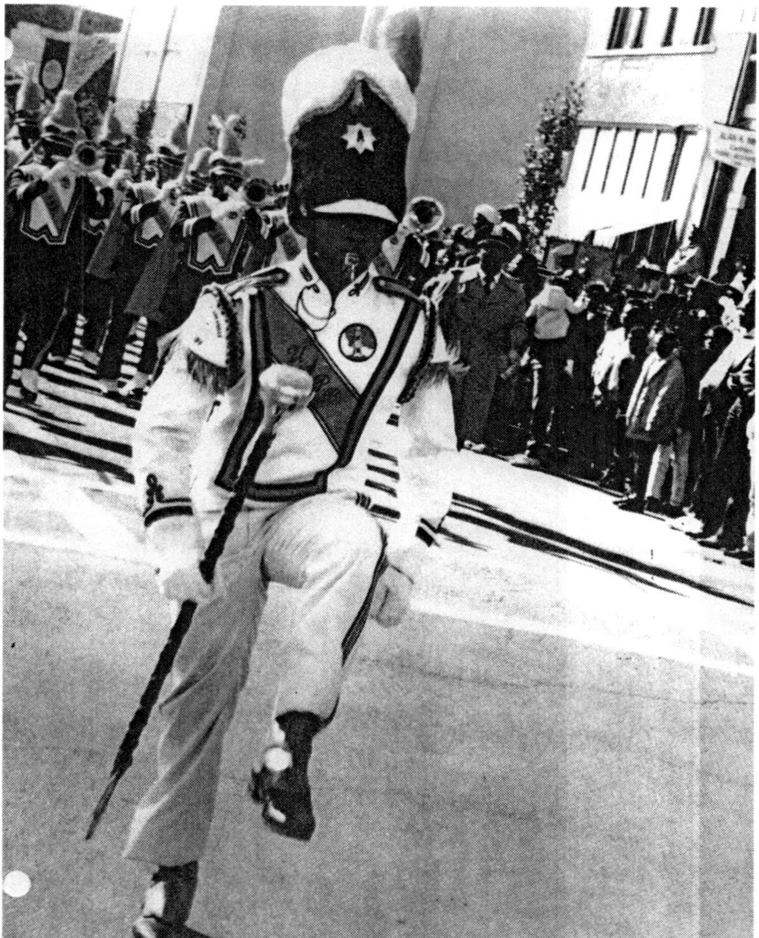

Sederick C. Rice

I contacted the university registrar regarding my application to UAPB, in the spring of 1990. I was offered a band scholarship of $700.00 per semester, but the registrar told me to wait until the band director sent the final list of new students, so my balance could be paid. In-state tuition, at UAPB, was $900.00 per semester, which left me $200.00 short. I needed to make more money to take care of the rest. Traditionally, young men in Arkansas are required to work during the summers to raise money. They either cut lawns, rake leaves, or wash windows. My father was adamant that I work during the summer months. He felt working would build character and help me learn how the real world works. My option for work was simple, and there was no better place than my grandfather's automotive repair shop, located blocks from our house.

I didn't need transportation to get there, but regularly borrowed my grandfather's Schwinn 10-speed bicycle to make sure I wasn't late for work. My grandfather paid me to be there and learn, while hoping that some lessons would stay with me as I got older. My work schedule was long; 7:30 a.m. to 5:30 p.m. each weekday and 7:30 a.m. to noon every Saturday. At the end of the week, I would gross $60.00. My grandfather would always staple the money together with a hand written note, before giving it to me. This was major money as a youngster living in the Bluff.

I worked at my grandfather's automotive business known as the *Shop*, every summer during my teen years. Ironically, his business was located one block away from the UAPB band room. I would always hear the beats and sounds that seemed to shake the windows and walls of our building, during their rehearsals. We were so close to the campus that we counted on hearing some form of music everyday. When I worked at the *Shop*, I had an opportunity to listen to spirited conversations about the condition of the city, county, state, and nation from people who came by for service, conversation, or a drink. My grandfather always mentioned his work/celebration policy: *"Never drink before 5 p.m., because we have work to do before then." "You will live a healthier, more productive life if you abide by this rule."*

The older men from the community, who spent a lot of time at the *Shop*, often watched and talked to me about education and how important it was to learn and achieve with the opportunities before me. I didn't feel tremendous pressure, but I did feel a sense of responsibility to live up to a standard that had been set by my grandfather, who graduated from college with a B.S. degree, and my father who earned an M.S. degree.

One day near the end of the summer, I was working at the *Shop* trying to find something to do to busy myself with before quitting time, when Mr. Fred Lowe, a community activist, got my attention as I swept the floor. He said very bluntly and surprisingly, *"You know your grandfather got his B.S. degree, and your father got his M.S. degree, and you are the third generation of Rice men, so you must get your Ph.D."* Mr. Jimmy Singleton, another good friend of my grandfather's, agreed with what Mr. Lowe was saying and in a strange and funny way gave me the same charge for my life.

This proclamation came out of the blue. Being young and idealistic, I couldn't even imagine why they saw into my future that way. I wanted to become a medical doctor and felt pressure to succeed, before I finished my first semester of higher education. My goal became to finish where my grandfather and father left off, and I quickly learned that success in education and life equals *"95% heart and 5 % talent."*

My summer job at the *Shop* was almost complete, and I was excited because this would be the first summer I had something else to do. I was also happy to be joining the UAPB marching band. All of my paperwork was complete with the admissions office, and the entrance letter to band camp stated that new members had to report one week before upperclassmen arrived. The organizers of band camp wanted new players to learn the fundamentals of marching, playing, and command structure quickly. I read the letter without much anticipation, since I had always spent the summers in high school playing music.

Mr. Fred Lowe

Four Tubas, a Guitar, and a Gallery of Cheerleaders

Freshman Year

I arrived at the UAPB band room at 6:00 p.m., on a Sunday evening in late July, for our first meeting. The upperclassmen section leaders and drum majors addressed the band, as well as the head band director, Dr. Joseph "Doc" Miller, a former assistant band director from Grambling State University. Doc Miller laid out his plan for the band year. His vision was clear but somewhat controversial because he had taken over from a musical legacy, Mr. Odie Burrus, who held the title of Director of Bands at UAPB from 1980-1989.

Freshmen students got instructions about what was next in band camp. I remember when the meeting was over and people finished their speeches. All of the new people got up and headed toward the door. Then, we heard three loud shrills from a whistle and immediately were yelled at and forcibly directly to sit back down in our seats. The head drum major stood on a chair and loudly said, *"We don't leave this room like that!"* with a cold stare and contempt for all of the new musicians.

I looked around to understand what was going on and was puzzled like the rest of my "crab[6]" mates. I was confident everything would be okay, since I had been through Mr. Lott's music program, saw his name embroidered on the wall, and thought I had seen and done it all musically. Then, someone prematurely asked, "What time do we report tomorrow?" The staff hastily and loudly responded, "five-o-clock," so I immediately thought they meant 5:00 p.m. In actuality, they meant 5:00 a.m., which was made very clear before we left the band room.

The drum major asked if there were any more questions. No one said a word, and then he instructed us on how to leave the band room after each practice. He said, "You only leave this room, when I blow this whistle in this fashion. Tweeeeeeet-Tweet-Tweet. Stand to your feet, and say 'U------A-------P------B' beginning from a parade rest position and ending at the attention position!" "Are there any more questions?" "Ok! Let's try it" "Tweeeeeeet-Tweet-Tweet. U-------A-------P------B!" He immediately stopped us and told us to do it again, because that try wasn't loud or good enough. The inflection in his voice changed. He was angrier with his commands and instructions. Tweeeeeeet-Tweet—Tweet. U----A-----P----------B now rang forcefully in unison from everyone in the room, but this

---

6 Crab- is a term given to first year musicians, which was indicative of the hierarchy in the band organization and a way to identify sophomore students in the band. Band students were called crabs until their second year in the band.

time we were so focused on making the statements loud that we forgot to come from parade rest to attention. We had to do it one more time.

Our group didn't take this exercise seriously and some people were laughing near the back of the room. This wasn't a good idea. The drum major made us all very aware that this exercise was no laughing matter. He told us "You think it's funny now, but it won't be funny tomorrow!" Most of us were first year college students, who were once were kings and queens of music in our respective high schools, but here we were often referred to in military terms as plebes, cadets, or crabs and could only speak or have something to say when addressed by our superiors.

We tried our exit from the band room one last time and we all nailed it, even though some of us were a little shaken by the fact that report time was 5:00 a.m. the next day. I thought that because I lived only five blocks from the school, it would be a piece of cake, but I didn't realize that band camp in the Marching Musical Machine of the Mid-South (M4) would forever change the way I approached music and life.

UAPB Band Camp

The next morning I arrived a few minutes early to practice. Everyone was dressed in black sweats and white t-shirts as instructed in the introduction package. No one really stood out. We lined up in formation by instrumentation, and marched in the early haze of the morning to our practice field. The practice field applicably named *The Dots*, was where we began one of the most grueling exercise and conditioning regimens I had ever experienced. We were musicians, but we trained like professional athletes. Each section leader was their squad's motivational leader. Drum majors worked to pick up the pace and encouraged us to do better each day. We did sit-ups, push-ups, running drills, abdominal crunches, stretches, and learned the *8-to-5 high-step marching style*[7].

---

7   8-to-5 marching style- is one of the most physically demanding of the marching styles and requires musicians to use an extended high-step that is then extended to the ground in a quick motion and alternated between legs. This form of marching was made famous in Big 10 schools such as Michigan, Ohio State, and Purdue. It is called 8-to-5 because if done correctly, the musician can take 8 steps for every 5 yards on the field.

Four Tubas, a Guitar, and a Gallery of Cheerleaders

I had come from a strictly *corps*-style marching[8] background, which was much easier on the joints and knees, when I carried the tuba. The transition to 8-to-5 marching was tough but exciting. Each day was a new challenge for all of us. We were disciplined as crabs to follow orders without question and be in top physical shape, in order to compete against rival bands. The conditioning exercises helped us build stamina and stronger diaphragms, which meant our lungs, could take in and control air more efficiently. This also helped us push air through our instruments more forcefully and create more sound.

Our band camp schedule was grueling. We arrived at 5:00 a.m., exercised during the early morning before the Sun came out, ate breakfast then focused on music in the mid-morning. We ate lunch, rehearsed again in the afternoon, ate dinner, and finally left the band room around midnight every day. The first couple of nights I was exhausted but upbeat. Even though I lived close to UAPB, I would have rather lived in the on-campus dormitories, so I wouldn't have to move very far when my alarm went off. Latecomers or no-shows to camp were severely penalized by doing extra conditioning under the watchful eye of the drum majors, who took personal pleasure in breaking the spirits of insubordinates, while others watched. Our bodies adjusted to the schedule over time, but our sleep patterns were messed up to the point that I woke up at night, went to bed at night, and couldn't determine what day it was. This was common among the first-year musicians.

We complained and moaned, but the discipline and conditioning made us better musicians and able to adapt to a rigorous travel schedule. Near the end of camp, our bodies and spirits were in tune. Now the task was to teach us how to make music together. It seemed as if everyone in the band came from somewhere else. I lost my hometown advantage. Doc Miller and his assistants recruited nationwide selecting people from Louisiana, Mississippi, Texas, Tennessee, Michigan, and Illinois. Only a few of us were from Arkansas.

Everyone was jockeying for positions, claiming to be the best at what they did, at their previous high schools. The biggest trash talkers were percussionists from Detroit, Chicago, and Houston. I was no exception, and felt there was no one better on the tuba, than me. There were so many personalities and

---

8   Corps style marching- is a type of marching that originated from military signaling units that differs from Carnival and Show Bands, which normally incorporate drum and bugle ensembles. This type of marching focused on precision, directional movements on the field, and was natural on the joints, because of the low impact of feet to the ground.

dynamics at play. The musical staff spent most of their time trying to get us all on the same page. They tried to get us to stop competing amongst each other, while Doc Miller organized the day-to-day schedules of the band.

The UAPB band was the flagship of the university, so Doc Miller spent his time interacting with university officials, city administrators and the general public. We never lost a step. Our band staff was organized similar to professional football teams' infrastructure. The head coach was Doc Miller, and he hired the proverbial offensive and defensive coordinators, and other coaching staff, who specialized in a particular musical skill.

We had people who were professionals in percussion, brass, woodwinds, auxiliary (flag line), and choreography. Doc Miller was in charge, but his second in command, Mr. Kelvin Washington or "Wash," composed the songs, designed the field shows for half-time performances, and rehearsed the band to make sure we interpreted the music he wrote correctly. Wash was in tune with the students because he dealt with them daily. His official duty was coordinating band camp, with oversight from Doc Miller. Wash was the brains behind our band and its performances.

"The Motivator and Teacher"
"Wash"

Wisdom Inspired by God

"Sed, play the song slow, until you get it, then play it at tempo or faster. If you can't play it slow, then you can't play it fast. You need to slow down and not let life take you too fast. You are moving at warp speed, but you need to take your time. I know you are young and impatient, but let me ask you a question. How long have you been working on a real job? Less than a year. I've been working for over 20 years, so we will never be in the same place financially or otherwise, so take your time. It will happen for you. You've got a good government job, so stay the course and make sure you get all of the experience you can. Don't let them encourage you to leave early. Get everything they have to offer."

I first met Wash during my first year of band camp. He was responsible for teaching the entire band, but he focused more on brass instruments because of his musical background. Wash was a tuba player like me, born and raised in Scotlandville, Louisiana, a suburb of Baton Rouge, Louisiana, and a devout alumnus of Southern University and A&M College. The first thing I noticed about Wash was his very deep and scratchy voice, when mixed with a strong southern drawl, created an interesting sound. He was a no-nonsense kind of guy, and most people in the band didn't fear or loathe him, but respected him for his skill and wisdom. We occasionally teased him because of his voice and glasses.

Wash is one of the most successful and famous students mentored by Dr. Isaac Greggs[9], who is known as one of the nation's most prolific Black College band directors. Dr. Greggs impacted multiple generations of musicians, students, and communities worldwide. The short list of African-American Bandmasters includes musical legends such as Harold S. Strong, Arkansas Agricultural Mechanical and Normal College (AM&N) now UAPB, T. Leroy Davis (Southern University), Conrad Hutchinson, Jr. (Grambling State), and William P. Foster, Florida A&M University (FAMU).

Wash talked about his experiences at Southern University, and he held the highest esteem for Dr. Greggs because of the significant impact he had on his life. I had an opportunity to talk with Dr. Greggs in 2004, before he retired from Southern University. I let him know that, "If Wash is the Father of music for his students; he would be the Grandfather." I respect him for changing the lives of so many people. Dr. Gregg's influence was circular, and his students related his teaching to so many others around the country and world.

I found out that Dr. Greggs stepped in to protect Wash, while he was in school. I thanked Dr. Greggs for his vision, because if he hadn't intervened, Wash's life at Southern, and the lives of those he taught may have been different. Dr. Greggs was a mentor and friend to Wash and supported him throughout his career. I love UAPB as my alma mater, but respect Southern University and their musical graduates, who have a

---

9   Dr. Isaac Greggs- is an African-American bandmaster who has impacted thousands of people around the world through music. Dr. Greggs also known as "Doc" has mentored some of the most successful musicians in the country and has always believed in the power of education in his students' lives. Dr. Greggs was honored with the Key of Life Award, during the 31st Annual NAACP Awards in 2000.

tradition of taking care of each other. Southern graduates often make sure that when they are in a position to hire, promote, and help their alumni, they do so. Dr. Greggs taught his students to love and respect music, but also to love their fellow musicians, which is one reason Wash was such an effective band leader.

Wash worked primarily in Louisiana, but I always wondered how he got a job at UAPB. I did some research and found that before Wash came to UAPB, he taught in Lafayette, Louisiana at *Holy Rosary*. After that, he moved to Detroit, Michigan and taught music at *Nolan Middle School* and *McKenzie High School* for two years, before being offered a job as a musical assistant at UAPB, by Doc Miller in 1989. Wash was very personable. During our free weekends, he allowed the band students and their friends, along with UAPB faculty and staff, to come over his house to fellowship. We barbequed, play dominoes, and sometimes watched marching band tapes of rival bands to scout their talents and weaknesses. Wash was a perfectionist and deeply serious about how music was interpreted and played.

I remember one day, during band camp, he asked all of the tuba players to clean our instruments. This wasn't a big deal because I thought that meant wiping off the bell and shining the base, with copper polish, as I had done in high school. To Wash, it meant taking the instrument apart, removing the valves and pads, filling the tuba with warm soapy water, rinsing it out with a water hose, and then tuning each slide. Wash was respected because he made us approach music differently. It wasn't the fact that we could play— *"Anyone can play the horn!"* was his favorite phrase— but it was more important that we were able to create music to make others around us sound better.

Wash was cool, but sometimes more straightforward with band students than the staff, or university expected. Most of us had a mystical view of what he did when he wasn't standing on the podium giving musical instructions. Because he was our musical and sometimes life mentor, it was fun fellowshipping with him outside of band practice. I had been in music most of my life and felt I was taught by the best, but he was the band director that first made us distinguish between *"rehearsal"* and *"practice."* Wash used to explain it like this, *"You practice on the instrument in your spare time, but you rehearse during class!"* It took me a while to really grasp what he meant by that saying. I learned that we should do the musical groundwork before rehearsal to smooth out the rough edges away from the larger band. When we came together as a unit, it was his job to fix the small glitches and problems.

When I spent time in the practice rooms going over musical pieces, he could hear me play. He often looked in and said, *"Play the passage slow until you get the feel for it, before you try to play it fast! You will never be able to play the passage fast if you can't play it slow!"* Somehow those words became a metaphor for my life. I wasn't his favorite student, and there were many times we didn't' see eye to eye, but I respected him. Wash knew I was the product of good training and could be one of the strongest tuba players in the band, if I approached the music a certain way. One of Wash's greatest talents was his ability to arrange and compose songs just by listening to them over and over again.

I was amazed at how he could hear the notes, phrases, pauses, key signature changes, and tempos, and then use a No. 2 pencil to write notes and rhythms on staff paper, with multiple instrumental parts and a score. He composed from sounds he heard in his head. Just as Johann Sebastian Bach, George Frideric Handel, Wolfgang Amadeus Mozart, Joseph Haydn, and Ludwig van Beethoven did in days past, Wash composed music using a concept called counterpoint[10].

Counterpoint is used in most forms of music, including marches, Rhythm & Blues, and even Rap or Hip-Hop, where melodies are established and proceed in one direction, while countermelodies travel in totally different directions. Wash normally used a piano to match tones for songs he heard on the radio. He could compose a complete score in two to three days, for our rehearsals and field shows, but was interestingly peculiar when applauded for his great talent.

Wash was modest and always downplayed his abilities saying, *"This is something I just can do, but the biology you study, I know is really hard."* He was always on top of his game, but didn't want too much adoration. Wash could also write songs without a lot of substance that only contained a strong beat and hook. He would add repeats to make the song seem to contain more musical content, which I know is one of the tricks of the trade for accomplished composers and studio engineers.

Successful composers and arrangers are able to adapt music to various instruments, groups, and styles. During the transposition of sounds and chords, recorded notes can be scored. Wash mastered this concept. No song request from the radio or television was too difficult for him to

---

10   Counterpoint- is an Italian musical term which represents point against point or note against note.

transcribe for us to play. The bigger question was if the recommended song fit into the scheme of our half-time performances. This shouldn't have been a problem, since the music in the early 1990s was made famous by *Boyz II Men, En Vogue, Mint Condition, Zhane, Janet Jackson, Keith Sweat,* and *Babyface.* The 1990s was a time when music was upbeat and popular with people young and old.

Wash did have his favorites, and just like most people who grew up in his era, *Earth Wind & Fire, Barry White, Al Green, Stevie Wonder, Rick James, James Brown* and *The O'Jays* were some of his greatest influences. Their style, flare, instrumentation, and chord structure influenced his approach to writing music for our band. Regardless of the occasion, Wash never forgot to include one or two classics from the Blues or R&B eras.

Wash also loved *Barry White* and his musical library. I remember playing *"You're the First, the Last, My Everything,* so much that even today when I hear that song I move my fingers in the same articulated way I did as part of the tuba bass line so many years ago. Classics such as *I Just Called To Say I Love You, Ebony Eyes, Fantasy, Serpentine Fire, Reasons, Love and Happiness, Give It To Me Baby,* and *Fire and Desire* were favorites of Doc Miller as well. Doc Miller and Wash used these songs to bridge the gap between the older and younger generations, during each half-time show.

Both made sure everyone in the crowd could take something home from the performance, often using *Down Home Blues*[11] as one of their strongest musical crowd pleasers. Their collective philosophies were that *"Great music was arranged and performed in the past, so why not use it now!"* I learned so much those first couple weeks about band, music, and myself that I tried to put it all together and be the best musician I could. I knew I was ready but the greater test was still to come.

Band camp ended near the end of August. All of us were primed for the start of the marching band season. I finally registered for my first semester of classes. Our rehearsal schedule lightened up some, but we still spent a great deal of time perfecting the music. I was interested in biology in high school and now it was my major at UAPB. My first semester, I enrolled in *Freshman Composition, Zoology, College Algebra, Developmental Reading,* and *Personal and Social Development.* I was also enrolled in a lower-level

---

11   Down Home Blues- is a type of rural southern music performed by artists such as Lightnin' Hopkins, John Lee Hooker, and B.B. King.

reading class due to my American College Test (ACT[12]) scores, which were right below the cutoff for remediation. I didn't want to take remedial courses my first semester at UAPB, but I had to comply. I probably went to the reading class three times, before the instructor realized I was more competent in reading and comprehension than the exam demonstrated. I was able to test out of the class, at the very beginning of the semester, which freed up more time for band.

Marching band on the university level was exciting. We prepared to travel and were ready to compete with rival bands from Grambling State University, Mississippi Valley State University, Southern University, and Texas Southern University. I was focused on my studies not wanting to get behind, because I knew band wouldn't let up. Every night, tired or not, I tried to at least go over the class notes from the previous day. Success in my biology curriculum was more important to me than band, but I did feel independent because I was financing my education with my musical skills.

Our football team was popular in the early 1990s, because of our coach Archie "Gunslinger" Cooley[13]. Cooley's style of coaching was exciting because he ran no-huddle offenses and used a Run-&-Gun set to get wide receivers open downfield. Cooley's presence stimulated great interest in UAPB and boosted the morale of faculty, staff, and students. He was also a great advocate for the band and viewed our presence as an important factor in the football team's victories. Cooley encouraged the administration to fund our travel to all games outside the state. Doc Miller took the lead and made sure we were ready for each school we faced, while Wash was busy composing songs and rehearsing the band.

The spirit of UAPB was high because the band had been reorganized and grew in numbers. Our football team was winning and getting national exposure, which made the administration and alumni happy. No expense was spared to support the football team, and our band boosters offered additional support, which allowed us to eat at the best restaurants when we traveled. Doc Miller was in constant contact with administration

---

12 ACT- is an exam that emphasizes thinking skills in English, Mathematics, Reading, and Mathematics in a testing format, and validates problem-solving skills. The ACT is used to measure the ability of students entering colleges and universities around the country.

13 Archie Cooley- was a college football coach who spent most of his career in the 1980s at Mississippi Valley State University in Itta Bena, Mississippi and was famous for coaching NFL great Jerry Rice.

officials and made sure we had the best goods and services, just like the football team. He believed that if the football team ate steak, we ate steak and we felt appreciated.

UAPB vs. Southern University

Our band operated as a multi-purpose unit and not only represented and encouraged our football team to victory, but also helped recruit additional students to UAPB. One of our biggest rivalry schools was on the schedule. We were scheduled to play Southern University in Louisiana. This was the game our band had prepared for all summer. We knew the reputation of Dr. Greggs and *The Human Jukebox*[14]. The rivalry between Southern University and UAPB dated back many years. This game was so heated and important for alumni bragging rights that when AM&N now UAPB won the game, they would suspend some campus activities and celebrate the victory. Our rivalry was strong and Doc Miller and his staff worked night and day to prepare us for this special musical battle.

As the game got closer, Wash was busy composing songs based on instructions from Doc Miller. Many students from Louisiana felt their loyalty was tested, while they marched for UAPB. This caused some rifts even among good friends. I was from the Bluff and really didn't care about the other band members' mixed feelings regarding Southern. I was excited and anxious because I wanted to challenge them with everything I had. When other band members bragged about Southern, but marched in the UAPB band, I was particularly motivated.

Our final preparation was complete, the equipment was loaded, and our mission was to represent the best UAPB and the state of Arkansas had to offer against Southern University. The bus ride was fun, but I was nervous. Many of the upperclassmen told jokes, while others slept. We arrived in Baton Rouge, in the early afternoon, before the game that night. I thought about how I was going to shine, and how this was a personal challenge for me. I warmed up and watched the section leader rouse the group. I was ready and knew the tuba section was ready.

The game began at 7 p.m. as the hot stadium lights illuminated both sides of the bleachers. Our old gold and black uniforms shaded the visitor

---

14 Human Jukebox- is the nickname of the Southern University Marching Band. This moniker also describes how the band's sound was compared to the power and clarity of a musical jukebox.

side for our fans. Southern University's light blue and white overlays lit their home side, to the point that the color schemes clashed. We opened up the musical battle and played our *"Fight Song."* Southern immediately answered with their fight song and the musical battle began. No one on our side was really concerned about the football game; what people came to see was the *Battle of the Bands* during half-time. We knew the real reason we were there, so we conserved our songs and energy. Doc Miller didn't want us to run out of music, before the fifth quarter[15].

Near the end of the second quarter, we went to the edge of the field to prepare for the half-time show. I was still nervous, but focused and tried to tune out everything around me and just concentrate on my steps, position, and music. This was the chance I was waiting for as a freshman student: to prove to the upperclassmen that I deserved to be in the band and could hang with the older musicians. We marched triumphantly and made beautiful music that night. We felt good about our performance, making sure we saved enough energy for the fifth quarter.

I don't remember if our team won the game. I was so exhausted from the half-time performance, I ran out of gas late in the fifth quarter, when it was really time to shine. The game ended and the musical battle continued. We played one song, then they returned a song, and sometimes they played the same song we had played, just to intimidate us before the next round. I remember we played our version of *Goin' Up Yonder*, a Gospel hit at the time, and they played their version of the same song as soon as we stopped playing. After playing six songs back to back with all my might, I noticed I couldn't feel my lips vibrate in the mouthpiece of the tuba. They seemed to be numb. I thought the horn had malfunctioned, because I patched a hole in the base and neck earlier that day to make sure no air leaked out. Unfortunately for me, my armature and jaw muscles were done. No matter what I did, no additional sound came out of the tuba. That experience taught me a lesson about my limitations on the instrument.

When I got back to Arkansas, I worked much harder to maintain consistent air flow in the tuba, by using daily buzzing exercises and long tones in the upper and lower registers to strengthen my armature. We stayed in the stadium during the post-game for nearly two hours until Doc Miller finally said we had played our musical repertoire to conclusion.

---

15 Fifth quarter- is a term used in a musical context to describe the battle between two rival bands after the football game has ended. Usually the band that wins has the best sound, the most music, and gets the crowds approval.

This ended the battle. There was no need to continue playing, because Southern seemed to have endless rounds of music to hit us with. We made our point. We were a young band composed primarily of first-year players, and we built our future success on that experience. This musical battle made us more competitive the following week and during the rest of the marching season.

Traveling with the band was fun but tough sometimes, because I had to study when I could and my major couldn't take a back seat to our football schedule. Classes were proceeding normally, so one day I decided to talk with Dr. Clifton Orr, then chairman of the biology department, about research opportunities in his laboratory. I was recommended to him by Dr. Shelton Fitzpatrick, who was a microbiologist and also a faculty member in the biology department. This wasn't our first meeting. I studied with Dr. Fitzpatrick during the previous summer, as a high school student, as part of a summer enrichment science program and decided to work with him during my first semester at UAPB.

My job in his laboratory was to study bacteria. I learned how to grow, manipulate, and sub-culture different types of microorganisms. Once my analysis was complete, my job was to use a high-pressure autoclave to dispose of the samples. One day I made a critical mistake, when working with live cultures I had been growing for a couple of weeks. I decided to take the autoclaved cultures with me to analyze them outside the laboratory work space, instead of making notes on the appropriate work bench.

This wasn't a good idea because Mrs. Mattie Glover, an Associate Researcher and coordinator of Dr. Orr's Cancer Biology Laboratory, saw me and immediately told me to return the cultures to their proper incubation chambers. I believe Mrs. Glover thought Dr. Fitzpatrick wasn't teaching me what he should have regarding proper bacteria storage and disposal. This really wasn't the case. I knew better, but I got lazy that day and tried to shortcut the process. Things could have gone much worse, but what came out of that situation was increased interest about my research potential from Mrs. Glover and Dr. Orr. I wanted to do research, but didn't know where to start.

Fortunately for me, UAPB was part of a network of HBCUs that participated in the Minority Biomedical Research Sciences (MBRS) and Minority Access to Research Careers (MARC)[16] programs, which were sponsored by the National Institutes for General Medical Sciences (NIGMS). Both programs were designed to increase participation of minority students in science and research careers.

I was really interested in MBRS and MARC because they included monthly stipends and an opportunity to travel to scientific meetings around the country. I also felt my acceptance would be impressive to medical school recruiters. The setup to work in MBRS or MARC was perfect because of my band schedule. This would also be the only opportunity I had to work during the day, because our band always rehearsed at night. Things seemed to be falling into place for me. I was thankful I stuck with biology.

---

16 The Minority Access to Research Careers (MARC) and Minority Biomedical Research Sciences (MBRS) programs were designed to increase the number and capabilities of minority scientists engaged in biomedical research, strengthen science curricula and research opportunities at participating institutions, and strengthen biomedical research capabilities of minority institutions.

Mrs. Mattie Glover

Dr. Shelton Fitzpatrick

I applied for a position in MBRS, submitted an application to Dr. Orr's office, and waited for a response. Dr. Orr received my application in November, evaluated my references, and then consulted Mrs. Glover about my potential skills and abilities. She agreed that I could be an asset to their laboratory, if I was interested in doing cancer research. Dr. Orr wanted to interview me first to determine my long-term goals, before he made a decision.

I received a letter stating that an interview was needed to complete the process, and I immediately thought about what I could say to "impress" him, so he would hire me. It didn't take long to come up with some of the boldest statements I had ever spoken to someone up until that point. I practiced and prepared for the interview, went over my tempo and words every day. The day of the interview, I arrived at Dr. Orr's office, which was located in the *Kountz-Kyle Science Building*, and waited about ten minutes before he was able to see me. When I greeted him, I shook his hand and sat down.

Dr. Orr mentioned that my references from Mrs. Whatley and Mr. Lott were very positive, and Mrs. Glover felt I had great potential to work in his laboratory. He read more facts in my application packet and then asked me "What makes you special and different from any other student that applied for this position?" I didn't think, I just spoke and told him that if he hired me, *"I will find a cure for AIDS before I graduate!"* I was obsessed with AIDS research and desired to be in a laboratory that did groundbreaking work in this field.

Dr. Orr paused and looked strangely in my eyes and asked me the same question again. I replied the same way, *"I will find a cure for AIDS before I graduate!"* Dr. Orr said, "Come on, I'm serious." I said, "I'm serious too!" with as much conviction as I had ever used in my life. Dr. Orr paused again and tried for a third time to get me to change my original statement, but I didn't. He then told me about his expectations for his laboratory students, and said he would let me know if I got the position.

I left the office feeling "proud" of what I said, hoping that it had enough "shock" value to make him listen. Years later, I talked with Dr. Orr about that conversation. He told me he was surprised I would say something so bold, considering the fact that I hadn't finished one semester of undergraduate work. He was also puzzled by my response, because world-renowned scientists, with medical and doctorate degrees, struggled to even understand how the human immunodeficiency virus (HIV) infects people, causes Acquired Immune Deficiency Syndrome (AIDS), and has led to a worldwide pandemic.

Dr. Clifton Orr

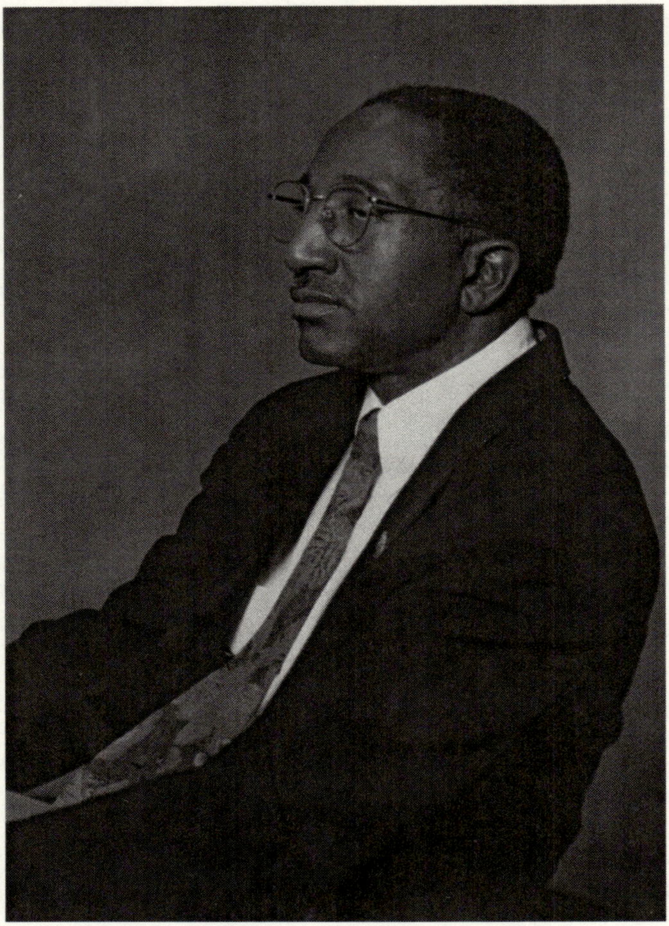

He said he couldn't believe I was so arrogant to think that I could accomplish a task of that magnitude, before getting my first set of grades on the university level. Dr. Orr also told me that he thought I was either crazy, or one of the most talented people he had ever seen. Lucky for me, he chose the other side of his judgment and hired me as a research assistant, during the second semester of my first-year at UAPB. Now, I had the best of both worlds. I was in the laboratory of the Chairman of the Biology Department, and my outrageous gamble paid off. This opportunity allowed me to get experience, money, and a sense of accomplishment I could brag about. I also felt more secure when other students talked about their reliability on band scholarships to pay their tuition and fees, knowing I had additional resources.

The first semester at UAPB, I did average work in my science classes and other general introductory courses. Band was easy because I was dedicated, so I earned A's in Marching Band and Applied Music. The travel schedule lightened up near the end of the marching season and one of our last performances was Homecoming[17]. I was musically exhausted from our schedule like most students, and looked forward to more relaxed rehearsals and time to study.

I finished my first semester at UAPB, with a 3.13 GPA, and was satisfied with my work and travels, but still felt the urge to be more active and involved on campus. I was still hung up on my limited fame in high school, as the band president. At UAPB, I felt like a long road was ahead of me to become more popular and achieve more recognition in a band dominated by upperclassmen.

I vowed to take a different approach, during my second semester, and was excited about our long Christmas break. The university winter break was more than a month long. I rested and thought about what the next semester would be like in the band and doing research in Dr. Orr's lab. I went to UAPB two or three times a week, during the break, just to walk the campus. I spent the rest of my time with my best friends from high school.

My closest friends started an organization called PBH, also known as Prosperity, Brotherhood, and Harmony. PBH's overall goals were to maintain close friendships; learn as much as possible about politics, history, education, science, and finance; leave Pine Bluff; and eventually

---

17 Homecoming- is an annual celebration by colleges and universities to honor their alumni. This celebration usually includes a ceremonial football game, parades, and parties.

return to stake claim on the city. I don't remember how I was chosen to participate, but think most of us had a common connection because we were in the band in middle and high school. We also didn't run in the usual cliques of more popular students.

We tried to do our own thing, and I was selected sixth out of eight people. Just like the *Beatles*, we all had very different personalities, in our private lives, and in the community. *Kevin* came up with the concept for PBH following our graduation from high school, in the spring of 1990. He was one of the most popular members of the group, although somewhat conservative, meticulous, and quiet. Kevin was talented and effective in public relations and responsible for organizing PBH, by selecting and endorsing members. He was also the most visible, because he often drove classic cars, and was one of our main sources of transportation.

Keith was principal founder and the brains behind PBH. He was an active leader and nicknamed us *Hustlers*, because we always tried to be innovative and find better ways to support ourselves and our community. *Leon (Jay)* was the spiritual one, who kept us grounded in a core belief in God, but was also politically minded and aware of current events. *Sedrick* was the flashy one, with a nose for finance, and whose personality and clothes were magnets for young ladies. Many women our age thought he was one of the most sensitive and caring guys they had ever met. Kevin, Keith, Sedrick, and Jay were PBH's four founders. Newer members were only selected by nomination from current members, led by Kevin's endorsement and Keith's vision.

Greg was selected next. He was a happy-go-lucky person, nonchalant about life, and never letting things get him down. He was also one of the smartest members of the group, a very quick learner and gifted academically. I was selected after Greg, following Kevin's endorsement. Years later, I discovered that they selected me because I was not deeply involved in any particular organization and was independent.

John was selected seventh and deeply involved in the military and R.O.T.C. in high school. He was focused on Aeronautics and wanted to fly jet planes off aircraft carriers. *Ralph* was the final pick and the only athlete selected. Ralph was unique because he played football, as a defensive lineman, and also sang in the choir. He was incredibly competitive in sports and in music. While the rest of the brothers played instruments, he used his voice to entertain. Ralph also had a powerful mind and ideas, as it related to history, politics, and religion. He could express relevant and timely facts as easily as he said his name.

Four Tubas, a Guitar, and a Gallery of Cheerleaders

When PBH discussed matters of state or the economy, Ralph could always offer us fresh perspectives on issues, without emotion, basing his arguments primarily on the facts, with an equal measure of common sense. PBH was the talk of many circles in the Bluff, as others tried to duplicate our chemistry. The eight of us were special. Our goal not to be in the normal cliques brought more attention to us. Spending time with PBH, during the break, helped me pass the time, and it was great fellowshipping with real friends. I was re-energized to start my second semester at UAPB.

The spring semester began in January and I began work in Dr. Orr's laboratory, under Mrs. Glover's direct supervision. I had an opportunity to be exposed, for the first time in my life, to cancer research and was happy that I could live up to one of my high school goals. I didn't have many laboratory skills and tried to learn as fast as I could. I was prepared to learn from great mentoring from Mrs. Whatley and Dr. Fitzpatrick. In Dr. Orr's laboratory, we worked with bladder cancer cells.

My project was to study the effects of anti-cancer agents on the growth of these cells in culture. We used high power microscopes and ultra-filtration units to protect the cancer cells from exposure to outside air and contamination before, during, and after they were grown. I thought the equipment was the coolest thing, because it felt like I worked for a biohazard facility, in the Centers for Disease Control (CDC).

Now that I worked directly for Dr. Orr, he was more involved in mentoring and advising my course work. We talked at length about my career goals and he recommended I take *Biochemistry*, as one of my core subjects, to prepare me for medical school. I didn't want to take this class, because I didn't like chemistry. The thought of biology somehow being merged with chemistry, didn't interest me at all. Chemistry to me was all about complex structures and formulas. I felt it would be hard for me to approach *Biochemistry* with *"any sense of purpose."* That semester, I registered for *English Composition II, Career and Life Planning, General Botany*, taught by Dr. Fitzpatrick, *College Trigonometry, General Chemistry II*, and the usual band classes.

Dr. Orr talked with me about why I enrolled in *Chemistry II*, before finishing *Chemistry I*, and to discover how my long-term plan and this course of action made any sense. I explained to him that I wanted to avoid chemistry all together my first semester. I was afraid that *Biochemistry* would delay my graduation date, if I didn't do well in the class. Dr. Orr paused during our conversation and shared some experiences he had in graduate school and was adamant about me enrolling into *Biochemistry*. I didn't budge and explained that I didn't like chemistry and would rather take Chemistry II and work hard to keep up, instead of taking *Biochemistry*.

Dr. Orr was disappointed with my decision, but allowed me to proceed and didn't override my course selections, which was well within his right to do. I was so headstrong that he couldn't change my mind. This was university work and I could succeed or fail based on my decisions. Dr. Orr left me with these words that still resonate with me today *"You will need Biochemistry one day, and if you don't take it now at UAPB, it may come back to bite you!"* I dismissed his words as another tactic to try to get me to take an elective course. I knew *"where I was going and what I was doing,"* so I enrolled in Chemistry II instead.

My schedule was now completely full with the band concert season starting and my new job in the laboratory. I was elated to have so much to do and now that the marching band season was over, the rehearsals were more relaxed. Wash was the concert band conductor and though the rehearsals weren't as long, they were definitely more rigorous and required more concentration. Wash's philosophy was "balance in sound" and he worked to get us to stop blasting through the instruments, as some of us did during the football season. Wash wanted more finesse in the way we played music. He instructed us to do more lip slurring drills and long tones to establish consistent sounds, in preparation for upcoming concerts.

Concert season was always fun for me because I could enjoy making music. By the time we settled into playing concertos and long concert pieces, our schedule changed and we began performing at public relation events. I thought marching band was over, but we geared up again for a parade out of state, to help promote the school and band. I traveled with the band before but our next trip was one of the most memorable experiences of my life. This trip was to the *Mardi Gras* celebration in New Orleans, Louisiana, as a participant in the Rex Parade[18].

---

18 The Rex Parade- occurs during the annual *Mardi Gras* celebration, was originally established in 1872, and follows the Zulu parade. The major route of the Rex follows St. Charles Street, in downtown New Orleans, Louisiana.

Four Tubas, a Guitar, and a Gallery of Cheerleaders

Marching in the Mardi Gras

Doc Miller acquired some resources for our trip to the *"Big Easy,"* and we prepared the best we could, after the marching band season. Doc Miller made sure we rode comfortably in chartered buses to the event. The trip wasn't as exciting as before, because I was used to traveling and performing with the band. When we arrived in New Orleans, I was happy but still a bit weary from a long marching season and rigorous concert band rehearsals. The upperclassmen tried to scare first year musicians, such as myself, by saying that the parade was ten to twenty miles long. The rumor was that the band wouldn't stop to rest, and the heat would be unbearable. I never thought a lot about what they were saying and lined up where the drum majors instructed. My goal was to give no more of my energy to the rumors, until I realized the parade was actually as long as suspected.

Before the parade began, the first thing I noticed was how hot and humid it was in New Orleans. Then I noticed how many people were lined up along the parade route, as far as I could see. There were miles and miles of people on both sides of *St. Charles Avenue* dressed in *Mardi Gras* attire. The *krewes*[19] were visible everywhere in the city. I learned then that all the shops and stores closed during the festivities, so everyone could attend the parades. Because of parade formation, the tubas were stationed at the back of the band for support, in front of the percussion section.

When the Rex parade began, I had so much energy and vigor that I couldn't fathom ever getting tired, due to my excitement. I was distracted by the pageantry and colorful costumes and masks worn by people. My bigger goal was at hand, and that was to finish the parade strong. I had marched in previous parades and saw this event no differently. The hand-decorated floats adorned in purple, gold, and green were some of the most beautiful and vivid colors I had ever seen. With each step, I realized that being in the marching band exposed me to one of the premiere parades of that year's *Mardi Gras* celebration.

I started the parade high-stepping fairly well, as we played *Do What You Wanna*, seemingly every other block, because of its popularity. The drum major kept calling that musical selection, but I wondered as we passed each block, when the parade would end. I just knew the upperclassmen

---

19 *Krewes-* are marching, walking, and masking clubs that participate in Mardi Gras celebrations and parades.

were joking with me about the length of the parade, but something told me that I was in for a long day's work. By the time we reached the half-way point, I was so tired I couldn't lift my legs. It was so hot that if we hadn't trained like professional athletes, many of us would have passed out and required medical attention.

My feet felt like they were on fire, my armature was gone, and if we played *Do What You Wanna* one more time, I was going to lose my mind. But we pressed on, and I remember that at some point we paused because the traffic ahead of us stalled. People on the floats were throwing beads and having a good time, but my biggest concern was to stop moving and try to figure out what was burning on the bottom of my feet.

I marched through the pain. Several miles later I finished the parade and realized that sometimes *"people give advice not to deceive, but to educate."* Many of my band mates were from New Orleans. They were unusually silent on the bus. I guess they were tired, but excited to get a free trip home. I think they knew what to expect and relished in the fact that many of us didn't. Marching in the Rex Parade, during *Mardi Gras*, was one of the most memorable experiences for me at UAPB and my first exposure to culture outside of Arkansas.

When we got back to the Bluff, time seemed to stand still and I was back to business. The rest of the semester went by pretty fast. I tried to relax and enjoy the concert band season and spend more time with PBH. I wasn't as apprehensive about my studies and still felt I made the right decision about the *Biochemistry* class. I did take for granted my previous mentoring relationship with Dr. Fitzpatrick, which was a mistake, and I didn't do very well in his Botany class.

The semester ended, and I earned a 2.76 GPA and a cumulative GPA of 2.94, for the year. I was concerned because I wasn't setting the academic bar high, as I first thought. On the flip side, I had a great set of friends, a band community, a job, and there was a 10:1 ratio of women to men on campus. I had no other real complaints, but vowed to do better academically the next year. I wanted to achieve something greater as part of my band experience and that was to become a member of the Epsilon Chi (EX) chapter of Kappa Kappa Psi[20].

---

20 Kappa Kappa Psi- is a national organization of band musicians organized in 1919 at Oklahoma State University. It's goal is to promote the betterment of college and university band programs. The Epsilon Chi (EX) chapter of Kappa Kappa Psi was founded on November 15, 1970 at Agricultural Mechanical and Normal College, now known as the University of Arkansas at Pine Bluff.

Sophomore Year

I was interested in Kappa Kappa Psi (KKΨ since high school. Mr. Lott was a member *Spring '78, Melodic 15*, and always had good things to say about their musical leadership in the band and around the UAPB campus. I also witnessed one of their step-shows, in the Isaac S. Hathaway-John M. Howard Fine Arts Center, which was so dynamic and rhythmic I wanted to join. KKΨ was about band, music, and having fun. No other fraternity encompassed more of my core values. As exciting as the possibility of joining one of the "Big Eight,"[21] I knew the men in blue and white, with a touch of gold, were a definite force at UAPB.

People wondered why KKΨ always won the step-show competitions and were so popular at parties and festivals. What these same people didn't realize was that KKΨ was already rhythmically sound, because they all were musicians. Movement with syncopation, choreography and style were rehearsed every day. I actually was bold enough to think that I could pledge as a first year student and prepared to do just that. Word around the band was that freshmen musicians should be spending their time taking care of academic issues, instead of trying to join a fraternity or sorority. I almost made the ultimate mistake by trying to join anyway, but our rehearsal schedules and my respect for my section leader changed my mind.

I really liked the KKΨ brothers because they would address each other by musical terminology, which was a reflection of their personalities. They called each other names such as *Poco Brion*, *Philharmonic*, *Dr. Largo*, and *Prince Pizzicato*. Members of the musical sorority Tau Beta Sigma (TBΣ) used names such as *Vivace d'Arco*, *Scherzo*, *Amoriso con Bravo Amore*, and *Dolce Con Brio*. Music has a language all its own, so this was a very innovative way to always be connected within the fraternity and sorority. I became well acquainted with *Moe Bass*,[22] an upperclassman bass saxophone player, and the older brother of one of my PBH friends. Moe Bass, also known as *Bass*, was an inspiration for me to join KKΨ.

---

21 "Big Eight"- is a Pan-Hellenic group of nationally organized Black fraternities and sororities including Alpha Phi Alpha, Phi Beta Sigma, Kappa Alpha Psi, Omega Psi Phi, Alpha Kappa Alpha, Delta Sigma Theta, Zeta Phi Beta, and Sigma Gamma Rho.

22 "Moe Bass"- is the musical nickname of Prince Appassionato. He pledged with the 14 Maestros of Sound in the spring of 1989.

Bass tried to caution me to know for sure that I wanted to go through the arduous membership process. I did, and was confident and patient, and waited until my chance finally arrived during the fall semester of my sophomore year.

Joining Kappa Kappa Psi

My first memory of the fraternity pledging process was the *Interest Meeting*, where current KKΨ members screened potential candidates, by asking them thought-provoking trick questions. Often the questions didn't have an answer, but they were used to see how the potential member would respond. I remember arriving thirty minutes early to the first session, and because I wasn't the only one in the band that wanted to join, we had a room full of people. They were just as passionate about music and scared as I was. The meeting began with an introduction and overview of the organization. Then, current members asked questions. Everyone seemed to get a different question and had to stand when answering. I was asked why I wanted to join the fraternity and immediately responded, *"Mr. Lott was my band director in high school, and he said this would be a good opportunity for me to grow as a musician at UAPB."*

The president of KKΨ was presiding over the meeting, looked at me with a smirk, thought about my answer, and told me to sit back down and went to the next person. I thought about how that may have been my only chance to try to "impress" the gatekeepers of a fraternity I really wanted to join. All I could think about in nervousness was the fact that Mr. Lott talked about KKΨ a great deal, hoping to use his influence to get me a chance at membership. After everyone in the room answered questions, the meeting ended and I waited about a week to hear from the fraternity. Fortunately, my gamble paid off. After band rehearsal the next week, I was informed that I met the qualifications to pledge with eighteen others, in the fall of 1991.

Seventeen Psionic Subtones

Fall pledge lines were always unique in the history of the EX chapter of KKΨ, because most membership intake processes took place in the spring of each year. Because of successful recruitment by Doc Miller and Wash, we had one of the largest freshman band classes in over ten years. So to capitalize on new blood, the fraternity wanted to select new members, who would join early in their college careers, and be around to work and support the greater vision of the band and KKΨ before graduating. Meanwhile, my new job in the laboratory was working out great. I saved more money the following semester than I had in years working at the *Shop*. The problem was my grades slipped and because I was still living at home essentially rent free, my father froze my spending privileges and savings. I knew this would be my first problem. In order to pledge any fraternity, the most important thing to have on hand is cash money.

Soon after learning I could pledge, I met the other members of the fall pledge class. Some of them I already knew in passing from band rehearsals. We met to discuss how this pledge process would go and our strategy for gaining membership. Our pledge line would not only be the largest membership class in the history of the EX chapter of KKΨ, but we had the most diverse group of young musicians in the band. Our line consisted of people from Arkansas, Illinois, Louisiana, Michigan, and Missouri.

During this first meeting, people were trying to figure out what would happen to us during the pledge process. I stepped up to the plate and made another bold and presumptuous announcement. I told the group that I had saved plenty of money, from the previous semester, so "we" would be FINE during the pledge process, knowing that I couldn't even get a check to write from my own account. The people in the room looked at me like I was crazy and continued talking amongst themselves about what would happen next. I felt like I had the right to say what I said and took the opportunity to do so. In retrospect, my announcement didn't help the situation.

Eventually, the consensus was that we needed to at least organize. Rumblings started regarding who would lead our group. This time I kept my mouth shut because I didn't want to seem arrogant and foolish. To my surprise, one of my new line brothers recommended me for president of the pledge line, also known as *Line Captain*. I was honored for the recommendation, but really didn't know what the responsibilities of a line captain were, until we met for the first time with our *Dean of Pledges*.

There was no preparation for this meeting. We were told to be at a certain place at a certain time. When we got to a house on the west side of the city, we rang the doorbell and asked to come in. As we walked to the top of the stairs, both drum majors were waiting with their arms crossed and a look of disgust on their faces.

We came into the room in a snaking pattern because there were so many of us. When we finally got organized, the head drum major assessed our large pledge class and asked, "Who is the line captain?" I triumphantly said, "I am!" after my impromptu inauguration. He said, "Do you know what that means?" I said, "Not really." He then described the duties of the position, one of which was being responsible for every other member of the pledge line. This meant that if someone was late, it's my fault. If someone doesn't make it to class, band rehearsal, or misses pledge club and does not act according to the principles outlined for membership in KKΨ, it's my fault.

As he spoke, I wondered if this was a good idea, but it was too late to back out now. The Dean of Pledges told us what to do next and then asked us to quickly leave his house. We were pledging and none of us knew what to expect. I didn't care because at least I was on-line and had an opportunity to become a *Loooooosenecking Humpbacking* member of KKΨ.

Even before we officially started, there were some problems with the pledge process. We lost two members for academic reasons, which affected us because we wanted to be the group that pledged *19 in 1991*, but we had to continue with the seventeen remaining people. So much happened during the pledge process that I couldn't possibly reveal in this book, so I will share an abbreviated version as it relates to my life. The most important thing that happened was the bond that grew between seventeen musicians, who worked hard to continue the legacy of the EX chapter of KKΨ.

Our line pledged for eight long weeks, during one of the most rigorous marching seasons I had ever experienced. We did everything before and after rehearsal; from cleaning the band room, washing cars to raise money for the band, singing songs to the big brothers' girlfriends, and be the best on our instruments. This meant additional hours of practice time each day.

The process required patience, and we were seventeen proud individuals who knew if everything went according to schedule, we would represent the largest line in EX history. What we didn't know was that the current members of KKΨ were frustrated with Doc Miller, as their only fraternity advisor. The older members approached Wash about gaining honorary membership, just so they could maintain their active status with the KKΨ National Office.

Doc Miller was a member of KKΨ, but he steered clear of any

involvement with the EX chapter because he felt it would be a distraction to the band. He also wanted complete oversight and control of all band activities that were once assigned to members of KKΨ. By fraternity law, Doc Miller was the head band director and the automatic advisor. Members scrambled to find a replacement because his future involvement with the fraternity was uncertain. Doc Miller wasn't supportive of increasing membership, in the short-term, which meant our pledge line was in jeopardy. The only other band staffer, who had the personality and charisma to relate to the students and fraternity and was in a musical position to get that responsibility, was Wash. I don't know what was said or how it was said, but Wash became the advisor, soon after becoming a member.

Wash actually joined KKΨ the same time I did in 1991, but he didn't have to do what other pledges did, because of his authority in the band. We were surprised, at one field show rehearsal, to learn that he had already finished the pledging process and was wearing the commemorative fraternity shirt, as an indication of his membership. Our line still had a few more weeks left, before we got our chance to "cross-over," and we stayed the course.

Our love of music and daily efforts to support the music program at UAPB weren't in vain, because on Saturday, October 26, 1991, we became members of the EX chapter of KKΨ and will forever be known as the Seventeen Psionic Subtones.

Sederick C. Rice

Kappa Kappa Psi
Seventeen Psionic Subtones, Fall '91
Largest and most diverse pledge line to date in EX history.
A Bionic Musical Style.
"As One Divided By None"
"It's Hard, But It's Fair!"

John Williams-	Deliristic Prelude	Percussion
Eric Epps-	Dr. Deuce	Trumpet
Kendall Perry-	Tre'	Saxophone
Sederick C. Rice -	Prince Serpentes "Bass"	Sousaphone
Antyonne Collins-	FREAKKΨ Hypedelic Fortismatic Con Fucco Funk Aeolian A# Minor	Saxophone
Morio Snelling-	Molto Mosso	Saxophone
Ledelle Turner-	Sotto Voce Affectuoso	Percussion
Christopher Giles-	Dynamic Exoticism	Clarinet
Ramone Brown-	East St. Louis Psi	Trombone
David Thompson III-	Count Bass "X"	Sousaphone
Dennis Johnson-	"D"-	Natural Trumpet
Donnie August-	FantaPsi	French Horn
Theodore Johnson-	Sir Fresco Virtuoso	Trombone
Arthur Johnson-	PΨmpy Psi	Percussion
Kenyan Rodgers-	Islamic Psi	Percussion
Akiem Scruggs-	Portporio Al Fine	Percussion
Maurice Posley-	Tail Psi	French Horn
Kelvin W. Washington	Advisor/Honorary	Band Director
Chris Neal (EP-EX)	Drum major "Beam Me Up Scottie"	Dean of Pledges

I was proud of my membership in KKΨ and role as line-captain. What didn't dawn on me was how I neglected my studies throughout the process. My role in KKΨ took a toll on my motivation to study. Dr. Orr really watched my progress in all of my classes that semester, because during the previous semester, I let my grades slip. He told me he was starting to wonder about his decision to hire me to work in his laboratory. All of my introductory classes were done, but I was still enrolled in *American Government, General Chemistry I, Health and Safety, Biological Research, Comparative Anatomy*, band classes, but still no *Biochemistry*.

Comparative Anatomy was one of my core classes for graduation and was taught by a very strict professor. I didn't take it seriously because of my time pledging. By mid-term, which was the bulk of my pledging period, I knew I wasn't doing well. Dr. Orr called me into his office and asked me specifically about Comparative Anatomy and how I was progressing. I told him I was doing "FINE," which in real terms means *Frantically In Need of Extra credit* because all of my test scores were low. Dr. Orr paused and said "OK," but in the back of my mind I knew I was lying.

I didn't realize that he was still the chairman of the department and had already seen every biology majors' mid-term grades, including mine, which was why he asked the question. I mulled over what I said to him and tried to work daily in the laboratory. We didn't have very much interaction after that, until my conscience compelled me to discuss the matter with Mrs. Glover. I told her what the situation was and she recommended that I write him a letter of apology, because I lied to him about my grades and progress.

Mrs. Glover also let me know that he already knew what my grades were and this situation wouldn't create a good work environment. I took Mrs. Glover's advice and wrote a heartfelt letter expressing my sorrow, guilt, and anguish about misleading and lying to him. I ended the letter vowing to work harder in the near future. I don't think Dr. Orr ever acknowledged that he received the letter, but I know he was disappointed in me, much more than I was in myself. This changed our relationship, but he was still supportive.

I couldn't rebound after the mid-term, and by the end of the semester I earned an F in Comparative Anatomy. This grade significantly changed my approach to college work because not only did I lie about my grades to the person that could help me learn to be a better student and write great letters of recommendation, but I failed a very important class. The semester ended and I earned a 2.29 GPA, and a 2.72 cumulative GPA.

This academic and professional mistake would be hard to recover from in the coming months.

By the time the spring semester began in January, I was back in band mode for concert season, but apprehensive about devoting too much time to music and the fraternity. I had already done irreparable damage to my GPA. It would take stellar work to bring it up to standards. I worked so hard to get into KKΨ, but now most of my line brothers and older members never saw me because I was devoted to my books and studying. I enrolled in *Genetics, Histology,* and *Intro to Social Science,* to stay on track for graduation. I really wanted to redeem myself. I did become more involved in writing and decided to take *Advanced Composition,* which was an upper level creative writing class.

Most of my writings were poems. I was able to combine words, syllables, and phrases that everyone in the class seemed to enjoy. I tried to tell stories with a rhyme, using my personal experiences as the material. That was a good time for me, because I just wrote whatever I felt and enjoyed the freedom to express myself on paper. Writing was also a great distraction from daily band rehearsals, as I worked diligently in the laboratory to make up for my missteps of the past year. I was finally more receptive for tutelage and advice from Dr. Orr.

UAPB vs. the NCAA

Across the campus, there was a buzz with faculty and students leading to speculation that our successful football program, led by Archie "Gunslinger" Cooley, had violated various NCAA rules. The fear was that the university would be punished accordingly. I never knew what the charges were, but after months of deliberation there was an announcement that UAPB had received the NCAA Death Sentence[23] and lost their football program for the next year. This news created a somber mood across the campus, as the football staff reorganized and people resigned, including Archie Cooley.

The band changed as well. Doc Miller and Archie Cooley were

---

23 The National Collegiate Athletic Association Death Sentence- was a reprimand to colleges and universities for violating the rules of order and conduct set by the NCAA. This ruling normally meant a loss of part or all of an athletic program for at least one year following an investigation of misconduct by colleges or university administrators and their coaches or players.

Four Tubas, a Guitar, and a Gallery of Cheerleaders

a package deal. They both gained considerable favor with school administration officials and accented each other. One developed a stronger football program than experienced in many years, while the other reorganized a marching band to act as an ambassador, for the university, and counterpart to sports programs. Miller and Cooley both received a great deal of support from the president of the university. When allegations of wrongdoing were verified, there was a shift in that support, to the point that some housecleaning took place. Doc Miller was one of the casualties just like Cooley.

The atmosphere of the band changed dramatically as assistants in the music department jockeyed for position to be the next head band director. I remember that although Wash was the driving force behind our musical success, he was stalled from getting the leadership position. We weren't happy about that decision. The tables were turning and as Doc Miller cleared out his office and made arrangements to relocate to another job, the fight for sovereignty within the band continued.

During the mayhem, one of the assistants tried to conduct band rehearsal, but the students refused to play. We tried to send a message to the rest of the band staff that Wash should be our head band director and we wouldn't accept anyone else. Wash returned to the band room and our rehearsal proceeded as planned, but I knew that our successes of the past didn't matter. We would have to establish a new legacy without a football team.

Wash decided to stay on as band director, on an interim basis. The bulk of Doc Miller's staff left. Wash was a lone soldier, who was now responsible for dwindling recruitment numbers because of the loss of football, and a lack of staff to support the marching and concert band programs. He embraced his new role. Students, including members of my pledge line, rallied around Wash and followed his instructions. Musically, we were actually much better as a band because we reduced in size to about sixty musicians. Wash was now able to concentrate more on the weaker players. We rehearsed balance and still could compete with larger marching bands. Unfortunately, even with our best efforts it would be more than a year before our small group would be able to say that we challenged another band.

I was disappointed about the chaos that pervaded the band, but was busy in the laboratory. Time moved slow as I prepared to travel to Washington, D.C. to participate in my first scientific meeting, organized by the MARC/MBRS program. I was excited about the meeting because it would be the first time I traveled by plane since high school, and the first time I visited Washington, D.C. I didn't present any work, but money was available for me to get exposure to the work of other MARC/MBRS students around the country.

Kevin was a chemistry major and member of MARC, so he also went on this trip. It was cool because we were roommates, so when sessions ended we walked around the city. Our meeting was the same weekend of Howard University's Homecoming, so the downtown area was buzzing with people. This wasn't the first time I experienced an HBCU Homecoming, which is always festive, fun, and memorable, but it was the first time I saw riot police march to disrupt crowds of African-Americans peaceably celebrating a yearly event.

I remember looking down from the window of my hotel room and saw bootstrap commandos in riot gear, brandishing clear plastic shields to push crowds of people away from the downtown business district. The police demanded that everyone leave the area immediately by loudspeaker, or they would be arrested. Eventually, the crowd dispersed and there were no other incidents.

I learned a lot that weekend about being in a different place and was more comfortable traveling outside the state of Arkansas. I don't know what was preventing me from wanting to leave Arkansas. I think it was because my friends and relatives were there and I knew that life would always be somewhat predictable. Fortunately, I got more opportunities to leave my comfort zone and experience more things in and out of the state. I returned to the Bluff and was more resolved about my experiences in Washington and anxious to grow on a social and personal level.

The semester ended. I did much better in classes than the previous term. I was gearing up for my junior year, which was a turning point and more than halfway to graduation. I was more comfortable in the laboratory and worked in the fraternity as the business manager. My first priority of the fall semester was to retake *Comparative Anatomy*. I wanted to replace the F earned the first time.

Junior Year

The start of my junior year was probably my most productive and rewarding at UAPB. I was more motivated to achieve great things and my goal to lead the fraternity was one step closer. I was nominated that year to be the vice-president of the fraternity, which meant I would also serve as Assistant Dean of Pledges. I felt if I played my cards right, I would one day become president. Our band schedule was really up in the air. We didn't have a football team and would only travel minimally out of the state. Wash was creative and made sure we at least played at events, to give our band some exposure, and keep the musicians interested.

During our improvised marching season, we played at small events around the city and state. We even did a half-time show at my former high school. Many of our events that year were designed for future recruiting. Our small band ensemble also took bus trips to Louisiana to perform as the featured band, in local *Battle of the Bands* contests. Most of our members understood that as soon as we crossed the Arkansas-Louisiana state line, the featured band was always *The Human Jukebox*. It was only respectful to pay homage to Dr. Greggs because of his influence on Wash.

That year, I was appointed section leader of the tubas, so I endured additional scrutiny from Wash to be the best on my instrument and make others in the section better. Wash knew I had been in the band for a while, and sometimes felt I knew more than he did. He made it clear that he was in control of the band and I was his student. He treated me fairly and expected me to maintain a high level of leadership and excellence, to be an example for others. The more responsibility I got from band, the more I was interested in experiencing different things.

I also spent more time with PBH because I wasn't traveling as much and the majority of my friends were still in the Bluff. Ralph, John, and Sedrick were the only members we didn't see often. We stayed in touch during school breaks and holidays. Greg, Keith, Kevin, Jay, and I also wanted to be more informed. Our collective interests turned to seeking information about the *Masons*, who we felt were the most connected and respected organization in the community.

We were nervous about joining because their work and influence appeared to be clouded in secrecy. I talked to Moe Bass about the Masons. I knew my grandfather was a member, but I didn't want to ask him about them. My grandfather never talked about what they did, so I thought one of my older fraternity brothers would be more informative. Unfortunately, Moe Bass was just as mysterious about the organization as my grandfather was. I was amazed at how even the slightest notion about the group was presented with vague allegories. Not knowing was exciting but stressful to us, so joining the Masons would be a learning experience.

Moe Bass told me he would bring up my membership in the next meeting and let me know what they decided. I found out afterwards that the only way to become a *Prince Hall Free and Accepted Mason* was to ask a member about the rules and regulations of membership. Some members donned bumper stickers that read, *To Be One, Ask One!* Becoming a Mason was definitely something I thought about a great deal. There was so much on my plate, that what I wanted to do had to wait for what I needed to do. I let the notion of my membership, in the Masons subside and turned my attentions to my studies and ΚΚΨ.

This semester, I was back in the flow of my biology curriculum and enrolled in *Comparative Anatomy* to repeat it. *Organic Chemistry I, General Psychology*, and *Special Topics* were the next courses I had to take. After learning from previous mistakes, I didn't let the fraternity or other outside influences change my new approach to my studies. I was the vice-president of ΚΚΨ and wanted to exercise my power, but my role was strictly for backup, in case the president couldn't fulfill his duties. The semester went by quickly. I did what I needed to do in all of my classes and learned a great deal about managing the fraternity. My hard work and focus paid off and I ended the semester with 3.31 GPA. My overall cumulative GPA rose to 3.02. I earned a B in *Comparative Anatomy*, which replaced my previous F. This was a great accomplishment, but my love for music was strong and I looked forward to the spring concert season.

Without football, the marching season was dull, but I knew the band ensembles would be more active. Wash liked marching band but really enjoyed directing concerts and helping us become better musicians. I was proud of my progress, for the fall semester, and knew that as long I stayed focused, I could maintain high standards. My mission was to push toward my long-term goals.

The spring semester began without any real problems. Concert band was in full swing and we sounded great. Our small numbers helped Wash divide more resources allotted for the music program. More time was also spent training better players. We worked daily on sound and balance. Wash required all of us to tune our instruments before each rehearsal. One day Wash approached me about a position in the instrument room as the caretaker. He said I would be responsible for cataloguing the instruments, before and after rehearsals. I told him I would do it under the condition that I would still be able to perform with the concert band.

It was kind of strange spending time in the instrument room, while the band warmed up. I didn't mind but was careful about the new position and tried to do it to the best of my abilities. To me it seemed elementary, but Wash and the music department was adamant about monitoring the use of band instruments. I never expected additional compensation for the work I did, but Wash had his own ideas.

Nearly two weeks into the semester, I remember when Wash spoke to his assistant, Mr. Elliott in the band room, as I catalogued instruments that had been checked in. As I stood there working, Wash walked up to Mr. Elliot and showed him a figure regarding my scholarship for the spring. Mr. Elliott acknowledged the figure with a smile, as Wash walked out of the room. The next week my band scholarship increased.

To me it was a great surprise and meant that I would finally have enough money, after paying tuition, to buy a car. I was so thankful for the money and grateful to Wash that I tried to do the best job I could in the instrument room. I used that money to help buy a red 1985 Toyota Hatchback. I never forgot the confidence Wash showed in me, and how the extra money helped a struggling college student be successful. Without that scholarship, my college years would have been very different and I credit Wash's generosity then and now as a major key to my success in life.

Things were going great in school and my mind was pretty focused. My feeling was that the worst was over and there was nowhere to go but up. I practiced and rehearsed my music and studied late into the night. My father was very critical of my time management skills and felt I spent too much time hanging out with my friends in PBH. I told him everything was **FINE** and that he shouldn't worry, because "I knew what I was doing." To ease some of his concerns, my friends began studying at my house, so he could see I wasn't wasting time. One evening after rehearsal, Kevin and I got some food and he dropped me off at home. I had a test the next day, so we talked about catching up later. When I arrived home, nothing was unusual. My father was gone and I had a quiet house to work and study in.

3 Knocks at the House Door

Around 9 p.m., someone struck the house door, with three distinctive and loud knocks. I wondered why they hit the door so hard, and why they paused after hitting the door three times in succession. I finally opened the door and it was Mr. Fred Lowe. I vaguely recognized him and he asked if he could talk with me. I invited him in as a courtesy, but he stood in the entrance of the door and said, *"It has been brought to my attention that you are interested in Freemasonry. I am here to inform you that your name has been submitted for consideration in our lodge."* Mr. Lowe stood upright and spoke with a powerful deep voice. His chest was stuck out, and his feet angled perpendicular towards me. Mr. Lowe spoke to me as if he had known me all of my life.

I didn't recall when I first met Mr. Lowe, but he reminded me that he knew my grandfather very well. Once he mentioned my grandfather, I remembered the conversation we had about my future. Our new conversation was brief, but his words and actions left a lasting impression on me. He demonstrated strength, knowledge, and secrecy in his demeanor. Mr. Lowe asked me to meet him later to talk, and told me to bring my friends, who were also interested in becoming Masons. He wanted to talk with all of us before we went further in the process. The next week, Kevin, Jay, and I met with Mr. Lowe. It was interesting because we thought the Masons were the most powerful organization in the city and more influential than the fraternities and sororities at UAPB.

Our meeting seemed to be an example of that because Mr. Lowe met us at UAPB and literally walked into one of my former professor's offices and said he needed to use the room. I presume the professor was a Mason, and remember seeing Masonic insignias on one of his rings. He acknowledged Mr. Lowe, left the office, and closed the door. Once things settled down, Mr. Lowe tried to explain to us what it meant to be a Free and Accepted Prince Hall Mason[24]. We asked several questions, most of which revolved around the secrecy of the organization. As Mr. Lowe talked, we knew it would take a level head and hours of study to become a Mason. I didn't say it, but was still a little skeptical and wanted to make sure I was doing the right thing. Kevin and Jay seemed ready, but I decided to talk to Dr. L.K. Solomon, pastor of Indiana Street Baptist Church. Dr. Solomon was very positive about the Masons and gave me some clear examples of their role in the community. He also explained how there were many rumors circulating about their activities, but for the most part they were distinguished and respected men in the city. Dr. Solomon's words were definitive enough for me. I was resolved to start the

---

[24] Free and Accepted Prince Hall Masonry- was organized by Prince Hall, who was from the British West Indies and responsible for organizing membership for Blacks in the Masonic order during the War of Independence. Now Prince Hall lodges number more than 4,000 worldwide and are active in 44 independent jurisdictions, with over 300,000 members.

process to become a Mason. It was cool because all of my closest friends would go through the process with me. Keith eventually joined us and we all registered at the same time. Once we were accepted into membership, we learned so much about God, family, and what it meant to be an upright man in the community. People often wondered why we studied so much and met so often at the lodge. So much happened during that process that it would be too much to mention in this book, and out of respect for the organization, I won't go into any more details.

What I will say is that the process took three months, from the time our initiation started, until we completed training. I did make one mistake, after taking the first steps in Masonry. Following our first meeting and education session, we learned about the first sets of tools a Mason uses, when presenting himself to other Masons in public. I was so excited to finally know something about the organization.

After that meeting, I went to my grandfather's shop to show him what I had learned. I was "green," but knew my grandfather was a Mason and hoped he would finally discuss the organization with me. I walked into his office as he sat there watching television. I told him I had just become an Entered Apprentice in *Haygood Lodge #407*, where he was a member. He slowly lowered the television volume and looked at me with a strange grin.

I didn't know what he was thinking, so I tried to show him what I had learned that night. I remember saying "Hey granddaddy, look at this!" I presented one sign that entry-level Masons give to each other to communicate. I just knew he would recognize it and share some of his Masonic wisdom. My grandfather did the opposite. With a cold stare he said, *"You are already doing wrong!"*

I didn't know how to take that and he never explained. What he was probably saying was that I didn't know enough to be "throwing signs" and expecting other Masons to respond. He gave me that infamous look which meant *"Boy you have so much more to learn."* I never did that again, but that experience helped me be more cautious and humble with the powerful and iconic symbols in Masonry. Kevin, Keith, Jay, Greg, and I were accepted as Entered Apprentices. We learned and were passed as Fellowcrafts, and eventually raised to the sublime degree of Prince Hall Affiliated Master Masons, in April 1992.

Becoming a Mason made me more focused on my image in the community. I changed the way I dressed, spoke, and worked. Eventually, I was appointed Treasurer of the Lodge, which was an honor for someone as young as I was at the time. The older members in the lodge, including Mr. Lowe, focused on the role of God, work, and family in our lives. The Masonic Order gave me the knowledge and tools to interpret the true meaning of KKΨ and other fraternities and sororities around campus. I was empowered to do great things. Joining the lodge was a great boost to my morale and focus, which was reflected in my grades. I ended my junior year at UAPB with a semester GPA of 3.06 and a cumulative GPA of 3.03.

The next semester I would be a senior, and was so excited. My first goal was to become president of the EX chapter of KKΨ. After hours of debate and deliberation, my dream came true. The brothers of KKΨ voted me to the highest post in the fraternity. Once the votes were in, I spent days thinking about the fraternity and how I would influence the band and my brothers in music.

Next year would be my last at UAPB, so my goal was to do big things. My first priority was to prepare for medical school and try to market myself as much as possible. I was confident in my abilities, but knew I didn't have the focus of some students and would have to work very hard to compete with them. I used band scholarships, my stipend from working with MBRS, and hard work to pay for my education up until that point.

Although I did well in classes during the semester and recovered from a few messes, I still felt there was so much I didn't choose to learn. I never enrolled in *Biochemistry*, which was a splinter in the back of my mind. I reflected on the words of warning from Dr. Orr, which served as a constant reminder of a decision that could have a much bigger impact on my life. As bad as I felt about that decision, my focus was to graduate on time and have fun doing it. I felt my senior year would be my defining moment as a student.

Senior Year

I started my senior year on a real high as president of KKΨ. My work in the Masonic lodge as treasurer was productive, and football was back at UAPB. I was happy to be able to end my college career in the band as it had begun, and my role as president was what I always wanted. I took the job very seriously. I felt my goals were clear and knew my experiences helped me understand the challenges the fraternity faced. Wash was busy with new band recruits, as KKΨ became a larger part of his support network. Wash was independent and lacked staff, but still tried to bring new students up to speed musically, as quickly as possible.

Some of my classmates felt upperclassmen pride and thought we were in a position to tell first year musicians what to do, without following the same rules. Wash made it very clear that tenure in the band is not an excuse for lax musical behavior. He made all the students feel apart of his program. Just because we had been in the band longer than the new talent, it made our responsibilities greater. Wash expected a higher level of excellence. Wash also depended on us to set the tone for musicianship. With this in mind, I spent more time in the band room and was more involved in the day-to-day operations of our musical program.

I felt I was neglecting my other work, and tried to stay busy in my classes and in the laboratory. That semester, I enrolled in *Cell Biology*, *Developmental Biology*, *Calculus I*, and *General Physics I*. My focus and plan was to try to do everything possible with the band. I led the tuba section and felt Wash was confident in my abilities to prepare other players for our performances. He allowed me to schedule sectionals to review difficult pieces of music, with other players, and gave me freedom to create and play new songs.

My Toyota hatchback was more useful than first imagined. I would take my instrument apart and place it completely in the back seat of the car, while I traveled back and forth to campus. I could practice anywhere my car could go, including the football field, park, or sometimes right in front of my house. My car was unique and useful even though my friends teased me because my front driver's side window didn't work. The window was held up by a wooden stick. When removed, the glass would drop into the door panel. Luckily, the window never broke. I didn't mind the teasing and jokes, because the car did what it was supposed to do; get me from point A to point B.

Later in the semester, I scheduled a meeting with Dr. Orr to discuss my future goal to get into medical school, as my undergraduate career was winding down. I hoped to take the Medical College Acceptance Test (MCAT) and apply for a slot at the University of Arkansas for Medical Sciences (UAMS), in the fall of the next year. Dr. Orr encouraged me to apply to UAMS, because he had some connections with the school, and knew they were trying to diversify their student populations. I thought it would be cool to go to medical school in Arkansas, primarily because I would be closer to home, family and friends. I lost ambition for USC and just wanted to go where I could get in, hopefully somewhere close to the Bluff.

One Saturday that semester the football team traveled out of state, and the band stayed behind. I had some free time to try to prepare for my future medical school career. I took that opportunity to drive to UAMS, which was located about forty minutes away, in Little Rock, to attend a meeting Dr. Orr set up for me, with the UAMS Dean of Students. I arrived on time and was prompt because I wanted to make a good impression. The dean's staff assistant asked me to wait about ten minutes, then ushered me into the office. The dean introduced himself and told me that he knew Dr. Orr very well. We made small talk for a couple of minutes, joked about the state of Arkansas and the Razorbacks, and then he asked me what I wanted to do in my career.

I paused and spoke with as much conviction as I had used since my first year at UAPB. I honestly said, "I want to cure AIDS!," which was still a passion for me, even though my science experience focused on cancer research. The dean paused, before he spoke in rebuttal. He asked me the same question as Dr. Orr had done three years prior. I continued to give him the same answer. I didn't know at the time how to articulate my desire to do AIDS research or become a physician specializing in Virology to study the HIV virus.

The one-sided conversation continued. I just knew my exuberance would be enough to "impress" the dean, so he would offer me a slot in the medical school. I was in for a shock, because I didn't understand how the medical school entrance process worked. Instead of encouraging my magnanimous dreams, he encouraged me to talk with some *"Minorities!"* At first I was waiting for the punch line, but it never came. I just looked at him with a puzzled expression, as he continued to ask me the same question related to eating and talking with some *"Minorities."* We never got past that point and eventually ended the conversation. I had nothing else to say. The dean ushered me to the door and kept directing me to go eat and talk with some *"Minorities,"* which puzzled me, so I declined.

As I think back now, and will give him the benefit of the doubt, I believe he was trying to encourage me to visit with students, who shared my background and experience, and were already engaged in the medical school process. I also think he wanted me to talk with people, who could answer my questions and help me structure my focus a little better for medical school. I didn't feel the same way, at that time, and felt he was dismissing my interests and dreams.

This was my first real interview outside of the protection of Dr. Orr's laboratory. For the first time in my life, the person I thought could make the decision about my fate didn't share my vision or passion and wasn't "impressed" by my words. This hurt my pride deeply and I remember driving back to the Bluff feeling discouraged, not really understanding why. I thought that *"passion"* was enough to get an *"opportunity,"* but I was wrong and learned a very valuable lesson that day.

When I talked to Dr. Orr the next week, he wanted to know how the site visit went. I told him it went **FINE**, which can have many meanings, including **F**eelings **I**nside **N**ot **E**xpressed, **F**ickle **I**nsecure **N**eurotic and **E**motional, or my favorite, which probably described my demeanor the best: **F**eeling **I**nadequate, **N**eeding **E**ncouragement. I quickly gave a summary of the weekend, changed the subject, and never mentioned going to medical school for the rest of the semester.

I thought about my appointment in MBRS and felt that people would always label me as a *"Minority."* I never really accepted it as a term to describe any group of people, not just African-Americans, but realized the program gave me great opportunities. I just kept my spirits high and concentrated on the positives. After the UAMS interview, I was more sensitive to being called a *"Minority,"* but tried to maintain an even disposition, if the subject ever came up. Now my life's ambition became cancer research and I wanted to earn a Ph.D. I needed to feel like I was helping to make a difference in the world. As much as I disliked being labeled a *"Minority,"* my travels to Washington, D.C., as apart of the MBRS program, helped shape my true ambitions and passions for science.

Two years prior at the MBRS Annual Conference in Washington, D.C., I went to a presentation given by Anthony S. Fauci, M.D.,[25] a leading researcher in the fight against HIV/AIDS. His speech inspired me to do biological research. I wanted the best of both worlds, so thoughts of earning an M.D., Ph.D., and becoming a physician scientist were churning in my mind. When I reflected and remembered his speech, I wanted to learn what he knew, and be connected in similar international research circles. The fire for research burned bright for me now. I was determined to learn as much as possible, before I left UAPB, under Dr.

---

25 Dr. Anthony Fauci- has been director of the National Institute of Allergy and Infectious Diseases (NIAID), a part of the National Institutes of Health since 1984. His background is in immune regulation, sexually transmitted diseases, and HIV/AIDS research.

Orr's guidance, so I prepared to present our laboratory results in every setting I could.

Arkansas Academy of Sciences

In the early fall, our laboratory was planning to attend the annual Arkansas Academy of Sciences Research Conference. I was scheduled to give a presentation. I learned some great techniques in Dr. Orr's laboratory and tried to stay up on current events in science. Because of my focus on extracurricular interests, I hadn't reached a level of scientific understanding necessary to give the best presentation. Mrs. Glover prepared me as much as she could for the talk and Dr. Orr prepped me for questions from the audience. My topic was "*The Sensitization of Human Multiple Transitional Cell Carcinoma Cells to Cisplatin by Anguidine.*" I presented it during the Biomedical Sciences portion of the program.

I was nervous from the beginning of the talk until the end. I spent the majority of my time trying to remember the key points of the research. When the moment came to recite my notes, I missed several very important facts. Dr. Orr recognized my errors and addressed them after the conference. He wasn't overly critical, but concerned and hoped I would improve in the near future.

I didn't feel as bad as I did during the UAMS interview, but worked diligently to try to catch up on materials I missed over the last three years. I was in this position partly because of my inability to accept "structured criticism" and "sound mentoring." I realized I hadn't taken my laboratory work seriously enough before now, and it was starting to show. I was determined to make myself more marketable, because the semester was about to end and I had one more semester to try to turn it all around. I was excited because I felt I had time to shape up before I graduated, but was distracted by community events out of my control.

Fitting the Profile

Many people have said I have a familiar and famous face. I always dismissed their comments as jokes, until one evening a local detective called my house and said he wanted to talk to me as soon as possible. I was disturbed by the contact, but eventually called him back. When we talked, he was very vague and encouraged me to come downtown to the police station, so we could speak in person. The first thing I did after our conversation was contact my Aunt Rae, who was an attorney, because I had no idea what the detective wanted with me. I knew I hadn't done anything criminally wrong. The call broke my focus for the rest of the night.

The next day I had a lot on my mind, so I decided to hang out at UAPB to try to clear my head. As I walked across the grounds, I remembered that one of my former science teachers from Pine Bluff Junior High, *Mr. Ray Woods*, was on campus helping coordinate a student enrichment program. When I saw him, I remembered how he sternly lectured us to "stay on task and out of trouble." I never felt such a high level of confusion, worry, and panic and thought he would be a good person to talk to.

I walked up to Mr. Woods and made general conversation, with that phone call in the back of my mind. I really wanted to talk about it, but was hesitant to do so. Mr. Woods was a teacher and could see that something was wrong with me. All the masking I did to try to "tell him without telling him," eventually dissolved into me explaining my trials and tribulations to someone I thought would listen. I hoped his wisdom could help me make sense of my situation and feel better. What I wanted him to do was tell me what to do, but he never did that. He listened instead.

Mr. Woods analyzed my scenario and helped me calm down and focus on the facts. He advised me like a lawyer, in his own emphatic way, to stay the course and to remember "If I didn't do anything wrong, stick with that point." I always liked Mr. Woods because he was a military veteran, disciplinarian, and deeply involved in science. When he taught, I believed he was an expert in science, life, and everything else. Many students were fond of Mr. Woods. During the summer months, me, and my friends used to walk in his neighborhood just to see how he was doing and "get our knowledge," as he would describe it. Every time he spoke to us, he always discussed a scientific issue he thought we needed to know about. Mr. Woods also encouraged Kevin and I to become trailblazing scientists and bring some energy back to Pine Bluff. I guess he saw potential in both of us.

He was proud of my work at UAPB and often lectured me on the state of affairs of his alma mater. One day I walked through by his neighborhood as usual. He was in his front yard and in a very jovial mood. He explained what was going on at the Pine Bluff Arsenal,[26] and his theories on how they were making and disposing of toxic nerve gases. Mr. Woods described how smoke and exhaust are created, when substances are burned, and the process of toxic gas management. Much of what he was saying was too technical for me at the time, but always made me think.

He posed this question to me, "Where will it go?" and then pointed to a white cloud of smoke that came from that area, as we spoke outside his house. I understood what he was trying to say. Where I'm from, when elders talk, youth listen and I was definitely listening that day. I asked him to tell me more about life and science and give me the answers to the mysteries of the universe. He emphatically and sternly said, *"I am not a knowledge-box— you can't just ask and get the answer to life's mysteries and idiosyncrasies!""You will have to learn some things on your own!"*

---

26 The Pine Bluff Arsenal was originally named the Chemical Warfare Arsenal in 1941 and designed to produce thermite and magnesium munitions. During WWII its mission changed to manufacturing, loading, and storing war gases. Now it stockpiles chemical weapons, for disposal through the Chemical Stockpile Disposal Program, which is monitored by the U.S. Army Chemical and Biological Defense Command. www.globalsecurity.org.

Mr. Ray Woods

I reminisced about those experiences from years past, as I looked into his eyes and explained my current situation. Mr. Woods was compassionate, gave me some advice, and offered to help me again if I needed it. I respected him for listening, and left the conversation feeling better. I went back home and waited to be contacted, but there was no word from the detective. We eventually played phone tag for a week. The detective then changed his approach and wanted to stop by my house to talk. I nervously told him that would be FINE, because I felt more comfortable talking with him at home.

He stopped by one afternoon and asked about my whereabouts on *July 3, 1993*. Someone identified me as the shooter and accused me of assault with a deadly weapon. When he described his reason for contacting me, I immediately defended myself. I had no idea what he was talking about. All I could think about was how an arrest, jail, and a record would affect my future. The detective was adamant in his assertion of my guilt and when my responses to his questions were consistent, he wanted to continue the conversation at the police station. Later that week, I got a call from the detective and he told me to come by the police station to give a statement. I decided to comply with his request and notified my Aunt Rae, just in case something out of the ordinary happened.

I went down to the station alone and wore a white oxford shirt with an emblazoned Masonic emblem on the shirt pocket. I arrived at the police station and was immediately ushered through several layers of security to the detective's offices. I remember seeing my former baseball coach in uniform, as I walked through the safety cages. He saw me but didn't speak. I wondered what he was thinking and wished I could let him know that I hadn't committed a crime. By the time I got to my last stop, which was really a hole in the wall at the end of the hallway, we began to talk about the alleged events.

The detective told me that SOMEONE said that I shot at them with a 12-gauge shotgun, on Sunday July 3, 1993 between 10 and 11 p.m. They said they knew it was me, because they saw my face. I immediately froze before I spoke, and adamantly said I didn't know who this person was or why they thought I would do something like that. The detective then asked me about my whereabouts on that Sunday. I told him I was at home. I never missed an episode of "Star Trek," which aired from 10 to 11 p.m. every weekend on Saturdays and Sundays. I made sure he included that piece of information in my statement, because in my mind, that established a clear alibi for me.

The detective dismissed what I said and tried to intimidate me by saying, *"He already told me you did it, so you might as well confess!"* I paused again and was so scared that I gave the exact statement again. I wouldn't say anything different, as I remembered what Mr. Woods told me. Then, I realized the detective was trying to coax a confession out of me for something I didn't do. All I knew how to do was to repeat my same statement over and over again. I never wavered from my original alibi. His next move was to try to convince me to be fingerprinted and photographed, as he alluded to in our earlier conversations.

I asked him why I needed fingerprints for something I didn't do. He went into this long drawn out story about how when he was growing up, SOMEBODY accused him of stealing from a grocery store. He hadn't done it, but had to be fingerprinted as a matter of protocol and it was never a problem for him. I just looked at him, while he reminisced with a nostalgic look in his eyes. I guess in his mind he thought that story would make me feel better and convince me to get the prints done. In actuality, I was weighing the implications of not doing the fingerprints and photo.

I didn't want to create more suspicion on my part and didn't want to be forced to comply, so I agreed. I left his office and for the first time in my life I was about to participate in a ritual I had only seen on television. As the camera recharged after each photo, my body trembled. I turned profile holding a registration number linked around my neck. My life flashed before my eyes. PBH wasn't there and the Masons weren't there. I was in the police station with God and my thoughts. I believed that I would never get my picture taken at a police station, or be fingerprinted in my life, but it happened. After stressing me for thirty minutes, the detective allowed me leave without further questions.

I didn't hear from him for a while after that. Two weeks went by and I decided to check with him by phone, just to follow up and make sure my records would be clear. The detective had forgotten all about the case he was trying to prosecute me for and casually said, *"I don't believe the other guy was telling the truth, and I don't expect anything else to happen from it."* Then, he ended the call. Afterwards, I thought about what it felt like to be accused of something I didn't do and almost go to jail on the word of SOMEONE I didn't know. I also thought about how the detective was trying to use "coercion tactics," which were evident in television shows such as *"New York Undercover," "NYPD Blue," "Law and Order"* and *"CSI."* His goal was to get me locked up to try to solve a case, for which he had no evidence. My Aunt Rae was stern and proficient, when she dealt with him and my case and let me know he didn't have any evidence. The fact he caused me pain, anguish, and wasted my time made me view the criminal justice system differently.

During that experience, I thought about how many other African-American (Black) men were coerced into giving confessions for things they didn't do. It made me more fearful of the police in my community. I tried to stay away from them as much as I could. It wasn't fun to watch television shows like *"Cops"* or *"Real Stories of the Highway Patrol"* or movies about African-Americans being incarcerated, no matter how jovial the writers and directors made jail seem.

It took me some time to refocus, after being accused of a crime that could have meant serious jail time, but I knew I could always turn my attention back to what had always been my lifelong support: Music. The UAPB band room became my new home away from home. I was so comfortable there that most other places seemed boring. Even after a brush with the law, I was excited by band and music and never forgot that experience.

The rest of the marching band season seemed uneventful. I was running the fraternity as I saw fit. Mr. Gerome Hudson, also known as *"Hud,"* was the full-time advisor of ΚΚΨ. He was one of the oldest members in the chapter (Spring 81). While Wash had his hands full with the band program, *Hud* decided to stop advising the fraternity. He was disappointed by the previous years' lack of respect for the band and music, and saw our efforts diminishing week to week. I talked to *Hud* and tried to get him to support me as the new fraternity president, because Homecoming and the "Round Up" were near. I also worried about organizing the annual *Dexter Baggett-Jackie Johnson Talent Extravaganza*[27] also called the *"Extrav,"* which was held during in the spring semester of each year.

I really wanted to do better than previous chapter presidents, but had my hands in so many fires, I knew there wouldn't be enough time in the day for me to coordinate the activities of the fraternity, rehearse, work in the laboratory, and sleep. Something had to give, and unfortunately it was my grades. I made a decision to focus on Homecoming and catch up on any assignments or study time I missed, before the end of the semester.

---

27 Dexter Baggett- Jackie Johnson Talent Extravaganza- is an annual celebration featuring musical performances and step-show, sponsored by the EX chapter of Kappa Kappa Psi and the ΔΠ chapter of Tau Beta Sigma. The Extravaganza is a yearly showcase and is dedicated to the memory of Dexter Baggett and Jackie Johnson.

It was easier for me to think about music and the fraternity because they were things I wanted to do versus studying, which was something I had to do.

Homecoming came and went without any major problems. The nostalgia and regalia of alumni returning to support the university and band wore off quickly for me, as I reflected at the end of the semester and was anxious about my grades. My semester GPA was 2.27 and my cumulative GPA dropped to 2.91. I realized I was out of time and couldn't rebound to graduate with at least a 3.0 average; which would make me marginally competitive for graduate school.

I was troubled about my GPA, but decided to register for the Graduate Record Examination (GRE) and MCAT anyway, just to have the experience of taking the tests. I received my scores from the MCAT first. They were low and nowhere near minimally acceptable for medical school. My GRE scores were a little better, but not high enough to warrant interest from any graduate program. I was upbeat but decided to try to use my last semester to be more open to whatever opportunities were available. I just hoped something would turn up for me in the spring.

Before the semester ended, I applied for an internship with the Robert Wood Johnson Foundation[28], as part of their initiative to increase representation of "minority" students in medical schools across the country. This organization was specifically recruiting students to attend medical schools in the Chicago metropolitan area.

When I completed my application, I was more cautious with my words and gave a real assessment of my abilities and goals, to the selection committee. I would have to wait until the next semester to determine if my writing sample and references were good enough for acceptance into the program. At this point, I didn't care what the opportunity was; I just wanted to be apart of something in the summer. My other classmates had already received word of their internships and selection to graduate and medical programs. I was silent because things hadn't worked out for me as I would have liked. I talked with Dr. Orr and we both waited to see what would be available, while keeping our fingers crossed that something would turn up.

---

28 The Robert Wood Johnson Foundation- is an organization whose mission is to improve the quality of care and support for people with chronic health conditions by promoting healthy communities and lifestyles .Their goal is also to reduce the personal, social and economic harm caused by substance abuse, tobacco, alcohol, and illicit drugs.

In the interim, I returned to music but the mood and atmosphere of the music department changed again. Although we had a very successful marching season and Wash had increased the quantity and quality of the band and entire music program, the administration and Wash were in constant conflict. The problem was that Wash was hired by Doc Miller and was the last remaining fixture of an era that had passed. I believe in the midst of his success as a mentor, composer, and leader, the administration still wanted to go in a different direction. They weren't shy about proving that. I noticed that our music budgets were slowly cut, and Wash didn't receive the same support from the music department, as he had in the past.

Wash wanted and needed more help with the music programs. At that time, Mr. Elliott and *Hud* were the only assistants available to help him coordinate the marching and concert bands. He hoped to get more support from the music department staff, but any new hires were selected because of their specialized talents. When new music faculty arrived, they focused primarily on one-on-one instrumental study. The fraternity tried to support Wash the best way we could. I led the charge by thinking long term, and envisioned a spring pledge line, to keep the fraternity going, in the midst of growing chaos. I hoped to "augment" the band with dedicated loyal members, just as my pledge line did in 1991.

Concert band was now in full swing. Instead of focusing on my studies, I was more concerned about the day-to-day operations of the band and Wash's future. I spent more of my time in the band room than I did in the library, but I kept up appearances in the laboratory to try to keep my promise to Dr. Orr. I asked *Hud* for some help to manage the upcoming events, but he was still so distraught with the current reputation of the fraternity, he literally told me to run the fraternity on my own. This was what I really wanted all along, but needed approval. I also wasn't mindful of what I wished for at the time.

Now, I had total control of the fraternity with no real oversight from any member of the band staff. Wash was busy trying to save his job and music program, and I took a leadership style where I didn't listen to those who opposed my views. After a couple of weeks experiencing my new approach, the brothers in the fraternity began referring to me as "Castro," because I acted like a dictator. They couldn't do anything about it, because I was in the right position at the right time, in the history of our chapter of the fraternity. I had my own vision of where I thought the fraternity should go and got tunnel vision. I eventually lost support from many of the members near the time of the "*Extravaganza.*"

I decided to start a pledge line and bring new members into the fraternity by myself, without the help or consent from the greater membership body. I was really out on a limb now, but I didn't care, because I was more concerned about longevity and the reputation of the fraternity. I talked with Wash and let him know what was going on, but didn't let him know what was happening outside of the band room. During one concert band rehearsal in the early spring, I decided to pick the members I wanted for the fraternity instead of announcing a campus-wide interest meeting. I tried to hand-select people I knew would be positive influences and hard workers.

I passed out ten letters and ten men accepted my offer to join. The only problem was that I was in complete control, so I had to spend time pledging them as well. My biggest goal was to prevent the older initiated members from disrupting the pledge process because of their angst over my leadership approach. I was going day and night. I ate candy every day to give me the energy to keep moving, not really motivated to eat a real meal. If I wasn't in the band room, I was in the laboratory. If I wasn't in the laboratory, I was somewhere on the campus negotiating with administration officials to make sure KKΨ got the best deals and building access for the *Extravaganza.*

Once I had everything organized, I turned my attention to the ten people I knew would revolutionize the fraternity and the pledging process began. During the first couple of weeks, I tried to instill values I learned when I pledged. With help of Akiem, known musically as "*Portporio Al Fine*" and one my fall 91' line brothers, we worked to give musical wisdom and a love for KKΨ to ten young men. No one was more supportive than Akiem and I was truly in over my head. But I knew if I could just get this line "crossed," I would have support for the *Extravaganza.*

I tried to make the pledge process brief and did my best to give the "clefs" as much information as possible. I was running out of time, until Akiem and I agreed the line had learned all they needed to know. I felt they were trained and ready to join and be accepted into the fraternity, but there was still opposition from the larger membership body. Akiem and I made a decision to bring the new pledges off-line sooner than expected. The brothers weren't happy about my decision and made it clear that I had gone too far with my powers as president. I just wanted the pledges to become official members so I could concentrate on other things, specifically the Extravaganza. Akiem and I made our final preparations for bringing in the pledges and prepared for the worst. One of my other line brothers Antyonne Collins known as "FREAKKΨ *Hypedelic Fortismatic Con Fucco Funk Aeolian A# Minor*," decided to help us finish the pledge process. The older brothers got word that new members would finish initiating that night and many tried to form a gauntlet and convince me one last time to stop the process. I felt a sense of loyalty to the older members of the fraternity for bringing me in, but also felt that this was the best solution.

We proceeded as planned. I was nervous and knew I was beyond the point of no return. The pressure was mounting and other brothers in the fraternity were dissenting angrily, when Wash stepped in and made sure the process concluded as it should have. The entire ceremony was lackluster for me because it was all business. I knew that our bigger challenge was right around the corner. That pledge line is known as the *10 Augmented Surround Sounds*.

10 Augmented Surround Sounds, Spring '94

Augmented Surround Sounds *-to raise and elevate new eras of musical sound.*

Adrian T. Sanders-	*Hyperdelic Half-Note*	French Horn
Donavan Riggins	D # Chromatic Sweet Tone	Trombone
Marlin Montgomery	Syncopated Brio Funk	Percussion
Donald J. Lewis	D-Solo Hypnotic Mystro'	Percussion
Calvin Exson	Monotonous 5	Percussion
Alzester Brown	Psicho Sousa	Sousaphone
Antwuane Wilburn	Overtone Ab Diminished 7th	Saxophone
Andre Bracy	Presto Phunk Matician	Percussion
Hugh Simmons	Count Gradioso	French Horn
Brian Williams	Pasante Grave # 10	Percussion

Now I had ten new loyal members at my disposal. Our next move was to prepare for the *Extravaganza*. The new members were ready to prove themselves, as the time of the event was near. They worked hard and the contacts we made across the campus helped us put on a great show. Many of the older brothers returned to experience the festivities; some were happy with it, while others were still upset with me about the condition of the fraternity and this new pledge line. It was mission accomplished in my book. We collaborated with our TBΣ sisters and with a minimal investment, the fraternity and sorority were able to share more than $2000.00 from the proceeds.

Wash arrived at the front door of the event and was monitoring everything. In his own way, he helped me protect the integrity of the fraternity. I never will forget that at the end of the event, he saw me counting the money from the door and showed me how to hide it, so I didn't get robbed before we were able to enjoy it. After the *Extravaganza*, the fraternity and sorority went to Wash's house to celebrate.

We counted the money on his dining room table before splitting all of the proceeds in half. I was happy and relieved for such a productive weekend, but had so many other things I needed to do I couldn't really enjoy it. When everything finally settled down with ΚΚΨ, I tried to get back into the flow of classes and have some fun, but it was too late for that.

After multiple advisement sessions with Dr. Orr, I enrolled in *General Physics II*, *Vertebrate Physiology*, *Computer Science*, *Computer Programming/Fortran*, and *Biology Seminar*. Successful completion of these classes would allow me to graduate on time. I had wasted time taking courses I wanted and didn't follow the curriculum schedule. I was proud because I would be graduating without taking *Biochemistry*. I was in no shape to finish the semester strong because all of my classes required what I didn't have the most, and that was time. I did my best average work in those classes just so I could get to graduation.

My efforts were truly average and I ended the semester with a 2.52 GPA. My cumulative GPA was 2.86, after taking more than 131 credit hours. I knew I wouldn't be competitive in any medical school and just hoped I would get an opportunity to participate in the Robert Wood Johnson Summer Internship Program. Meanwhile, I passed the baton of fraternity leadership to one of my line brothers and was nostalgic about my experiences as president, but ready to let it go. The next week I received word that my application to Robert Wood Johnson Program was accepted. I would be going to Chicago, Illinois. I thanked God for answering my prayers.

I called the program coordinator soon after I got my letter, to find out where I would be stationed. There were several sites in Chicago available. He was cordial and told me that information would come in my award letter and asked that I be patient during this process. I checked the mail every day until the letter came nearly two weeks later. I was assigned to Northwestern University, one of the most prestigious universities in Chicago. Now, my goal was to prepare to leave the state of Arkansas for the first time, for more than a weekend.

During the remaining days of the semester, I anticipated finally leaving the Bluff and never thought I would be so emotional about it. I graduated on May 14, 1994, from the University of Arkansas at Pine Bluff, with B.S. degree in Biology. I remember standing in line during the convocation, before the program commenced. I listened to the concert band's version of *Pomp and Circumstance*, as Wash conducted.

Wash led the band as he had done so many times before, but it felt strange and I was sad because I wasn't performing. I quickly composed myself, took my seat. When they called my name, I quickly walked across the stage to the cheers of my parents and family members. I always thought that right after graduation I would party all night long. But after seeing my name etched on a degree, I went home and thought about my next stop in life, which would begin in Chicago, Illinois. I didn't realize traveling to Chicago for eight weeks would be a big adjustment, but I reminisced more about my band bus trips and experiences in Washington, D.C.

Chapter 3.
Chicago, Illinois

> I will love thee, O LORD, my strength. The LORD is my rock, and my fortress, and my deliverer; my God, my strength, in whom I will trust; my buckler, and the horn of my salvation, and my high tower. I will call upon the LORD, who is worthy to be praised: so shall I be saved from mine enemies
>
> **Psalm 18:1-3 (KJV)**

Four Tubas, a Guitar, and a Gallery of Cheerleaders

The Robert Wood Johnson Program was slated to last only eight weeks, but I packed all the clothes I owned into four large bags. At that time, airline passengers could take four to five large bags and additional luggage on the plane, without question or fees. I was a little nostalgic, but prepared for departure and said my goodbyes to my family, the PBH brothers, and the state of Arkansas. As I rode to Little Rock to board the plane, I thought about new experiences outside of Arkansas and how much I wanted to learn in Chicago. The path to the terminal was clear and as I walked to my seat on the plane, I became more nervous. When the cabin door was sealed and the plane backed away from the gate, I felt totally on my own, and was excited to be that way. As I sat on the plane and watched the ground disappear underneath the clouds, I thought about what it would feel like to live in "Chi-town" and the new challenges I would face. I dozed off for what seemed to only be a couple of minutes, when the pilot spoke on the intercom informing us of our initial descent into *O'Hare International Airport*.

When I finally stepped off the plane into the terminal of the country's busiest and most crowded airport, I was overwhelmed and didn't know what to do next. Fortunately for me, I had family members living in the city, and they had been instructed by my father to take care of me. My first cousin *Harold*, son of my father's oldest sister, lived in Chicago with my aunt. He offered to give me some guidance and help me adjust to Chicago living, which wasn't fast paced, but faster than what I was used to. I stood at the end of the terminal, near the transportation level, when Harold walked up and greeted me. I was so glad to see him, only remembering his face from my days in Arkansas as a young boy. *Harold* stepped up where my father left off and began to show me some of the things his uncle had shared with him.

My first big hurdle was trying to get to Northwestern University with all those bags, while on the city's rail cars that were packed with people. I managed to make enough room for the other passengers and reminisced about riding the bus with my baritone, as a boy. *Harold* knew where we were going, but I was busy trying to see outside the train windows and not fall down from the constant jerking of the train. I flashed back for a moment, but then came to reality and paid more attention to my new surroundings to learn how to navigate in an unfamiliar place. I really appreciated *Harold* for his time and family care. I think about those experiences now and realize how important his patience and attention were in my growth and development. I eventually had many other issues to deal with while in Chicago, including trying to "fit in," meet new people, and manage my life with a consistent lack of funds. *Harold* recognized the correct stop and we got off the train near the North main campus, where my dormitory and the famous Magnificent Mile[29] were located.

I actually arrived six hours early, before any of the other students. *Harold* asked me where I needed to go on the campus. I gave him the address, which was on Michigan Avenue facing the waterfront. We arrived where we should have and I gleefully approached a guard at the front desk of the dormitory, to ask about checking in for the program. The guard wasn't as enthusiastic as I was with his response and he asked me where I needed to go.

I gave him my award letter and he grudgingly read the details. He looked at the letter and offered no additional information. The guard then recommended I call SOMEBODY to find out where I was supposed to be. *Harold* stepped in and asked, "Can you call and find out for us?" with a stern look of determination. The guard grudgingly made a call and found out where I could pick up my keys and which dormitory I was assigned to. I thanked *Harold* for advocating on my behalf.

---

29 Magnificent Mile- is the description of North Michigan Avenue in Chicago, Illinois. This street is famous for shopping, culture, dining, and tourism.

Harold

Sederick C. Rice

I was so glad to be off the plane and train that I would have sat there for hours, until the other students arrived. *Harold* knew the mentality of his fellow Chicagoans and was happy to help me learn the motivations and interests of people in his city. Time passed by quickly as other students arrived. All of us were directed toward a conference room, for a quick head count. After a brief orientation from the program hosts, I got to see my room, which contained a twin mattress on a twin frame and a desk.

I knew coming into the program that I wouldn't have a television or refrigerator in my room, but I didn't realize what an inconvenience this would be during the heart of one of the hottest summers on record. I unpacked and thanked *Harold* for his help, as we walked back to the train station. When *Harold* left, he told me to keep in touch and that he would visit me from time to time.

Later that evening, the remaining students arrived. I didn't get a chance to meet and greet them, but saw them moving in down the hall. Tomorrow would be my big day to start a new chapter in my life, hopefully preparing me for medical school. Participating in this program was my second chance to become a doctor, in spite of my GPA and lack of preparation, so I prepared to do my best.

The first day of the program I met several of my cohorts, who had come from all across the country. The student facilitator gave us our first mission, which was to look at the person next to us and describe them to the rest of the group, as part of our meet and greet ice- breakers. The chain of responses went around the room and when it was my turn, I tried to be as descriptive as possible. I wanted to "impress" the young woman sitting next to me. I used words like *vivacious, bubbly, stimulating,* and *provocative* for someone I really only knew for a few minutes. She described me as fun, charismatic, and thought I played football.

On our first day we met *Ms. Lorraine Bogan*, our site coordinator. She was accompanied by several medical students, who decided to help with the program. Ms. Bogan laid down the law. She told us why we were in Chicago and her expectation that all of us conform to the rules of order regarding work site assignments and enrichment goals of the program. The structure of the program included matching students with Northwestern University medical faculty and staff. This would allow us to get experience working in the field of medicine. We also took courses and practice exams to prepare for the MCAT.

It was a rigorous process. The time our group spent together bonded us as a small family. I tried to be the dominant one as I did in PBH and

KKΨ, but this didn't work, because there was an older woman in the program everyone looked up to. She was military trained and the only one who had a car, so no one else in the program could compete with that. There were days when I tried too hard to "fit in," and those were my toughest moments there.

I didn't have the close friends I was used to in the Bluff. My biggest support network now seemed broken. Kevin was at Florida State University; Sedrick was at the University of Illinois at Urbana-Champaign; Ralph was at the University of Arkansas at Fayetteville; John was in the Navy; and Greg, Keith, and Jay were still in the Bluff working in the community, to bring about economic and social change. I missed PBH the most, but realized it was time to try to learn as much as I could, so when I returned to Arkansas I would be better person than when I left.

When the program started, I was matched with a pathologist. Every morning I would walk down to his office from my dormitory. He gave me and another student specific learning goals each day. Most of our time was spent in the library researching current medical articles and doing literature reviews. I learned how to research bibliographies and other sources of information manually, which is significantly different from how information is managed and retrieved today. There were no web-based search engines. Some days I was able to watch doctors diagnose and assess tissue samples removed from people, who were still on the operating table; other days the tutors spoke to us about careers in medicine.

I was happy with my work assignment, because we had weekly seminars and classes to prepare us for medical school. Mid-way through the program, we participated in a mock medical school interview. We were critiqued on our ability to answer typical medical school entrance questions. I learned that interviewing was a big part of the medical school acceptance process. Even if my grades weren't as good as they should have been; interviewing well could give me another opportunity. I took this exercise very seriously and prepared for my interview for about a week. I knew that if I could get this right, I would be one step closer to becoming a doctor and maybe UAMS would give me a chance.

On the morning of the interview, I dressed appropriately and was my usual confident self as I entered the room and met the interviewers. The program directors decided that instead of interviewing one student at a time, a panel would be assembled and two students could be asked the same question. Responses were judged on creativity, clarity, and factual content. I was matched with a female student and we were interviewed by two medical school faculty. The question session began and we alternated our questions and responses. I often listened to my peer's answers and sometimes she listened to mine. We were judged accordingly. The format seemed very informal. They asked us everything from current events in the news, to controversial health-related issues. I will never forget that my question was related to Euthanasia[30]. Both reviewers asked me how I felt about this multi-faceted subject.

I paused when I first heard the topic, gave my opinion, and answered against the use of Euthanasia. I remembered reading about the *Hippocratic Oath*[31] that doctors take and I thought it directly forbids physicians from aiding in the death of people they treated, regardless of the circumstances. I gave it a good try, but had misinterpreted the oath in my thought process and didn't look further into the question for a real example. I also answered the question based on my limited knowledge of the subject. There was no "right" or "wrong" answer; the reviewers just wanted to hear how I would compose and defend my answer and views. The reviewers also asked me how I relaxed in my free time. I spoke about my tuba, and how music was a big part of my life.

About a week later, I got my critique back and my scores were low from one reviewer and much higher from the other. I was disappointed because I thought my answers were more consistent than revealed by my scores. I went back and forth about my performance for a couple of days, and tried to figure out how to do better. I eventually looked on the bright side and was happy to at least have had my interviewing skills assessed. I congratulated my cohort on her high scores and prepared to start working with a plastic surgeon, in conjunction with the pathologist the next week.

I worked with a pathologist in the mornings and afternoons and then walked up the street to intern with a plastic surgeon. I appreciated the Robert Wood Johnson program because I learned more about practical medicine. My plastic surgeon mentor actually interacted with patients. He was cool and would brief me before each person came to their appointment. He actually made me feel like I was one of his colleagues in medicine. He was about to retire from practicing medicine and allowed me to learn some cool techniques used to do skin grafts and reconstructive

---

30   Euthanasia- is a process that tries to end life in a painless way.

31   Hippocratic Oath- is a traditional oath taken by physicians, where they vow to practice medicine in an ethical way.

surgery. This work assignment ended before the program finished. I spent the remainder of my time studying MCAT practice exams in my dorm room.

That summer in Chicago, the temperatures were hot every day and without a refrigerator, it was difficult to store any food in my room. I tried to improvise and bought a Styrofoam ice chest that I filled with ice, lunch meat, milk, and cheese each evening. By morning, the ice was melted and the cold water warmed up during the day, but I was still able to save some food. Without a television, I began to read more than I ever had in my life. I read the *Chicago Tribune*, which became my source for news, sports, entertainment, and culture. I bought a small radio, but the only station that came in clear enough to listen to was conservative talk radio. I didn't share any of the views of the commentators, but the clarity was so good that I listened each day.

My weekly schedule was simple: Each day I worked and in the afternoons I studied to take practice MCATs, at Malcolm X College. I was productive, but still didn't know what I was going to do when I returned home. My back up plan was to try to get a job, retake the MCAT, and apply for medical school at UAMS. I was already low on funds and the Discover™ card I got at UAPB, was just about maxed out. Every two weeks we received a small stipend for living expenses. I sent small payments to Discover™, to protect my credit, and keep some room on the card just in case of an emergency.

We had an ATM in the dormitory and I would get cash advances in multiples of $20.00 bills. This would give me enough funds to make the next payday. Living in Chicago really taught me how to budget my money. I was frustrated and broke, but too proud to ask for money from home. I was on my own and wanted to make it on my own.

The program had gone more than six weeks, and many of us were getting weary of the same routine every day and every weekend. *Harold* visited me several times. We would normally venture out into Chicago by foot. He was a former taxi driver and knew the city very well. *Harold* used his street-by-street experience to show me several Chicago landmarks up close. I appreciated the culture, history, and museums in the city. I always wondered where the Oprah Winfrey show was filmed, but we never got a chance to find the location. I got a chance to get out, but other students weren't so lucky, so program coordinators tried to help eliminate our boredom. Ms. Bogan scheduled fun sight-seeing events, but many of us were so homesick and ready to take the MCAT, that we just wanted to finish the program and enjoy the rest of our summer.

I did get a chance to visit the Dusable Museum of African-American History[32] and was reminded of the pain and suffering caused by Slavery. Visiting the museum motivated me to continue to want to excel in education with the opportunities that were available. I also experienced the "Taste of Chicago[33]" and sat on the dormitory lawn, which faced Michigan Ave. I saw more cars and traffic than I had ever seen in Arkansas. These were my most memorable experiences in Chicago, but I still missed home and was ready to leave. A combination of the heat, a lack of money, and the monotony of the same daily schedule were taking a toll on me. We had more than two weeks left, so I tried to stay busy.

Another enrichment activity was organized by the Northwestern University medical students. They decided to give us a mock interview, which was designed to assess our progress and growth, after the midway point of the program. In this exercise, medical students asked the questions and critiqued our answers. Sessions were one-on-one and this time, I tried to learn from my previous mistakes and show some growth and maturity.

One of the medical students asked me what my long-term goal was and how that goal was benefited by participating in this summer program. I paused as several things ran through my mind at once, then answered as I had done before with as much conviction as possible and said, *"I would like to get into a good medical school, earn an M.D., Ph.D., and be able to mentor 100 students to do laboratory and clinical research."* I waited for the looks of awe and surprise, and braced myself for what was familiar to me in these situations.

There were no obvious objections to what I said. I immediately felt my assertion wasn't bold enough, because of the lackluster response. The medical students just wrote notes and discussed my answers, before asking me to step out of the room. One senior medical student, who worked closely with the summer program, stopped me in the hall after

---

32 Dusable Museum of African-American History- was established in 1961 and is the first and oldest museum dedicated to the preservation of African-American history, culture, and art.

33 Taste of Chicago- is a 10-day celebration, established in 1980, and held annually in Chicago before the 4th of July. The Taste highlights the world's largest food festival and includes live music, food vendors, and cuisines from restaurants around the city.

the session. He told me I did a good job and to try to be more confident when answering questions for review panels.

I felt pretty good about my overall performance and glad I adjusted my goals into something I felt was more reasonable. The senior medical student was positive, but cautioned me about my response and said I should say what I said, only if I truly believed that was what I wanted to do. I told him I was being honest.

He thought my goals were admirable, but questioned whether they were real. I assured him that the response was the way I felt and the mentoring program made me feel that way. I learned to be confident and my past experiences motivated me to always stick to my guns, regardless of what other people thought or said. Now, I believed I could articulate my goals and then defend them from skepticism.

That afternoon, I decided to go play basketball down the street from the dormitory, to blow off some steam. I tried to keep from going back to my boring dorm room. I arrived at the court and waited in line to play a pick-up game of 21. Like most occasions, people from the city as well as medical students, played against each other on the courts. I sat on the bench and watched the game right before mine and could hear someone in the distance cursing profusely and talking trash. He screamed, "Foul!", "Walk!", "Ball!", "I'm Open", "Shoot It, and Damn It!"

I just looked at the guy, who was about 5'7 and thought he must be one of those guys from the Chicago area, who show up to play basketball. I had already stereotyped him because of the way he was talking and dressed. As the game progressed, he seemed to become more creative with his profanity, to the point that one of the players from the other team got in his face and wanted to fight him.

They were separated and both apologized and went back to the game without further incident. When the game was over, I wasn't picked to play and this loud and rude individual came over to the bench and sat down to rest. I said hello and noticed that he was wearing a short-sleeve smock, with a Northwestern University medical school logo on it. I wanted one of those smocks and had seen other students in the program with them. With bravado in my voice, I asked him where he got it and stared at him, until he gave me an answer. I felt privileged to be in a program at Northwestern University and was curious about his background. He wiped the sweat off his forehead and said *"I'm a neurosurgeon at Northwestern and decided to take a break on the basketball court, before my next surgery."* I was stunned and amazed and got quiet because of how I stereotyped another African-

American male, as a street thug with a foul mouth, and an ugly jump shot.

All I could do was sit beside him quietly hoping to be called into the next game. Then, he asked me some questions and wanted to know who I was. I told him about the Robert Wood Johnson program and my experiences in Chicago. He offered me some free advice and told me to *"Never let these people make you feel like you can't become a medical doctor!" "You can do anything you set your mind to; just work hard and it will come for you!"* He talked about his experiences in medical school and the challenges he faced as an African-American. He was candid about how he had to be twice a smart and work twice as hard to get the same opportunities. I was really motivated after talking with him. His story was inspirational to me because I still didn't know what my next move would be after the program ended.

I finally felt my perception of the world wasn't always correct and that was a good thing. Meeting him was a turning point for me, because it made me think *"out of the box"* and was a further indication of why I needed to get more exposure to different people and places. Before he left, he encouraged me keep pushing and study hard. I never got his name. He reminded me of Dr. Benjamin Carson, whose philosophy is *"Be the best in everything you do regardless of your circumstances, or racism."* I never saw that neurosurgeon again, but was more inspired at that moment than from any other seminar or workshop I attended in the last six weeks. God setup our meeting that day. I met an incredible person that was a true inspiration.

The program was winding down, and I was aching to return home, but still didn't have a clear plan. One evening during the final week of the program, I received an unannounced call and voice message from Dr. Hazell Reed. Dr. Reed was the Dean of Graduate Studies and Research, at Delaware State University in Dover, Delaware. He later told me that he called me based on recommendations from some of my former instructors at UAPB. I still don't know who gave him my name, but I believe it might have been Dr. William Willingham, who was the Dean of Arts and Sciences and coordinator of the MARC/MBRS programs. It also could have been Dr. Orr; I just didn't know.

Dr. Reed left me a message as an introduction and asked me to contact his office about an opportunity at Delaware State University (DSU). I didn't know what the opportunity was, but I called him back promptly, because I still wanted to go to medical school. I knew I needed to improve my interviewing skills and MCAT scores, to be competitive in the upcoming fall semester. My feeling at that time was that any new opportunities were worth pursuing. When I talked to Dr. Reed briefly on the phone, I was *humble, attentive,* and *motivated* to know what he had to offer. Dr. Reed told me he was spearheading and recruiting for a program to encourage students to pursue a Master's of Science degree in Biology at DSU, and I was nominated as a potential candidate.

Dr. William Willingham

Chapter 4.
$20.00 Bill

> For wisdom is a defense, and money is a defense, but the excellency of knowledge is that wisdom giveth life to them that have it. In the days of prosperity be joyful, but in the day of adversity consider: God also hath set the one over against the other, to the end that man should find nothing after him.
>
> **Ecclesiastes 7:12-14 (KJV)**

FEDERAL RESERVE NOTE
THE UNITED STATES OF AMERICA
TWENTY DOLLARS
EG 04086695 E
SERIES 2004

THE UNITED STATES OF AMERICA
IN GOD WE TRUST
TWENTY DOLLARS
20

The twenty-dollar bill is probably the most common and useful denomination of money in the United States Treasury. There is something about twenty dollars that makes a person feel like they have money. Maybe it's because of its crisp and neat value, or how when broken or exchanged there can be multiple money combinations of change. My favorite combination is twenty $1.00 bills, because together they appear to be worth more in bulk. I think the twenty-dollar bill is popular because most people have the ability to get twenty dollars and use it to pay for important things such as a haircut or car wash. It also makes an excellent tip for a deep-tissue Swedish massage. It's a great bill for paying a tithe or giving a love offering to a minister or pastor, for providing a well-organized and inspirational sermon.

The twenty-dollar bill has a following like no other piece of currency. Many banks have now decided to only dispense twenty-dollar bills from their ATMs. Whatever the combination, the twenty-dollar bill is a powerful monetary tool. It is used for *a note of legal tender for all debts public and private* according to United States Treasury guidelines. The most important message printed on each piece of currency, especially the twenty-dollar bill is "IN GOD WE TRUST." I had to learn to look for spiritual guidance from God to shape and mold my life and can honestly say that twenty dollars changed my life

---

Sed- "Good morning, Dr. Reed, how are you?"

Dr. Hazell Reed- "FINE, and you?"

Sed- "I got a message to contact you regarding an opportunity at Delaware State University."

Dr. Reed- "Thanks for returning my call so soon. Listen, I'm the Dean of Graduate Studies and Research at Delaware State University. I would like to offer you an opportunity to get a Master's of Science degree in Biology, starting in the fall. The program is two years in length and could lead to you obtaining a doctoral degree, at the University of Vermont."

Sed- "Sounds good to me. What do I need to do?"

Dr. Reed- "Send me *twenty dollars*, along with the application, and we can start from there!"

I was so excited to get that call that I waited anxiously for the next two days, until the application packet arrived. When the package came, I opened the mailing and read about the DEVELOP[34] program, and the twenty dollar processing fee that had to be sent with the application. I felt pretty good about my chances, because of the way Dr. Reed contacted me. It felt like someone from the Bluff was helping me and I was so grateful. The only problem was that I didn't have twenty dollars, which was secondary to the fact that I needed more than that to make sure the application reached its destination.

The application fee had to be a check or money order and I wanted to ship the package the fastest, using overnight mail. My only hope was to go to the ATM in the dormitory and try to retrieve the money from an already maxed out Discover™ card. I really needed a $20.00 bill and decided to try the ATM, with hopes that one more transaction would go through. I already knew I was over my cash advance and spending limit, but had faith the Discover™ card wouldn't let me down.

I went downstairs to the ATM, inserted my card, punched in my cash advance access code and prayed that by some miracle from God, money would come out of the machine. There was a brief moment of silence then I heard the ATM tick as if money was being counted and dispersed. This is when I knew I may have a chance to get some money. The noise stopped, the drawer opened, and a crisp $20.00 bill came out. I was so elated that I punched the access code again and tried to get another $20.00 bill. Money was dispensed again.

I was thinking I was on a roll, knowing that my credit account was already maxed out. I punched in the code again. My third attempt was denied, but I was thankful for the two $20.00 bills. The money allowed me to buy a money order and send my application to DSU, using express mail. It took me nearly five years, after that day, to pay off the Discover™ card balance, primarily because of the late and over-the-limit fees. I haven't had another Discover™ card since. It was fitting to use that card, based on its name, because I was about to embark on a new journey. Discovery was ahead of me outside the state of Arkansas.

---

34 DEVELOP- was a bridge program designed to foster cooperation and a partnership with an HBCU. The University of Vermont supported their new diversity agenda by collaborating with an HBCU. DEVELOP was funded by the federal government. Students accepted into the program would work on their M.S. degrees at DSU, and then enroll at the University of Vermont for their doctoral work.

Three days later, Dr. Reed called and let me know he received the application and I was accepted into the DEVELOP program. I was so ecstatic to have a real opportunity in the works, that I didn't think long term about living and working in Vermont. I focused on the first steps of my journey into Delaware. All I knew was that I had always been taught to look for and take opportunities as they arose. I was ready to finally accept a *"bird in hand"* that could expose me to so many different and exciting things.

The last couple of days of the Robert Wood Johnson program went by fast. Ms. Bogan was busy planning our final banquet and farewell celebration. Most of us were emotional during the ceremony, but I was thinking about DSU and Arkansas and felt I had learned enough to pass the MCAT. Students, coordinators, and medical students said their goodbyes. Many of my program classmates had strong leads for medical school admission.

The next day, I packed up my things and prepared to go back to the airport. I called *Harold* and thanked him again for his help in Chicago and told him how much his presence made the difference. He told me to give his regards to my father. I said I would.

As I sat in the cab going back to the airport, I reminisced about Chicago, but was anxious to see what PBH, KKΨ, and Wash were doing in my absence. I hoped Wash had reconciled with the administration and they recognized he was a valuable asset to faculty, staff, and students. I was ready to share stories about my experiences with people from the Bluff. I left Chicago tired, but renewed, and returned to the Bluff ready to go to Delaware. I was a bit apprehensive, but excited to leave Arkansas, because I always felt that there was something more magnificent beyond our city limits.

When I got back to the Bluff, I spent most of my time resting and visiting friends. Nothing had really changed in the eight weeks I was gone. I stopped by Wash's house to fellowship with him. He was preparing to find another job and I bugged him incessantly about his plans for the future. He was emotionally down, because he felt he was forced to leave a job he put his heart and soul into. Wash did have some leads and was talented enough, that several band directors were interested in his skills. Most schools wanted him to come and help improve their growing musical programs.

The next day I was hanging around the band room, as Wash was trying to finish up some paperwork. We both walked outside together and he told me he wanted to talk with me in private. As soon as we left the perimeter of the building, Wash told me he may have a potential job in Delaware and wanted to know if I wanted to go with him and march in the DSU band. Wash had contacted the Director of Bands at DSU, Mr. Randolph "Ricky" Johnson, another Southern graduate trained by Dr. Greggs, for an interview. I was honored that Wash was still trying to help me in the midst of his unsure future. I will never forget when he approached me that day, not knowing that I was already headed to DSU.

Wash told me not to discuss his potential move because he didn't want any negative attention towards his new position. I finally told him I had already been accepted to DSU and thanked him for looking out for me. If I didn't have an opportunity, Wash would have helped me. Wash was a man with integrity and a very big heart. These characteristics were what I appreciated about him the most. When I asked him years later about his troubles at UAPB, he told me that in the midst of everything that happened, "*leaving was the best thing that ever happened to me*," because he learned how to work in hostile environments and still do his best.

I bugged Wash every day following our conversation, to find out if he got the job at DSU. He still welcomed people into his home, but was clearly depressed because he knew he was leaving. I tried not to press the issue much more, after I saw his mood, and later learned that he didn't get the job. He was offered an opportunity by another Southern University alumnus, for an assistant band director position at Howard University, in Washington, D.C. Wash sold his home near the end of the summer and left Arkansas for the nation's capital. I was happy for him and wished him well, but hoped to stay in touch with him.

Meeting Dr. Reed

Meanwhile, I spent the rest of my time preparing to leave Arkansas. Money was the only thing on my mind. One afternoon, I decided to go to the bank to deposit some money and check my account. While I was in the bank, I heard a voice that was faint but familiar to me. One of the branch managers was having a meeting with an older gentleman, with a strong southern accent, snakeskin cowboy boots, and a very big smile. I thought I heard his voice before and turned around, as the gentleman was leaving. As I walked in the direction of his voice, I asked him, "Are you Dr. Reed?" He responded, "Yes, and who are you? I told him my name and he smiled. I stood in the bank astonished to have randomly met the man behind the distinct southern accent and the Dean of Graduate Studies and Research at DSU.

Dr. Reed never seemed flustered by our chance meeting. I found out why he wasn't shocked to meet me, when I learned he had known me most of my life. Interestingly, he watched me grow up at the *Shop*. Dr. Reed joked about how my grandfather hired me, but was cautious with what he would let me do. He spoke about how my grandfather watched me closely, all the time, to make sure I didn't "drop a jack" or leave lug nuts loose on tires I changed or fixed. My grandfather's biggest concern was that I would hurt myself, by not paying attention.

I asked Dr. Reed what he was doing in Pine Bluff, since I only knew of his position in Delaware. He told me he travels "home" all the time, and was there on business. Dr. Reed said he only traveled by plane, when his schedule prevented driving, and he loved riding in his truck. I wanted to talk more, but he told me he was returning to Delaware in the next couple of days. He said he would contact me, when he reached his office. We shook hands and I left the bank feeling as if God's destiny for my life was beginning.

The next week, Dr. Reed called me at home to finish discussing the details of the graduate program. I inquired about traveling to Delaware and how I would get there. I wanted DSU to provide a plane or bus ticket, for my own convenience, but was prepared to ask my parents for money. Dr. Reed told me to save my money, because he was returning to Pine Bluff from Delaware, to link up with another student chosen for the program.

He said I could ride back with him. Dr. Reed made sure I was serious about going to school in Delaware and wanted to guarantee both of his prospects reported on time. I took Dr. Reed up on his offer and he picked me up on that fateful morning. This was when I listened to one of the most prophetic and timely conversation between my father and Dr. Reed regarding my life.

Sederick C. Rice

Men and Conversation

3 a.m. Pine Bluff, Arkansas, July 1994

Father: "Good morning Dr. Reed. How are you?"
Dr. Reed: "FINE, and you?"
Father: "Good, good. Sederick, do you have all of your stuff?"
Sederick: "I do!" (Loading bags and clothes in the back of a two-door, two-seater, blue Ford pickup truck)
Dr. Reed: "Are you ready to ride?"
Sederick: "Ready to go!" (Dr. Reed and my father shake hands briskly)
Father: "How long is the ride to Delaware?"
Dr. Reed: "About 17 hours, give or take."
Father: "Are you stopping to spend the night?"
Dr. Reed: "We only stop for gas, and will try to get as much highway done as possible before dark."
Father: "Have a safe trip and be careful." (Anxious and nervous about son leaving home for good)
Dr. Reed: "Alright!"
Father: "He is Kinda Green!"
Dr. Reed: "I Understand!"

"Father Figure, Mentor, and Wise Counselor"
Dr. H. Reed

Wisdom Inspired from God

"Send me $20.00 for Delaware State University's Graduate Application fee and once admitted do your work. Sederick, everyone has to mature and you are no exception. Think about yourself now and then in ten years. You think you are good now, but in ten years, you will be much better. Keep your eyes open and your mouth shut and you will be ok. You need to be ready to respond to the challenges of the Ph.D. program. If you still want a Ph.D., get to Vermont. I'm certainly glad that you didn't quit when it got tough in Vermont, because that is what they would have wanted you to do. Let me know when you will defend your doctoral dissertation, and I will make sure to be there." Sederick, don't just take any position because you are nervous about the future, be patient. You are highly trained and will have a long time to establish a great career. Just Be Patient!" Don't allow others to inspire anger inside of you, because once that happens you may lose control, make even more mistakes, and damage your character and reputation. Always keep your cool and stay professional regardless of the situation or conflict! I have two mentors Fred Paige and Dr. S. J. Parker whose influence has helped me even after his death. All people need is a chance and my philosophy is if you can't help someone else during your lifetime, there is really no reason to live."

When I first talked to Dr. Reed on the phone in Chicago, I listened intently to what he was saying and tried to paint of mental picture of who he was as a person. At the same time, I tried to predict how we would interact, when we finally met. I respected him because of his position as Dean of Graduate Studies and Research and because he offered me an opportunity to leave Arkansas. My experiences in Chicago changed my unchallenged views of my abilities, and I was more willing to learn. Before we met in the bank, I had no idea what kind of person he was and how he handled business. I did know after our brief conversation that I wanted to try to learn as much as I could from him.

Dr. Reed, at first glance, seemed stern, principled, and driven, which was a familiar characteristic of older men in the south. He, like my grandfather and father, felt young men had to go through a process to earn the title of being called a "man." An honor only bestowed when males in the family reached a certain level of maturity. I worked hard in the Bluff to be recognized as a "man," but didn't realize transitioning into manhood is a lifelong process. This is probably why I felt so shocked when my father told Dr. Reed I was *"green,"* as a strong reference to my immaturity and lack of experience.

How could I be *"green,"* after finishing four hard years of higher education, becoming a Prince Hall Free and Accepted Mason, and living in Chicago for eight weeks. What were they thinking? *"Men and Conversation"* kept running through my mind, as I loaded up the rest of my things in the back of Dr. Reed's truck. When we pulled away from my house, I was anxious to prove my "manhood," and dispel the belief that I was *"green."*

Chapter 5.
Dover, Delaware

> It is better to hear the rebuke of the wise, than for a man to hear the song of fools. For as the crackling of thorns under a pot, so is the laughter of the fool; this also is vanity. Surely oppression maketh a wise man mad, and a gift destroyeth the heart. Better is the end of a thing than the beginning thereof: and the patient in spirit is better than the proud in spirit.
>
> **Ecclesiastes 7:5-8 (KJV)**

Four Tubas, a Guitar, and a Gallery of Cheerleaders

Dr. Reed and I left around 4 a.m. traveling east toward Memphis, Tennessee on Interstate 40 (I-40). We were trailed by another student, who also accepted an opportunity to study at DSU, but decided to drive his Jeep. I rode in the passenger seat of Dr. Reed's truck, and really had no concept of the length of the trip in hours. I was more focused on what my father told Dr. Reed and obsessed about their words. My excitement was building as we left the Pine Bluff city limits, but I decided to hold my exuberance, until we crossed the Arkansas-Tennessee state line. I made the most of the time by trying to remember highway landmarks and attempt to converse with Dr. Reed. He was down to earth and had a big sense of humor. I quickly learned he wasn't easily "impressed" by what I thought were major life experiences on my part.

We had driven for nearly three hours and approached the Memphis, Tennessee city limits. I sat in the passenger seat trying to fight the urge to go to sleep, after staying up anxious about the ride. I asked Dr. Reed how he was able to stay awake when he traveled long distances. He told me it takes "experience," "will power," and "chewing gum." I thought he was going to drive the entire way, but he let me know that at some point, I would have to drive. This made me nervous because Dr. Reed never told me when he wanted me to drive.

I really wanted to take a nap in the truck. But growing up, my father taught me to stay awake, while riding in the passenger seat, just in case there was an accident, or I needed to help the driver navigate. My mind changed about sleeping. I didn't want to be snoring, after only three hours on the road. I knew that would probably make me look *green* and immature, at least to highway driving.

We finally reached Memphis and stopped at a convenience store for gas. I purchased some NōDōz ® to help me stay awake, in preparation for my drive, not realizing that the excitement of finally leaving home would eventually produce enough adrenalin to keep me awake. I grabbed the NōDōz ® box and then read the label, which indicated it contained concentrated caffeine. I wasn't a coffee drinker, so I thought it would really pick me up. I tried to swallow the large pill, but couldn't get it down for fear of choking. Instead, I broke it in half and chewed it. It was the worst thing I had ever tasted. My expectation was to feel different instantly. The true NōDōz ® effect was delayed for a couple of hours.

After our stop, Dr. Reed and I got back on the road. The plan was to follow I-40 out of Memphis and travel through Nashville, then Knoxville, and change to I-81 near Bristol, Tennessee. Once we got out of Tennessee,

Dr. Reed wanted to drive straight through Virginia. The Sun had risen and I could see the road more clearly. I was "wired" and began asking questions. Dr. Reed wanted to get us to Nashville, which was about 200 miles away, then let me drive while he rested. Meanwhile, I tried to find out more about Dr. Reed.

He casually mentioned how he knew me as a boy, and that my grandfather repaired his cars on many occasions. He told me he was from Hughes, Arkansas, which we passed before entering Memphis, and was trained as a *Plant Science Physiologist*, in the field of Horticulture. He mentioned learning at AM&N/UAPB, the Tuskegee Institute, Pennsylvania State University, and the University of Arkansas at Fayetteville, where he received his doctoral degree.

I thought because of his background he was only involved in farming, but he served as chairperson of the UAPB Agriculture Department and worked actively with the Cooperative Extension Service[35] for more than seven years. I wondered why I never remembered him from the *Shop* or saw him on campus. Dr. Reed seemed interested in telling his story. He told me his last position, at UAPB, was Vice Chancellor for International Affairs and Title XII Officer. After he left, he accepted a position as the Dean of Graduate Studies and Research at DSU.

We had some lively conversations and talked about everything from politics to religion, conspiracy theories related to the Los Angeles riots, and other major events in U.S. history. We did have some things in common and I felt more comfortable. He was at least interested in what I had to say. We dialogued for the rest of the trip to help shorten the drive. By my calculations, there were 700 miles to go. Unfortunately, we were still in Tennessee and I was running out of things to say. We both seemed tired of talking, so we listened to some of his cassette tapes and the radio.

Our next stop was Knoxville, Tennessee. This is where we gassed up again, as part of our driving strategy. Now it was my time to drive. I jumped in the driver's seat, put on my seatbelt, and pulled off toward the highway signs. Dr. Reed pointed me in one direction toward the east exit to get us back on I-40, but for some strange reason the highway signs confused me. I drove toward the west exit. Dr. Reed tried to steer me to

---

35 Cooperative Extension Service- is an educational program funded by the U.S. Department of Agriculture and designed to improve the lives of people through research-based programs, agricultural awareness, youth services, and community based initiatives.

Four Tubas, a Guitar, and a Gallery of Cheerleaders

the right exit and thought he made the directions clear. I kept going the wrong way and eventually had to make a U-turn in the street.

When I finally got back to where I was supposed to be, I could see the confusion on Dr. Reed's face. I just knew he was wondering whether he should let me drive again. He just looked at me and said *"Lord,"* with a strong southern gasp, which meant that he and I needed understanding from GOD in this situation. I tried to play it off, but understood what his temperament meant. My *"greenness"* was clearly evident. I just drove and kept my face pointed forward trying to make sure I didn't make any more obvious mistakes, before he took over the drive. My stretch of highway was smooth. The more comfortable I got behind the wheel, the faster I drove.

Dr. Reed reminded me to watch my speed then told me a story about how he got a ticket on this same highway for driving faster than he should have. After about 200 miles, he asked me if I was tired. I said no, and he let me drive the length of I-40 into Bristol, Tennessee, where we picked up I-81 North heading into Virginia. Once we got to Bristol, we crossed over the Tennessee-Virginia state line and the landscape changed.

We had driven through the *"Smoky Mountains"* for most of the morning and early afternoon. Now we were traveling the *"Tobacco Roads."* Both sides of the highway were lined with acres of tobacco plants. I drove another stretch into Virginia through Christianburg and then into Blacksburg. Dr. Reed told me to bypass Roanoke and follow I-81 through Harrisburg, Virginia to Front Royal, where we would pick up I-66[36].

It was late in the evening. We stopped to get something to eat and gas up again. Dr. Reed told me he would take us into Washington, D.C., after our rest stop. I could finally relax the rest of the ride. We were still about two hours outside of Washington and four hours from Dover, Delaware. As it got darker, I felt a sense of accomplishment for driving as long as I did with no major foul-ups. My mind was focused on what I would see next. We rode I-66 for about an hour into Arlington, Virginia. As we came out of the city limits, I could see landmarks of our nation's capital. The highways were dark, but the lights from the approaching city illuminated the pavement. I was overwhelmed by the historic buildings and architecture. I realized that this was the same city where the President of the United States lived; Congress convenes and make laws for the entire country and home of my favorite NFL team, the Washington Redskins.

---

36 I-66- is the only major highway that allows travel from Washington, D.C. into Northern Virginia.

I was always a Redskins fan growing up, but never thought I would ever see where they were located and played home games. Once we came off I-66, we followed I-395 into Washington, D.C. through *Constitution Avenue*. I felt a joy at that moment that I have never felt since, because my eyes recognized the beauty, majesty, and history of Washington, D.C. I was proud to be a Black-American living in the United States of America. As we quickly drove through the city streets, the historic buildings slowly disappeared from view, and the city lights dimmed. Afterwards, I felt more empowered to make the best of my opportunities at DSU and was ready to get to our final destination.

The ride to Dover seemed short after sitting for more than fifteen hours. We followed *Massachusetts Avenue* out of the city, through U.S. 50 East into Annapolis, Maryland. My anticipation grew and I noticed that Dr. Reed was tired of driving. I could tell because he kept chewing more pieces of gum. He then began talking to me about the challenges that lay ahead in graduate school. He told me he would do what he could to support me, but expected me to focus and concentrate solely on my graduate studies. Dr. Reed's words reminded me of the speech my grandfather gave me every day, when I worked at the *Shop*. "*Keep your mind off those girls and concentrate on those books!*" "*Once you get those books, the girls will still be there and you can do what you want!*" It felt good to reminisce and think about how my grandfather established a strong work ethic within me.

I almost forgot about traveling to my new home, when I saw a sign that read "City of Dover 5 miles." Out of the darkness, flickers of light cut across my field of view. As our speed diminished near the city limits, I thought about how far we had traveled in a day's time. We finally arrived in Dover around midnight. Most of the city was shut down because of the time and weekend. The city reminded me of a small country town in Arkansas. I didn't get a chance to explore my new surrounding because it was dark. We headed straight to the campus dormitories.

Dr. Reed dropped me off at a brand new housing complex and made sure T.S. and I got our keys to open our room. I got my stuff out of the back of the truck, shook Dr. Reed's hand, and said thanks for getting me there safely. He showed me where his office was on campus and told me to come see him the next day. I finally talked with T.S., who trailed us the entire way alone. I remembered him from one of Dr. Fitzpatrick's classes at UAPB. T.S. helped me with some of my bags and when we got to our room, we talked for a while. Both of us were still pretty wound up. I let my parents know I made it safely to Dover and went to sleep.

Graduate School at DSU

The next morning T.S. and I went to Dr. Reed's office and met Mrs. Givens, his executive assistant. We talked about the next steps in the DEVELOP program. Mrs. Givens was responsible for making sure we settled in and had everything we needed to be successful. Dr. Reed explained more about the DSU graduate school, and how incoming students chose mentors. After our conversation, we met the rest of Dr. Reed's staff. He escorted us across the campus and gave us a brief tour of the buildings, laboratories, and infrastructure. I liked the campus because it reminded me of UAPB, but appeared to be more spread out. It was bigger than most HBCUs I had seen.

During our conversation, I asked about the marching band as we passed by the Fine Arts building. Dr. Reed knew my musical background and mentioned to the band director that I would be coming to DSU, and had marched at UAPB. The band director wanted to meet me. Dr. Reed told me that the director wanted to know if I was interested in joining his band. He had already given me a word of warning, before our pending conversation, and said he would have to talk with Mr. Johnson about that. Dr. Reed felt I was brought to DSU to do graduate work and band rehearsal and travel might interfere with my studies. I had no intention of joining the band and actually tried to avoid talking with Mr. Johnson until classes started.

My goal was to have a good excuse when and if asked about joining. I did stop by Mr. Johnson's office to say hello. I was a little curious about the band and his program. Mr. Johnson gave me a tour of the music department and told me more about his role as band director. He was very persuasive and reminded me how much fun it was to march in the band, but my mind was totally focused on graduate work. I appreciated but declined his offer. I did tell him I would come to the first game of the season, to see the band and the football team. In the back of my mind, I did miss music and the excitement of performing, but wanted to focus more on my career in science.

I tried to work on my feelings of nostalgia for the band in my spare time, because I needed to make the most of my new opportunities in graduate education. We ended our conversation on a good note and as I was leaving his office, I asked him where he went to school. Mr. Johnson told me he graduated Class of 75', from Southern University. He talked highly of Dr. Greggs as his mentor and now I understood why Wash was offered a job at DSU. Dr. Greggs' philosophy was still influencing the hiring of Southern University alumni. I was glad we had our conversation because I planned to meet with some potential advisors, before the end of the week, and wanted to make sure my schedule was clear.

I went back to the dormitory and talked with T.S., as we both prepared to meet with the biology faculty in the morning to choose our permanent work sites. We devised a strategy for both of us to work in the same laboratory, so we could help each other and make sure we graduated in the two-year time frame outlined by the DEVELOP program. The next day we met with the chairpersons of the biology and chemistry departments and toured their laboratories. Dr. Reed informed us that a faculty member in the biology department, who worked with proteins, was very interested in taking one or two students in his laboratory. T.S. and I met with him the next day and did a walk and talk with him across the campus.

He asked us what kind of research we wanted to do. I said "FISH," presumptuously. He looked at T.S. for a moment and then gave me a puzzled expression and facetiously asked if I wanted to go fishing. I told him, "No!" and said I wanted to do some "FISH." He still didn't understand what I was saying, until he asked for an explanation. When we got to his laboratory, I told him that when I was in Chicago, *"At Northwestern University!"* I was introduced to a technique called *"Fluorescent In Situ Hybridization"* also called FISH. This technique was used to determine chromosomal abnormalities, in developing embryos before they were born, and screen them for potential birth defects.

This was the best example I could think of to explain what FISH meant. He seemed to understand, but explained that on the graduate level, students normally work on projects related to the principal investigator's expertise. His expertise was in sodium channel proteins and electric eels. He talked with both of us for about an hour, sometimes going off subject and mentioning things around the campus that we were two new on the scene to understand.

Even though he talked off subject, we were optimistic about our futures in his laboratory. We told him he was recommended by other administrators on the campus. He seemed to enjoy being sought after. After we talked, we told him we would think about his offer for a week and let him know as a follow-up to discussions we were having with other faculty members in the department. He agreed with this plan of action. I left his laboratory feeling inspired, but also cautious because he seemed indifferent and I really didn't know what to expect from him.

Meanwhile, the first game of the year was approaching. That weekend was the kick-off for classes that would start the next week. Game day was busy and thousands of people showed up, which seemed to overwhelm Dover. I was familiar with HBCU football games and got my ticket early, so I could find a good seat. I tried to sit where the band would be so I could reminisce about ΚΚΨ and my former musical life. Then I heard "Tweeeeeet-Tweet-Tweet-Tweet-Tweet as thunderous bass, snare, and tenor drums began playing a marching cadence.

I immediately stood up to try to see what the band looked like, as they got closer to the viewing stands. I could see them marching. When they came around the turn toward the stadium, they opened up musically. I felt like I did in the Marching Musical Machine of the Mid-South and a surge of emotions pulsed through my body. I couldn't help but move to the beat. The stadium shook as the band filed into the stands next to me.

Each musical section filed in row by row and I remembered how the tubas at UAPB came up the stands last, swaying from side-to-side with the *"ugly look"* on their faces. Our goal as *Tuba Dogs* was to intimidate rival bands, but more specifically their tuba section. I was mesmerized by the drums and beats and didn't realize the game was about to start. When the pre-game ceremony began, I looked at the "youngsters" in the band and wished for my glory days again, but was proud of their opportunity to march.

Mr. Johnson saw me in the stands and waved while he was conducting, as the pre-game ceremonies began. The band played *Lift Every Voice and Sing*[37] and the DSU Fight Song. I never heard an HBCU band perform the *"Black National Anthem"* at a football game. I was so proud that DSU had a rich sense of history and African-American culture. As soon as the military color guard left the field, the game started and the band stood in the stands during the kick-off. Mr. Johnson wasted no time cranking up the band's sound.

My eyes were transfixed on the tubas and I looked for who I believed was the strongest player in the section. I spotted a guy at the bottom of

---

[37] Lift Every Voice and Sing- is often referred to as the Negro National Anthem and Black National Anthem. It was written as a poem by James Weldon Johnson and set to music by his brother John Rosamond Johnson in 1905.

the row and my guess turned out to be correct. I could hear that he was the strongest player in the section and knew he was the section leader. He had the tubas rocking. When he shouted commands over the percussion beats, his section immediately followed his instructions.

The football game was boring and by the end of the first half, Mr. Johnson called up musical arms again. The band played a spectacular rendition of *Africano*, by Earth Wind & Fire. I remembered that song, because it was one of Wash's favorites. Mr. Johnson reminded me of Wash, by the way his managed his musicians. When they played their first song, he motioned for them to conserve their energy. The musicians were really excited and fed off the crowd's energy and participation.

I reflected because Wash was all about balance and he never liked to hear one section overpower other sections, especially the tubas. We could always overpower any group of musicians, regardless of their numbers, but he taught us to have a "strong but considerate sound." There were times when Wash allowed us to really give some power, and there was nothing like hearing a strong bass line support and balance the other sections.

Mr. Randolph Johnson

The second quarter started and the band wasn't as active, but I knew they were preparing for their half-time show. The game clock wound down slowly and play was stopped at the five-minute mark, for an official time-out. The band began to file to the sideline and my anticipation and anxiety increased. I didn't think anything was wrong with me, but I couldn't sit still. When the tubas passed near me, I saw their bells glistening in the Sun. I told the section leader to *"Give 'Em the Bass!"* He already had a pretty ugly demeanor, but when he saw me he made an even uglier look on his face, as he left the stands and huddled his players. The second quarter ended and the band was finally lined up and ready to go on the field. The public address announcer introduced the staff of the *"Approaching Storm"* Marching Band.

Mr. Johnson signaled a drum roll and downbeat into the theme, from the movie *2001: A Space Odyssey*[38].The trumpets and bass drums introduced the piece through their rim shots, which shook the stadium. As each part of the song was played, Mr. Johnson reacted violently as though he was evolving with the music. By the time the song climaxed, he had thrown his hat and acted as though he was physically exhausted.

He really sold the entrance skit, which became his trademark, and the crowd went crazy. This opened the field show, as the drum major blew his whistle in repetitive succession and the musical showcase began. The band marched on the field and performed several classic tunes and one popular radio hit. I watched carefully in the stands how they marched and what kind of sound they produced. I was "impressed" by the field show, but felt an "aching" for music again. As soon as the band returned to the stands for the second half, I tried to let that feeling go.

I tried not to think about my musical past and just wanted to be an interested spectator. The crowd was huge and it almost seemed like "Homecoming Weekend." The band took a break after half-time and when they reassembled at the end of the third quarter; they warmed up for the fourth quarter. As soon as the referee blew the whistle to stop play, Mr. Johnson motioned the tubas to play. I saw the section leader hold up two fingers and then they played a "riff.[39]" The whole crowd started to bounce and move in rhythm to the tuba bass line. It was over for me. I

---

38 2001: A Stereo Space Odyssey- is a science fiction movie directed Stanley Kubrick in 1968 that chronicled what life would be like on earth in the 21st Century. This movie has been called by many as the "greatest movie ever made."

39 Riff- is a repeated chord progression that musicians use to emphasize a memorable musical phrase.

stood up and looked directly at the tubas, as they rocked from side to side feeling every note. Then, I got this nasty look on my face, just like the tubas on the field, and that moment felt like my experiences at UAPB. I didn't want to control my emotions because I was really into the music.

Their sound hit me deep. I felt like I was in a trance. The music *"Shook me up inside,"* but at the same time was *"Charming My Soul."* People next to me were trying to get my attention and making fun of my odd movements, but I didn't care. I was totally engrossed in the band's sound. After the tubas finished and the crowd was more animated, Mr. Johnson sent the band into a medley of songs, during each stop in play.

It was almost too much for my senses to hear *"Skin I'm In"* by Cameo, *"Zoom"* by The Commodores, *"Before I Let Go"* by Maze, *"Stairway to Heaven"* and *"Backstabbers"* by the O'Jays, *"Ribbon in the Sky"* by Stevie Wonder, and then *"Can You Feel It"* by The Jacksons. All the songs had heavy bass lines and the tubas supported the rest of the band with "Power!" All I could do was close my eyes and let the music travel through me.

When I opened my eyes, Mr. Johnson was looking directly at me. He smiled and then motioned with his fingers like he was playing an instrument and swayed from side to side. I knew exactly what his gesture meant. I nodded in the affirmative and said, "Yes!" He went back to directing the band. Then, I started thinking about how my band uniform would look and wanted it right then.

I couldn't believe I just joined the marching band, but all of my actions since leaving Arkansas and settling in Delaware probably could have predicted this move. The time away from music was hard for me. I knew what challenges lay ahead, but I needed music and was determined to make it work. After the game, I followed the band back to their band room for the *"Go Down[40],"* and told Mr. J. I had to join. I didn't think about what I would tell Dr. Reed, but at that moment, it didn't matter. My head was pounding from listening to the drums up close. I wanted to be in that number. I thought about the game and my decision all weekend, until I literally had to face the music.

On Monday, I went to Dr. Reed's office and cautiously told him I joined the band. He paused and looked at me with concern and reminded me of my duties in the DEVELOP program. I told him that band wouldn't

---

40 Go Down- is a term used to describe how the band marches back to their band room following a home game. Spectators and fans usually follow the band until the music stops and this is a time to highlight each musical section one last time after the game.

interfere with my studies, but he still wanted to have a conversation with Mr. J. Meanwhile, I tried to adjust my schedule that hadn't really started yet and knew that my studies would have to be my priority. When I left Dr. Reed's office, I felt the right decision was made and the thought of marching again gave me a sense of purpose and peace. T.S. and I made a decision to study proteins. We made preparations to spend more time in our new advisor's laboratory, before we enrolled in graduate classes. Our majors were General Biology, but the *DSU Graduate Curriculum and Courses* were agriculturally based.

Once we finally settled in Dover, Dr. Reed invited us out to dinner to talk about our transition from Arkansas to Delaware. He tried to measure our motivation for what was to come. Dr. Reed always checked on us like a father would his children often opening his home for us. We were happy about our living arrangements, but more concerned about our stipends and how we would pay for food and living expenses. When we found out we had to pay for our own housing costs, we were surprised and disappointed.

Dr. Reed reminded us that this is how it works in graduate school and within the DEVELOP program. It was funny, because I had already counted my stipend money as gross and planned to do some shopping for clothes, shoes, and other items, in a sales tax-free state. I had to learn to budget money I hadn't received yet, which was just another learning experience, in the next phase of my life.

We prepared for classes on the following Monday. One of the classes we took was taught by our new mentor, and it would be our first opportunity to try to understand his teaching style. From the brief conversation we had with him, we learned he was originally from Mississippi and a former riverboat captain. He was an avid *Marilyn Monroe* fan and respected her accomplishments. The graduate classes seemed straightforward, but I waited to discover how much more work I had to do to keep up.

T.S. and I would always review the materials as soon as classes were over and then go to the laboratory to receive instructions from our new advisor. We both worked on tandem projects and our goal was to help each other finish strong in the two-year time frame. I didn't have a car, so I walked to local stores and took full advantage of Delaware's sales tax-free culture.

Meanwhile, I was fitted for my band uniform and Mr. J. gave me the music to learn for the next field show. The first day I was introduced to the band, I was a bit nervous. Mr. J. put me on the spot because he let

Four Tubas, a Guitar, and a Gallery of Cheerleaders

everyone know I was a graduate student and excited about the band, from seeing their first performance. There were already eight tuba players, so I had to choose one of the last instruments available.

I learned the marching steps quickly. Mr. J. surprised me because he would hand out all the steps and formations for the field show prior to rehearsal. I was used to learning the music first, then the steps, and finally incorporating all the components, before the end of the game week. I tried not to compare and contrast the difference between his style and Wash's, but found myself holding on to what I learned at UAPB. I eventually had to accept that this was a different band and band director, so I needed to follow his lead.

Mr. J. was a strict disciplinarian and in total control of his band. He loved Earth Wind & Fire. Most of the band's playbook came from their albums. I understood his vision for band and liked the fact that he expected us to play the music, just as he had written it, without omissions or additions. One day during rehearsal, someone was playing the musical passages and rhythms differently than Mr. J. wrote them. He stopped the band and barked toward the trombone section and pointed to the person and said *"Who is messing up my music? Stop messing up my music and play the music like I wrote it!"*

This was funny to me because I felt more mature than everyone else in the band and understood that the "youngsters," fresh out of high school, were getting a taste of the intensity related to the seriousness of Black College Marching Bands. Mr. J's attitude made me more diligent during practices and rehearsals. I eventually started competing with other tubas in the section. I wanted to take my musical skills to another level. I got into a rhythm with the marching band and was pleasantly surprised that practices were held only on certain days during the week. This was cool because it allowed me to study.

The first couple of weeks were easy because we didn't travel, and the home games were fun. When I marched into the DSU stadium for the first time under the banner and colors of the *Approaching Storm*, it felt strange. My original band colors were black and gold, but now they were red, white, and blue. I thought about how a week earlier I was sitting in the stands looking at the band, but now was in the band. I was happy and fulfilled and knew that as soon as my "chops[41]" were ready, I would be a better player.

---

41 Chops- refer to the level of musical skills a person has and is also slang in jazz genres for the ability to make music effectively.

I felt I did well during the first game. I didn't miss any steps and my music was on par. Dr. Reed was at the game and he greeted me afterwards and smiled, when he saw my uniform. He reminded me to stay focused and I told him I would. I don't remember if we won the game or not, but 1994 was one of DSU's most successful football seasons. I do remember that when we marched back to the band room for the *Go Down*, I was really into it. When my turn came to showcase how the tuba could be twisted, bent, and turned, as if it were a fixture on my body, I made sure not to let the crowd down. I was out of breath, sweating, light-headed, and hoarse, and knew that music was what defined me. I felt I couldn't ever let that feeling go.

After our first game, we were given the rest of our marching season schedule, which included travel to Liberty University, and a game in the Philadelphia Eagles' stadium against Florida A & M University (FAMU). Their stadium was open due to the NFL strike. The last game of the season was at Howard University, in Washington, D.C. I was looking forward to all of the away games, because I remembered how much fun it was to travel with the UAPB band. My greatest attention was on FAMU. That was one band I always wanted to face. I only heard about the "*8 Wonders of the World,*[42]" but knew FAMU had a rich musical tradition established by Dr. William P. Foster[43]. My goal for the next couple of weeks was to study hard and practice more than I ever had, just to be ready to travel. I felt the younger tuba players had more energy, but I had more experience and knew that during long marching seasons, experience is what counts the most.

When I returned to the dormitory, I took a nap and when I woke it felt like I had been running for eight straight hours up hill. I was sore everywhere and every one of my muscles tensed. I was glad we had the weekend to recover because on Monday, T.S. and I would start learning our thesis goals in our new mentor's laboratory. My goal was to take it slow and develop a competitive pace in the band and in classes. I became

---

42 8 Wonders of the World- were a set of eight drum majors that marched with FAMU and known for their style, rhythm, and ability to excite crowds.

43 Dr. William P. Foster- is an African-American Bandmaster, known amicably as "The Law" and "Maestro," who worked at FAMU from 1946 until his retirement in 1998. Dr. Foster served as president of the American Bandmasters Association and was inducted into the Florida Arts Hall of Fame, The National Association of Distinguished Band Conductors Hall of Fame, and the Florida Music Educators Association Hall of Fame.

very neurotic about studying because I remembered how my lack of preparation cost me a competitive GPA at UAPB. I loved music, but science was my priority.

During my first semester at DSU, I enrolled in a *Basic Biology* course, *Statistics*, for my math requirement, and *Cell and Molecular Biology*, a core elective taught by my thesis advisor. The first thing I noticed about graduate courses was that they were much longer than undergraduate courses and we met less often. I enjoyed the extra time to study, but had to really work on my attention span. After three hours of lecture and laboratory, my mind started to wander.

The course load wasn't bad and a good start, while I adjusted to doing more hands-on laboratory research. T.S. and I tried to arrange our laboratory schedules with our class schedules and eventually developed a good balance. We really wanted to do well in our advisor's class and I felt more pressure to quickly get up to speed to do thesis research. We only had two years to complete the program and then transition to the University of Vermont, so both of us didn't want to waste any time.

Our advisor met with us once a week to get updates on our work, after his initial speech outlining the laboratory's research focus. He was interested in proteins and wanted both of us to do similar projects, but with different research outcomes. I was just excited to work with an electric eel and really disappointed when I found out that we would only be using the extracted tissue for experiments. During the day, we read research and review articles, while our advisor encouraged us to learn key protein isolation techniques.

I wasn't an avid reader, but liked to write, so I made notes from the lectures and discussions instead. I thought my band schedule would interfere with my studies, but rehearsals were not a distraction, because Mr. J. was organized and to the point. I had never been to a rehearsal that lasted only two hours, including field show work. We learned our music for an hour then drilled the show steps on the practice field for the remaining time.

The next home game (Towson State) wasn't very interesting because the rival band didn't come with the football team, but we did a good show for our crowd. I continued to practice and learn the "ins and outs" of Mr. J's program, and when my *chops* were in shape, I was ready to support the section leader. I respected Mr. J. because he was focused on band music, but also stressed education.

Once a week he told us to *"Use the band to help you with school, but don't be used by the band!"* He saw band as an opportunity to do something you loved and get a good education, from your hard work and dedication. Mr. J. wanted everyone in the band to have good grades and measured his scholarship amounts based on that fact. He required weekly study in the library, every Tuesday night, and made sure we were there by ushering us into the building.

By the end of the semester, sixty percent of our band was on the Dean's list. Education was always top priority. I understood how Mr. J. became so successful at DSU, in such a short period of time. He would talk with me from time to time because I was older. He let me know that he wasn't there to make friends with the band students. His only job was to make sure students got good training, teach good music, and help them achieve their goals. He also believed that *"Bands make and mold positive people!"*

My experiences in the *Approaching Storm* band were unique. Normally graduate students, who aren't music majors, don't participate during the marching season. I felt differently and wanted to connect with the younger students, but found it difficult. They were just starting their musical careers and I had re-embarked on a very familiar journey. Over time, I found a way to connect with others in my section first, then the rest of the band. I met and interacted often with the saxophone section leader *Diana Duckett*. She was the most intense musician I had ever seen marching in the band. Diana was friendly off the field, but when marching, she was all business. I saw her a lot because she worked in Mr. J's office. She was just as intense as I was about the band and music.

I still wanted more interaction in the band, but there was no KKΨ and I hadn't been there long enough to find a Prince Hall Masonic Lodge to attend. I followed the section leader and tried to grow musically with the other band students. Mr. J. felt that the *"Band was a fraternity and sorority all in itself,"* and nothing was greater than a family of musicians. I bought into this idea. Band was my support group, but I needed to feel more involved.

Liberty University vs. DSU

After the first four weeks of the marching season, we prepared for our first road game against Liberty University, a predominantly white university in Lynchburg, Virginia. This was the famous Christian university led by

Reverend Jerry Fallwell. Mr. J. organized the ranks and we set up a nice field show early in the week. By Friday, we were ready to go to Liberty, and I was caught up in all of my courses.

The next morning we loaded the buses and headed toward Lynchburg, Virginia. The bus ride was cool, but I still felt older than most of my band mates. The conversations they were having were some of the same ones I had many years ago. I tried to connect with them in any way I could, by embracing their views on education and life, knowing that I had a little more experience.

I was more focused during this trip and while everyone else was listening to music or talking, I was reading books and preparing for my next exam. The bus ride took about six hours. By the time we got there, I was tired and decided to rest before the game. I went to the hotel room and went over the field show and music in my head and on paper, to make sure I didn't make any mistakes.

Mr. J. was very good at field show arranging. He normally used the same template from the previous week, but changed the formations, dynamics, and music to create different visual effects. I was curious how Liberty's crowd would embrace our music and marching style. Suddenly, I flashed back and thought about how Mr. Lott was under significant pressure to design field shows, at certain Catholic high schools in Arkansas that differed from our usual show formats. In high school, we learned to perform more conservatively. I didn't understand or care at the time. All I knew was that we didn't play or perform like we were accustomed to. Mr. Lott explained it to us like this, *"There is a time and place for everything so let's not let other situations place us in a small musical rectangular box and limit our capabilities." We are a diverse band with diverse strengths and talents."* Mr. Lott spoke prophetically then. Now, I understood what he meant.

I was curious if Mr. J. had to face similar dilemmas or pressures, on the college level, to change the band's music to fit certain audiences. I found out later that he was always concerned about going to Liberty and sought advice from Dr. O'Neill Sanford[44], another Southern alumnus and the first African-American band director of a Division I band program. Dr. Sanford knew that Mr. J. always created shows with style and class. Mr. J. would make shows he said "my mother can watch and enjoy." Dr.

---

44 Dr. O'Neil Sanford- is one of the most prolific music educators in the nation. He currently is Director of Bands at Norfolk State University and has been involved in music and music education since 1965.

Sanford told him to bring in the same show styles he had always done before because they would inspire the football team, as well as entertain the crowd. Mr. J. listened by improving the show from the previous week and was confident our band would be well received.

When we arrived in Lynchburg, we got off the bus and checked into our hotels. I was glad to finally stretch and within minutes, my band roommates and I unpacked the equipment. I decided to try to get some work done and something to eat in the hotel. The other students wanted to eat at McDonald's or Wendy's using their travel allowance. I didn't want to eat like I ate in my undergraduate days, so I decided to eat in the hotel's restaurant.

While I was sitting there, Mr. J. and his entire band staff entered the restaurant and acknowledged me. I guess we all had the same idea about where and when we wanted to eat and tried to find a quiet place to unwind. He invited me to join him and his staff for lunch and I did. This was the first time Mr. J. and I talked up-close because I was always busy trying to learn the music, steps, and band personnel. I noticed, from joining their conversation, that his staff was passionate about the *Approaching Storm* band. I could tell that Dr. Gregg's philosophy instilled through Mr. J. was rubbing off on his assistants. We talked band for a while, then I excused myself and went to the room to get some rest. I was tired of studying and used the rest of my time to think about tomorrow's game.

I rested well and before game time proudly assembled my band uniform and prepared for another musical battle. We really didn't have to worry about being late because the stadium was across the street from where we were staying. We also knew Mr. J.'s philosophy which was *"If you are with me, then you aren't late."*

The Liberty-DSU game was so popular in years past that hotels in the area actually competed for our band to stay with them. They seemed glad to see us drive up. After the morning introductions, we lined up by instrument ranks, the drum major blew the whistle, and we loudly marched into the stadium kicking up our heels, as dust flew into the air. Our routine and music were still the same for the half-time show. My concerns weren't as important as I first thought and the game began.

The first half was uneventful. The crowd was more subdued than other rival crowds and our football team was winning. The time quickly approached for half-time. Mr. J. gave us his pre-half-time instructions. We knew he would do his traditional entrance, after the drum roll, but I wondered how the crowd would receive it. As was his style, Mr. J. excited the crowd with his rendition of *"2001: A Space Odyssey"* and both sides cheered. Our sound was clean and the entire band didn't miss a step or beat. Even our dance routine was received with cheers and praise. I knew then that Mr. J.'s system was polished and he was a very good band director. We finished our show and exited the field, while Liberty's band prepared to perform their show.

Most of us were winded. I noticed that I wasn't as tired as I was the first couple of games and happy to be close to regaining my previous musical stamina. After half-time, we removed our overlays because of the heat. The Liberty band shared cold drinks with the entire band and staff. The game was exciting and our team won by a small margin, so we had reason to celebrate during the ride back to Dover.

Later that evening, we went back to the hotel and rested before our return home the next morning. I felt pretty good about band, but was still cautious about the future. The ride home was lively and because we rode on chartered bus lines to our performances, we could watch movies. Some people brought their own videos. One of Mr. J.'s favorite movies was "The Wiz[45]," starring Diana Ross and Michael Jackson, which seemed to always make it on the bus viewing list. Once I got back to the dormitory, I told T.S. about my experiences and went to sleep. By the time I woke up, it was Sunday afternoon. When I finally got up, I prepared to go back to the laboratory and continue classes on Monday. I had fun traveling with the band, but wondered where my weekend went.

T.S. and I were now working and spending the majority of our time outside of class in the laboratory. I was somewhat unclear about my goals as a graduate student. Our thesis advisor had tunnel vision regarding how our research should proceed. During the first couple of months, my protein isolation experiments didn't work. I immediately questioned the research approach. My concern was whether my experiments would disrupt my graduation timetable. At that time, I didn't realize how graduate level research progressed, but quickly learned that repetition and patience are key ingredients for experimental success.

I needed some help, so I looked for more guidance from my thesis advisor. I realized he wasn't Dr. Orr and I would have to learn how to make things progress in the laboratory, when experiments didn't work. It was a learning process for me. Being independent, created more stress

---

45 The Whiz- is a 1978 movie, based on the original "Wizard of Oz" starring Diana Ross, Michael Jackson, Nipsey Russell, Mabel King, Richard Pryor, and Lena Horne. It was created to capture the African-American experience and culture.

than I first thought. Meanwhile, Dr. Reed was planning a trip to Vermont to discuss the progress of the DEVELOP program and to introduce us as the first graduate students from DSU.

I had never been to Vermont and couldn't point it out on a map. Dr. Reed briefed us about our visit and wanted us to use that opportunity to try to network with other faculty, staff, and students. I was excited to go because it would be a nice change of scenery. The DEVELOP program staff, at the University of Vermont, were interested in T.S. and I. This was no ordinary weekday getaway.

First Time in Vermont

Dr. Reed, our new thesis advisor, T.S. and I took a chartered van to the Philadelphia International Airport and flew into the Burlington, Vermont International Airport. The first thing I noticed was how small the airport was in comparison to Baltimore Washington International (BWI), and other airports I had seen. The second thing I noticed was how no one in the airport looked like me. I already had stereotypical views of the state anyway, but was really shocked not to see one or two black people anywhere in the airport. I thought I would see a black flight attendant, or airline customer service representative, but that wasn't the case. I was glad to only be there for a couple of days. Quaint Dover wasn't looking so bad now.

When we arrived at the University of Vermont, we were greeted with smiles and warm conversation. T.S. did most of the mingling. I sat quietly and thought about what it would be like to live there. I did talk with some people, but was more distant than anyone else. I had never been in a place where I felt so different. Dr. Reed saw me sitting alone and told me to interact more with the graduate students and faculty, who were there to discuss their research and career objectives.

I complied and realized that I would have to develop a more outgoing personality, in these settings, to be successful in this place. I didn't open up fully because of personal shyness, but was glad Dr. Reed recognized the need to encourage me to interact with others in the room. I was able to talk with other students, about their careers, and found out we had common strengths and weaknesses. We also toured the campus and became familiar with some of the laboratories and their directors. Our last stop was a meeting with Dr. Brooke Mossman, a tenured professor who was also the Director of the Environmental Pathology Training Grant. She was a dynamic researcher, fundraiser, and speaker, hailing originally from New York State.

Dr. Mossman was well connected in many research circles at the University of Vermont (UVM) and around the world. She was deeply involved with the DEVELOP program and worked closely with Dr. Reed to help establish a network with DSU, to support graduate student education. She showed us her state-of-the-art laboratory in the pathology department and invited T.S. and I to really consider UVM for graduate work. Dr. Mossman encouraged both of us to apply for the Environmental Pathology Training Grant, which would give us stipends and research money.

If we chose that path, we could choose the laboratory we wanted to work in and not have to worry about funding for the first two years. I was interested in that proposal because I wanted to be flexible where I worked and felt that having research dollars already in place, would make me a more competitive graduate student. By the time we left Burlington, I was more excited and comfortable with UVM and glad for some exposure to other cultures and areas. Now when asked, I could honestly say I had been to and know where Vermont is on a map.

When we got back to Delaware, T.S. and I talked strategically about future opportunities in Vermont. Both of us tried to paint a best-case, worst-case scenario about our academic futures. I still had a "*bird in hand*" mentality and wanted to make sure any opportunity at UVM wasn't wasted. T.S. felt differently and was still holding out for other options. He wanted to be closer to his family in Arkansas and Texas. We debriefed with Dr. Reed and he felt we did a good job marketing the program, but wanted me to improve my networking skills. I understood what he said and tried to work on being more open and articulate with my friends and colleagues.

FAMU vs. DSU

My next big event was the football game against FAMU in Philadelphia. Because of contract disputes among the players and owners of the NFL, players were locked out and the 1994-1995 seasons were disrupted. This gave two HBCUs an opportunity to play a Classic[46] game involving rival Mid-Eastern Athletic Conference (MEAC) opponents, in a normally occupied professional stadium. We were all excited to be performing in the same stadium as the Philadelphia Eagles and knew that exposure would be good for DSU and the music program.

Mr. J. was tenser that week than I had seen any band director during my musical career. He was focused on every aspect of the game. Not only did he have to deal with the promoters for the game, but also had to negotiate with Dr. Foster regarding the schedule of events for that weekend. Mr. J. knew the reputation of FAMU and understood that they would be the featured band in Philadelphia. All of the advertisements and flyers used the tradition and rivalry between two MEAC schools, to hype a monumental event. We were the home team and there were major discussions about who would perform first.

Organizers from FAMU's camp decided they wanted to do a pregame, half-time, and post-game show. They introduced those ideas to Mr. J., who thought about it and agreed, but told them that we would do those same shows too. We never knew what was going on behind the scenes, but Mr. J. was trying to give us as much leverage as he could, before we went up against a powerhouse band. After promoters and organizers finally reached an agreement with the two schools, the bands were scheduled to do much more performing than usual. The pre-game, half-time and post-game showcases between the bands were set. We also had other public relations appointments in Philadelphia.

This was a big weekend for DSU alumni and fans. We were scheduled to perform the day before the game at a pep rally in the downtown Philadelphia Plaza, and that night at City Hall, made famous from depictions in *Rocky* films. The most famous scene depicted Sylvester Stallone's character Rocky Balboa running up the City Hall's steps, to train for his big title fight, while *"Eye of the Tiger"* released in 1982 by the American rock band *Survivor*, played in the background. The event and atmosphere was appropriate for our band, which felt like Rocky's character and had to overcome seemingly insurmountable odds.

The buildup and hype, during our rehearsal week, was filled with

---

46 Classic Football Game- is a game associated with HBCUs who compete against each other in neutral cities, which can accommodate larger crowds than their stadiums can hold. These games also promote rivalries between schools and serve as community events that stimulate fan participation and positive publicity for participating schools.

Four Tubas, a Guitar, and a Gallery of Cheerleaders

anticipation. A former member of the FAMU band brought his old uniform to remind us of the colors we would see a lot that weekend. I was familiar with FAMU, but never faced them in musical competition. Their reputation for size, power, and style preceded them and was their trademark along with their historic band director.

Behind the scenes, Mr. J. was still negotiating with promoters and Dr. Foster regarding the order of events during that weekend, in the city, and during the game. Because we were the home school, we were scheduled to perform after FAMU. Mr. J. didn't want us to follow FAMU and he worked hard to make another deal. He knew FAMU typically marched over 300 people and didn't want our band, which marched 112 instruments and 16 auxiliary, to feel intimidated.

Mr. J. negotiated with Dr. Foster to allow us to go on first, by reminding him that FAMU was the featured band. He made FAMU's staff feel like they were the only stars of the show, while protecting our musical interests. Mr. J. convinced Dr. Foster that allowing us to perform first would be *"saving the best for last."* Dr. Foster agreed, at the strong behest of one of his top assistants.

His assistant wanted FAMU to go on first, but Dr. Foster sided with Mr. J. After that hurdle was crossed, Mr. J. turned his attention and our focus to the three shows we would perform during the game. Because we had so many home games and did a new show drill every week, we had several formations we could rearrange to fill the three slots. Rehearsal was intense that week because we knew we were *"David"* and wanted to figuratively take out *"Goliath."*

Every one was attentive and focused. As soon as we knew what songs were chosen for that weekend, we rehearsed them constantly and tried to polish the field show music. Our goal was to finish the music first, so we could work on the show drills. Mr. J. always had us spell things on the field such as DSU or other short phrases during half-time, but this week we were rehearsing to do the scoreboard drill[47]. I always wondered how band directors created the exact numbers on the field to match the half-time score. Sometimes it seemed like the bands were clairvoyant and knew what the score would be, but as I watched and learned from Mr. J.'s musical playbook, I realized there was a logical explanation.

Mr. J. began charting scores, as a high school band director. When he outlined formation steps, there were always gaps caused by low band

---

47 Scoreboard drill- is a marching drill designed to create the current football game score on the field in big block letters.

numbers, which prevented an accurate presentation of the scores drill concept. Mr. J. organized the shows on paper and then drilled them to correct mistakes. He could always find errors on the field that weren't evident in the charting process.

Mr. J. told me that when he used angles at ground level, those same angles were different when seen in higher fields of view. This is when he realized that charting paper didn't give the correct perspective. From that point on, Mr. J. always viewed show drills from high in the stadium, so he could see how the dimensions and formations matched the concepts on paper. He used this technique to teach us how to create half-time scores.

As an interesting backdrop, when Mr. J. was younger, he was an amateur magician and made extra money by creating illusions for small audiences in his home town. His goal was to re-direct attention away from what people believed to be important and relevant, to something that may not or may not be as important. This created the desired affect. When he did the score drill, people asked him how he knew what the score would be. He jokingly told them he was dialed into *Dionne Warwick* and her *Psychic Friends' Network*. The goal was the illusion and he pulled it off very well.

Marching a Score Drill

In order to teach us how to make scores, Mr. J. taught each section of the band how to collectively make numbers **(0-9)**. We learned to make any combination of numbers, including a dash, to distinguish the two. I was amazed the first time we made a score because I only occupied one spot, but in the collective whole helped create two large numbers and a dash. We drilled the scores concept every rehearsal. Mr. J. would allow students to create fictional scores such as **(57-19)** in our favor, for practice, and we would create them on the field. Mr. J. had a bigger vision for the score drills during half-time. He always planned on meeting his alma mater in the Heritage Bowl[48], which featured the SWAC and MEAC football champions.

Mr. J. told me he loved Southern University with all his heart, but really wanted to face them and show his mentor and the *"Human Jukebox "* that he could do the scores drill on the field. Mr. J. also wanted to

---

48 Heritage Bowl- is an annual football game featuring the winner of the Southwest Athletic Conference (SWAC) and the Mid- Eastern Athletic Conference (MEAC).

take this game's performance to the next level. He wanted to send a message to Southern University, by creating the current temperature, and a description of the weather, such as "67° F," and include the letters "PC" for partly cloudy.

He never had the personnel to do the half-time scores in high school, but now wanted to showcase that skill if DSU made it to the Heritage Bowl. If DSU beat FAMU in Philadelphia, the stage would be set to finally face Southern University. Everyone in the band was in a different zone by Wednesday of that week. Our instruments were tuned and shined, our uniforms were pressed, and our canvas spats were clean and white. Mr. J. kept reminding us to *"Do your talking on the field!"*

The big day was finally here. We loaded our buses and traveled to the *"City of Brotherly Love,"* which was less than two hours from Dover. We arrived early in the afternoon. Our first stop on that Friday was a pep rally in downtown Philadelphia. It started to rain, but we had a scheduled performance so that didn't matter. We got off the bus and marched around the business district to promote the football game and showcase our talents. When we finally lined up in the plaza, we played two or three songs for the crowd. I was surprised when Mr. J. called me out to lead the tubas in a riff we had just practiced the night before.

This was Mr. J.'s style. At any time he would call you out to play or perform, so your objective was to always be ready. I was nervous about the riff because we had just practiced it, but was ready to do my best. The tubas broke rank, lined up in front of the band, and we literally *"Blew the walls down."* The bass was strong and the syncopated beat with the percussion created a dynamic sound in downtown Philadelphia.

The atmosphere was unique because of the tall buildings that seemed to reverb every note. The band was excited and danced to our song. I was pumped, because it worked out very well. Mr. J. signaled the drum major to cut us off and we walked back triumphantly to our designated ranks near the percussion section. After a few announcements, we left the downtown area and went to the hotel to rest for our performance at City Hall.

The time seemed to fly by and before I knew it, we loaded the bus again to go to our next event. Once we got to our destination, I remembered that scene from *Rocky* and felt nostalgic because there was so much history and culture in Philadelphia. Once we lined up, we warmed up and played a few songs for a small crowd and did several sound checks. This event was all about publicity and we had some fun. Mr. J. was not as tense as he had been earlier in the day. As we played, the crisp night air helped our sound cut through the city streets. The tubas really carried a strong bass line. I always liked playing in cold weather because it would make the band's sound more sharp and crisp.

We played a couple of songs on the steps of City Hall and then we saw in the distance, one lone FAMU musician adorned with their traditional green and orange overlay uniform. I guess they sent a scout to critique our sound, so we tried to make an "impression" and send a message that the *Approaching Storm* was ready to battle. I believe they were scheduled to play at City Hall as well, but decided to rest before the game. We stayed in our positions for another thirty minutes, as Mr. J. went through our music list late into the evening. He tested dynamics, articulation, and power. Once our assigned repertoire was complete, we loaded the bus and went to the hotel to get some rest.

I was in a pretty good mood and remembered the Southern University game, four years prior, and made sure I was ready to redeem myself. The other tubas were just as focused as I was. We took some time to go over a riff called *"Fright Night,"* now known famously from *Transformers* cartoons and movies. We wanted to challenge their tuba section or be ready if they challenged us. I didn't care that they had twenty-five tubas and we had nine.

All I cared about was giving our band the best chance to showcase our talent. I had never performed in so many different settings, during a weekend, and made sure I rested my "chops" and mind. I didn't want to miss a step or note during the performance. Back at the hotel, some people decided to get something to eat, but I stayed in and enjoyed the room. There was less than twenty-four hours to go before show time, so I found peace and fell asleep.

My rest was good and when my alarm clock went off, I knew it was time to do what I had done for so many years in Arkansas. We suited up and prepared to go to the stadium. Once we got there, we lined up in parade rest formation to do our final checks. No one really said a word before we got to the stadium. Even people from Philadelphia seemed to place their connection with the city in the background until after the show. Before we entered the stadium, we stretched and warmed up. Some of our band members were looking for the FAMU band, but our resident expert on their tactics reminded us that when they got to the stadium everybody would know. Three hundred people would be hard to miss, especially with instruments.

Four Tubas, a Guitar, and a Gallery of Cheerleaders

The drum major blew the whistle and we marched into the stadium and prepared for our pre-game show. As we were adjusting our ranks, we saw one bus, then another bus, then another bus, then another bus, and another bus pulled up beside the entrance gate. The doors opened and their green and orange uniforms meshed together to form the *"Marching 100*[49]*"* as their ranks organized right behind us. Spectators were transfixed on them, while most of us were still thinking about the pre-game show.

I just wanted to see them up close and hear their much hyped sound. Their drum major blew his whistle and they jolted from parade rest to attention. Soon after four drum taps, I heard why they were so respected as one of the most innovative HBCU marching bands. I guess they were trying to send us a message, because before entering the stadium they opened up. Their sound was truly *"Stereophonic."*

I had to give them their props because a band that size, with a sound that clear, demonstrated to me that they were all about sound teaching, musicianship, and discipline. I listened for just a moment, just to get a taste of their persona, and then turned my full attention to my duties on the field. I wasn't impressed by FAMU anymore and only concerned about giving my all for Mr. J., his staff, and the *Approaching Storm*. I felt like I was representing DSU and the state of Delaware. I was so proud to be wearing the red, white, and blue uniform.

Once things settled down, we did our pre-game show. Our first song was *"I Belong To You,"* by Toni Braxton. We made large TONI letters on the field. Out of the TONI formation, we made a large DSU to represent our school, and then played *"For The Cool In You"* by Babyface, for our dancers. Then, we created the letters COOL. This was our big warm-up for the rest of the game. We ended the pre-game with our *"Fight Song"* and *"I'm So Glad,"* as we approached the side lines. There were no mistakes and in my mind I was thankful that one set of drills was done.

I was ready for the start of the game and when we finally sat down, we could see FAMU's band, which covered a large portion of the visitor stadium seats. After the pre-game, they fired against us first, but we were more subdued and knew that our main concern was half-time, so we conserved our energy. The excitement was in the air and though they tried to coax us into playing, Mr. J. wanted us to be ready to entertain our DSU fans first. Soon after the kick-off, FAMU wasted no time pumping

---

49 Marching 100- is a nickname for the FAMU Marching Band. Some historians state that FAMU was the first HBCU marching band to successfully integrate 100 instrumental players on the field.

up the stadium. Our side responded in-kind with our trademark " **D------** You've got your **D----** You've got your **D, S-----** You've got your **S---** You've got your **S, U-** You've got your **U,** You've got your **U-** What's that spell **D---S---U.**"

Our fans sang the phrases in unison and we knew we had home town support from Dover. FAMU continued to try to challenge individual sections, during the first quarter, by motioning and mocking our players, but Mr. J. opted to use the percussion section to represent the entire band and allow us to rest. Our percussion and their percussion traded heated rudimental challenges. Though we were much smaller, we had more flair when we played. Eventually, the FAMU band director ended the constant challenges and both bands watched and supported our teams throughout the first quarter.

As soon as the quarter ended, FAMU watched our side and waited for us to play our first set of songs. Mr. J. had waited long enough before sparking up the band and the crowd, who had anxiously waited to hear us play. We played another popular radio song and the crowd sang along, which helped us sound much bigger than we were. FAMU wouldn't be outdone and quickly played the same song to try to establish their musical superiority. We just laughed and felt our circumstances were just like *"David vs. Goliath."* We knew that the end of that biblical story was a victory for David.

The second quarter was almost over. I ran the field show through my mind a hundred times, and tried to make sure I didn't forget a step or note. I literally tuned everyone else in the band out. Mr. J. gave us our assignments and we filed down the stairs to our sideline posts, before the clock hit (00:00). I focused my mind because our field show was dynamic. Once it began, it didn't stop until the end. Four drum taps later, the half-time show commenced. The pride, spirit, and honor rested on our shoulders, as musical ambassadors for DSU. Everyone was on point and the steps, formations, and music were perfect for our show. Our first song was *"Can't Keep Going"* by Take 6, then we played *"Before I Let Go,"* by MAZE, and the breakdown song was Aretha Franklin's *"Deeper Love."*

Our sound was strong and clean, and when we made a large DSU on the field, the crowd was amazed. I was amazed myself because I couldn't fathom how all those formations were created in a matter of minutes. I had new respect for Mr. J. and all other band directors, especially at HBCUs, because of their ability to organize hundreds of people, at the same time, and have them march in different direction to music; ending in the same place on the same note. Marching band directors' talents are truly *"Gifts from God."*

By the time we arrived at concert band formation, we were ready to excite our fans with music and dance, as part of the HBCU half-time tradition. The tubas didn't let up and I felt stronger the longer we stayed on the field. I could hear my old sound. The blending of the baritone and sousaphone was back for me. I followed the lead of the section leader, as he asked all the tubas to give the section more power. I was happy to comply. For our dance routine, we played, Prince's *"Let It Go"* and then did the *"Tootsie Roll."* We did very well on the field and I was proud of our performance.

As we marched off the field, the FAMU band lined up to present their show to their fans and tried to upstage our performance. When they finally marched onto the field, they were huge and seemed to fill the view from one end zone to the other. They were about business. When they opened up for their first selection, their sound shook the bleachers. I wasn't in awe, but did respect their musicianship.

After their show, I felt our music and performance was better, even though FAMU had an awesome sound and incredible instrumentation. FAMU performed well and represented the state of Florida and the MEAC with professionalism and class. Both crowds gave our band the crown. I was ecstatic and ready for the post-game show, because we all knew FAMU had to respect the *Approaching Storm*. I think they underestimated us a great deal. All of our players were fine tuned that weekend, so our efforts were designed to beat a larger musical opponent.

The second half was livelier than the first. We traded songs back to back with them, until the fourth quarter. I guess they wanted to try to prove their dominance in the stands, but we had done what we came there to do. We still had to do another show. Our focus was on making the end game score, using a new set of music and steps. I don't recall the final score, but believe DSU lost 22 to 15. Our post-game show was just as lively as the pre-game. There were a few mistakes due to fatigue, but we had accomplished our mission.

We played *"Because of Love"* by Janet Jackson then a C.C. Penniston song called, *"I'm Not Over You,"* and ended with Heavy D's *"You Got Me Waiting."* We received a lot of praise, but I think the crowd had seen enough marching bands for a day, so their response to our music was ok. When FAMU performed, the crowd was much more subdued. After the game, we packed our things for the bus ride back to Delaware and I remember being emotionally and physically spent. This was one of the most exciting events that happened to me, up until that point. Now, I could finally say I performed against the legendary *"Marching 100,"* and helped my band win the musical battle.

The bus ride home was quiet and I looked forward to the weekend to rest and prepare for an exam on Monday. When we got back to Dover, the city and campus were quiet because everyone was in Philadelphia enjoying the festivities. By the time I made it to my room, I was so tired I fell asleep in my uniform and didn't wake up until Sunday afternoon. When I woke up, T.S. was gone. I really enjoyed having the entire room to myself.

Later that afternoon, I wanted to do some things in the city, but didn't have a car. Dormitory living wasn't what I thought it would be. I did enjoy the convenience of being on campus and the meal plan, but felt I was too old to be staying in the dorms. This prompted me to start looking for an apartment. My goal was to have my own place by the spring semester or early summer. The rent was pretty reasonable in Dover and because of the state's tax-free status; a lot of my money was freed up to do other things.

I talked with Mrs. Givens about apartments in the area. She gave me some very good leads near Dover Air Force Base. Mrs. Givens also told me she would give me a good recommendation and to let her know if I needed any additional help. I really liked Mrs. Givens because she was a humorous and fun person to be around. When I stopped through Dr. Reed's office, I spent the majority of my time with her; if he was in a meeting, or not there. She treated me like her son and tried to provide me with as much guidance as she could. I appreciated her nurturing and she and her husband made me feel at home in Dover.

I talked with T.S. about getting an apartment, but he decided to become a resident assistant (RA)[50] instead, to save money. He prepared to move out of the dormitory in the spring, while I was still looking for a place of my own. My laboratory work was going FINE, but I concentrated more on my classes. I settled down and was more familiar with the city and began venturing out more. The first thing I did was try find where the Prince Hall Masons met.

I wanted to stay connected to the brotherhood. There was one spot in Dover called the *"Square Club,"* where most of the Prince Hall Masons

---

50 Resident Assistant- is a student who lives in a college or university campus housing facility and provides a support network for students living on the campus. Resident assistants work as counselors and mentors to first and second year students.

spent their time. The first time I went there, the older masons quickly challenged me to make sure I was legitimate. I felt pretty good that I successfully passed the tests and they embraced me as a brother. Now I had another place I could go to when I missed home, but Dover was nothing like the Bluff.

I was still happy with the band, but the rehearsals and my study schedule were starting to clash. The season was fun but long. We had five games left. Fortunately for me, we only had to travel to the final game of the season, at Howard University in Washington, D.C. I was looking forward to this game for a number of reasons. It was also our last game and I wanted to catch up with Wash to see how he was doing.

After traveling to Liberty University and finally meeting FAMU, I felt I had satisfied my urge for band music and seriously contemplated my future with the *Approaching Storm*. I knew I still had a passion for music and the band, but living in the dormitory and marching in the band, as the only graduate student, made other interactions difficult. I wanted to do something different than what I experienced in the Bluff, so after hours of contemplation I decided that this would be my last season of marching band.

I guess the fatigue and disconnect I sometimes felt, by interacting with a group years younger than me, made me feel out of place. Once I finally made my decision to retire from HBCU marching bands, I felt better and knew I could immerse myself in my research, which wasn't going well. I also knew to break clean with my decision, so my feelings for band would only inspire me to be an avid supporter of Mr. J. and the *Approaching Storm*. My biggest issue was transportation. I needed a car. T.S. was cool and would always give me a ride to Wal-Mart or the grocery store whenever I asked. I didn't want to wear out his generosity, so I started thinking about a car and how I would get one. My old car was wrecked, right before I left the Bluff to go to Chicago, and I had to use the insurance money to purchase my plane ticket.

I talked with Dr. Reed for some advice about buying a car. He told me he was satisfied with his Ford pickup truck. I told him I wanted a new car because I thought my graduate student stipend would cover a monthly car payment. Dr. Reed looked at me and paused before saying, *"Don't buy a new car son; get a used one. Right now I hope you don't get a new car because it will only give you a note to pay each month."* He then asked me what I was doing for Thanksgiving. I told him I had no real plans.

Dr. Reed said he wanted to go to Arkansas, during the Thanksgiving break, and if I wanted to go, I could ride with him. I was happy to get the request because it would be a cost-effective way to get back home and another chance for me to show him I understood more about highway driving. I felt pretty good because I had some plans lined up for the holidays and was excited about getting back to Arkansas. The next couple of weeks went by slowly. The majority of our games were at home. Two games were too far for us to travel to, so we took those weekends off. By the middle of November, I was worn out with band and graduate work, but happy to still be connected with music.

The last game of the year was finally here. It was sentimental for me because I knew this would be my last time in a marching band uniform. We traveled to Howard University to put on a good show for our fans and alumni. During the game, we used some of our best drills during the season. Mr. J. put together a nice collage of songs.

He reprised the "2001: Space Odyssey" skit, but added a royalty song, which represented Great Britain, and used traditionally in Buckingham Palace to announce the monarchy. Mr. J. added that song to advertise the jazz band's trip to England in January. He was more animated than he had been before. Both sides of the stadium went crazy to his antics.

We played songs from Toni Braxton, Babyface, Janet Jackson as well as *"I'm Not Over You"* by C. C. Penniston and Heavy D's *"You Got Me Waiting,*" while making TONI and COOL on the field. We also did a drill to the tune *"Going in Circles,"* and were surprised that Howard's band did the same drill. This wasn't uncommon among band directors trained at Southern University, who often referred back to Dr. Gregg's musical playbook.

I didn't get a chance to see Wash, but knew he was in the area. I decided to try to catch up with him another time. Once I got back to Dover, I hung my uniform up and almost kept it, but knew the university would probably charge me with theft by receipt. I checked it in and pondered my immediate future, without the marching band. Normally, I would have participated in the concert band, but knew if I did, I would be back in the saddle and never want to let music go again.

I finished the semester with a strong GPA and was ready to get to Arkansas to see what all of my friends and family had been doing in my absence. Dr. Reed reminded me that he was going home and I was ready to help him drive. A day before Thanksgiving, we left around 5 p.m. and arrived in Pine Bluff, at 11:00 a.m. the next day. Traveling with Dr. Reed was cool.

Four Tubas, a Guitar, and a Gallery of Cheerleaders

This time, I did most of the driving while Dr. Reed rested. I knew he liked *Blues* and I was into it too, so I brought some of my father's tapes to appear more mature. I also had some *Rap*, but was afraid to put the tape in the car's player, because I didn't want to offend him with some of the more explicit lyrics. I was surprised during this trip, because I fully expected him to be monitoring me every minute. He just told me which direction and highway to take and left the driving up to me. He trusted me with his life and then went to sleep.

Every couple of hours a noise on the highway or in the truck would wake him and he would ask me if I was ok. I was more than "ok," just because he showed more confidence in my abilities. I wasn't going to let him down. We did our usual plan and only stopped for gas. Because I did most of the driving, he was more rested and refreshed going and on the way back.

The first thing I learned on the drive back to Arkansas was why they called the mountains in Tennessee, the "*Smoky Mountains.*" By the time we got there, it was near midnight. In front of the window, was a thick fog that seemed to hover on the highway. I was tired but more alert and realized that this fog wasn't going to leave like the morning mist. It was heavy for miles. I sat up in my seat, tightened my seatbelt, and slowed my pace. One side of the highway, was the road leading traffic in the other direction and frequented by large 18-wheeler trucks. The other side was a steep cliff.

There was no way I would fall asleep under these circumstances. I was too afraid. By the time we got out of the "*Smoky Mountains,*" the fog lifted and Dr. Reed was ready to relieve me. I don't know if I would have let someone my age and lack of experience lead me through one of the most dangerous stretches of highway in the daytime, let alone at night. I was glad he was mentoring me like my father would and I continued to respect and grow from his experience.

We only stayed in Arkansas for four days, but it gave me a chance to see some old friends and get telephone numbers to try to stay in touch. I missed home, but was glad to have been out of the state and experiencing new things. Most of my close friends were gone. The only PBH brothers in town were Jay and Keith, so I spent the majority of my time trying to see what they had been up to. Nothing really changed about the Bluff, so going back wasn't easy, but it wasn't that hard. After our brief holiday stay, Dr. Reed and I headed back to Dover, the same way we came. This time we made good time. Both of us were well rested and I was more familiar with the road ahead.

The time I spent home sparked a fire in me to try to do something unique to connect me with the Bluff. Music was always the key. My dream was to write a book about my experiences in the marching band. I also wanted to write about the love I have for KKΨ, after a confrontation with one of my older fraternity brothers, known affectionately as "*Chico.*" This brother was one of the most unique and wisest men I had ever met. Though I didn't know it at the time, he sparked a desire in me, during my UAPB days, that helped give me purpose when I no longer marched with the *Approaching Storm* and felt isolated in Vermont.

When we got back to Dover, the rest of the year was cool. I rested and planned for the spring semester. T.S. was getting ready to move out and live rent free, while I relished in the fact that I could have the entire room to myself. Dr. Reed said he was going home for Christmas, so I tagged along again, but this time we stayed two weeks because of our long semester break.

It was fun being home during the holidays. Most of the PBH brothers returned to be with their families and we were able to fellowship. I got used to riding home with Dr. Reed and he appreciated the help with gas and driving. He would often call me up, at the spur of the moment, and ask me to help him drive to Arkansas. I didn't care and was actually grateful, because it was another way for me to get home and often more convenient and cost-effective than flying.

Spring 1995

I began the spring semester more focused on classes. I still supported the band and Mr. J., as they prepared to travel to London, England. Most of my classes were specialty courses including *Immunology* and *Methods in Experimental Biology*. Now that band was over, my time in the laboratory was more intense. T.S. and I felt like the laboratory was our second home. We spent our days and nights there. Our advisor wanted me to do more protein chemistry experiments and try to collect better results.

My mind was caught between research and the void created by the lack of structured music in my life. I really missed Arkansas and had saved some notes and lots of materials from my college days. One day, I decided to go through those notes to reminisce and found pictures and writings from my junior and senior years at UAPB. I remembered my research experiences in Dr. Orr's laboratory, but my fondest memories were of the band.

I thought about my role as fraternity president and remembered the *Extravaganza*. As I turned the pages and straightened crumpled papers, I had an "epiphany" and wanted to write a unique book about my experiences in Arkansas, and highlight my musical fraternity. At first, I laughed at the thought of writing a book. Then I saw an old photograph, which was clipped from a yearbook page highlighting the brothers of the EX chapter of ΚΚΨ.

I was in front holding my first fraternity hat and looked serious. That picture helped me reflect on the love of music I had in Arkansas and Delaware, which for me was still unsatisfied. I knew that going back to the marching band wasn't an option. Not because I lost the desire, but because my focus was now more academic. My greater goal was to achieve a Ph.D. in science.

I organized those notes and eventually found more and decided to write a book, but didn't know where to start. I brainstormed and thought about the fraternity pledge lines that came through our chapter and used those as a marker to build my story. Initially, I was only going to write about the fraternity, but decided to include the sorority, to make sure their influences were shared as well. I had this great idea, but the materials I needed to finish the project were in Arkansas. One fraternity tradition that always intrigued me was the fact that historical records were always kept in the band room, which included all of the pledge lines for our chapter of ΚΚΨ. This was a requirement for each line that crossed and designed to create a lasting monument to their achievement in music.

I realized then that the Seventeen Psionic Subtones (SΨS) didn't have a pledge board in the band room. My mind began churning. It was time to complete my pledge line's musical board. I knew when I pledged ΚΚΨ that the tradition was that once a line of musicians finished, they would offer a gift to the fraternity. This gift would be a permanent marker of remembrance in the band room, in the form of a pledge board, with the names of pledge line members. SΨS was such a large line and had so many diverse people on it that once we joined the fraternity, we went right to work and never completed our board.

My first goal was to create our line board, which would be labeled with our real and musical names. I knew Dr. Reed would be going home often, so I made sure to offer my services as co-pilot, because I really wanted to go to that year's *Extravaganza*. I planned my trip accordingly and knew if I could get home and into the band room, the entire history of the fraternity was stored there. That would be where I started.

The day I decided to write a book was the day I merged my musical side with my academic side. I know now that the mission was inspired by God, because it took me years to complete the project. What started as a hobby, eventually saved my academic life. Excitement aside, writing was still on the back burner for now.

This semester at DSU was slow. By the end of the first quarter, T.S and I were both tired and wanted a break. My mind was focused on writing a book. I felt I could do it because I liked to write. Ideas for the project kept coming. Our advisor was in and out of the laboratory and left most of the research decisions up to us.

I learned more that semester about research and why it often doesn't work, than I've learned in my entire life. We all were frustrated. I just wanted a project that worked, so I could write my thesis. I talked with my advisor on many occasions and let him know that I was concerned that the protocols, used for protein extraction and characterizations, were not yielding reproducible results. I'm sure he felt it was because of my work ethic, but I needed more guidance.

Every day was an experimental roll of the dice. Our research was innovative and "cutting edge," so there weren't many examples to learn from. Not many laboratories worked with electric eel tissue. We were in a good position to compete for major research dollars. I didn't panic about the research because I was living and doing well. My advisor was satisfied with our intentions to discover something new. I was more pessimistic and he knew that, which is why we clashed from time to time. I was young and still very new to this type of research. My philosophy had always been *"Work hard at it, and it will work itself out."* But this time, hard work wasn't enough.

On the graduate level, research takes more thought, planning, and execution, which was a new concept for me. I talked with Dr. Reed about my experiences, with my advisor, and he explained to me that, *"This is how research works, and the only way you will be successful is to try, try, and then try again!"* I believed Dr. Reed because he had an extensive research background in agriculture and had been where I was trying to go. I used his talk to motivate me to work harder and longer to try to get the job done. Meanwhile, T.S. moved to his new location on campus and we talked less. I stopped by a lot to try to catch him, but he was busy mentoring students and organizing events for the dormitory. We kept in touch, but weren't as close as we used to be.

Getting around for me was still slow. I needed a car, but I had to get some help from SOMEBODY. I talked to my father about transportation. He was prepared to help me get a vehicle, through a connection my grandfather had at the *Shop*. I knew whatever I got would be used, but was concerned. My experiences with used cars could always be described as "*fix-it-until-it-quits.*" I talked to Dr. Reed about a car and he encouraged me to wait until later to get something new. Now, I had two frustrations. One was transportation and the other was the laboratory, which eventually became secondary in my mind because the *Extravaganza* was coming up in about three weeks, and I was ready to go.

During the next couple of weeks, I rearranged my room and prepared to go to the *Extravaganza*. I was out of fraternity attire and tried to find some regalia, before I went home, to make sure I represented well. I looked all around Dover and couldn't find any stores that did short-order embroidery of fraternity insignias. I tried to wrap up all of my research assignments. By the time we were preparing to leave, I was caught up in classes and in the laboratory. As was a usual tradition, Dr. Reed and I left around 5 p.m. heading south toward Washington, D.C. and Virginia. This time our ride was quite different. We drove a *Mustang 5.0* that Dr. Reed had purchased for his daughter.

The comfort level in that car was totally different than in the pick-up truck. I was excited to get a chance to drive it. By the time we made it to the *Smoky Mountains*, it was my turn to drive. As usual, Dr. Reed gave me the keys and went to sleep. As soon as I touched the gas pedal, I knew I was driving a very good car. The acceleration and speed was amazing.

The car seemed to hug the road, when passing other cars and going around curves. I averaged 80 miles per hour, but the car rode so smoothly that when I gazed at the speedometer, I was going 90 miles per hour. I quickly knew to slow down. Dr. Reed seemed unfazed by how fast I was going. That was the first and last time I drove a car like that and understood why so many people loved Mustangs. Our ride to Arkansas was fairly quick. I truly believe it was because of the car. It was mid-morning when we arrived. Both of us were energized to be home. Dr. Reed dropped me off at my father's house and told me when he wanted to leave. I thanked him again for ushering me back to the Bluff and he said "no problem."

My father had been very mysterious about my coming home and just encouraged me to make sure I made the trip. I thought it was because he found me a car to drive. That was on my mind the entire drive. I let Dr. Reed know that I may be getting a vehicle and would probably have to trail him back to Dover. He said "no problem." To my surprise I was right, and sitting in the driveway was a red 1988 Chevrolet Cavalier. I was like a kid at Christmas trying to get to the biggest present first. I walked up the steps and beat on the door to get inside the house, as soon as I could.

My father answered and said "Hey, Boy!" and I said "Where are the keys?" Dr. Reed drove off, my father handed me the keys, and I ran to the car and opened the door to my new ride. When I first looked at it, I was somewhat disappointed and told my father that I wanted a new car and questioned why he bought that one. He angrily asked me, *"Why do you want a new car that you have to pay for each month? That car outside is just fine, so be satisfied with that!"* My "greenness" was really showing. If I had known then, what I know now, I would still be driving that car. I also thought about how Dr. Reed had given me the same advice weeks earlier.

As soon as I opened the door and turned the ignition, I fell in love with that car and apologized for being so immature. I sat outside my house revving the engine, before it was warmed up, to try to duplicate the power I felt when I drove the Mustang. My father stepped outside and told me not run the engine up that high because I was creating a lot of smoke and could "throw a rod" and tear up the car, before I got a chance to drive it. I settled down, but my excitement was overwhelming.

I took a drive over Keith's house, to show him my new car. My next stop was the UAPB campus and I headed straight to the band room. I wanted to see what my musical brothers and sisters were doing. I knew they were preparing for the *Extravaganza*. The members I pledged before leaving Arkansas were now in key leadership positions, so I was very happy.

My musical brothers and sisters greeted me with love. I felt more connected to what was really important to me than ever before. We shared stories about the fraternity and band. I really missed music, which is why my focus on writing a book about the musical fraternity and sorority grew into a passion. I knew my time was limited, so I gathered as much information as I could about the history of the fraternity. I spent the majority of my time writing down present and former members' real and musical names. This was my journal and the first step in my writing process. Once I finished, I had my start to the book project and was happy to have come home to begin my research.

I worked so hard to try to talk with people and get as much information as possible, that I almost missed the opening of the *Extravaganza*. When the lights came up and the fraternity and sorority were introduced, it took me back to my best days at UAPB. The show was dynamic and exciting. One of my fraternity brothers dubbed his copy, before I left, and I took the memories of that event with me back to Delaware. I was lucky to get a copy of the performance because it was so popular.

The next couple of days I spent more time with my family and planned to trail Dr. Reed back to Dover. I knew I was following him and very familiar with the route, but decided to read a few maps and outline my drive back anyway. I learned a lot about exits and directions and was ready to take my car back to Dover. Dr. Reed's schedule changed and he decided to leave earlier than expected, so we could maximize our daylight driving time.

I followed him closely, until we got out of Tennessee, then I backed off and enjoyed the ride. The hardest part of the drive was over for me, once we passed the *Smoky Mountains*. Later in the evening, as the Sun was going down, I could see Dr. Reed ahead of me enjoying his Blues. We still had about two hours to go before Dover's city limits and one more gas stop. I knew the drive would be over soon. The drive was cool and I felt independent coming into Dover with transportation. We finally made it back to Dover and I thanked Dr. Reed for helping me get back safely.

The next day I was back in the laboratory and in classes. Driving fatigue set in near mid-week. I was ready to have a weekend with no big responsibilities. I decided to go to the *Square Club* to fellowship with other Masonic brothers on Saturday night. We talked about Masonry and I asked them about apartments and housing in the area. I stayed up late that night. The brothers kept me laughing, until early in the morning. My other goal for that weekend was to go to church, because I hadn't been since moving to Dover.

Growing Up in the Church

I grew up in the church and was always actively involved in the service during "Sunday School," "Youth Days," and "Vacation Bible School." As I got older, my role in the church changed and I spent more time with older adults. The Deacons and Trustees of the church assigned me to pray for the "*Tithes and Offerings*," during every youth service. They were training me to be a good steward in the church. I remember the times I prayed using the same scriptures more experienced Deacons used. I could only paraphrase, because I would always forget the entire scripture passage and commonly repeated what I heard others say. A senior member of the Deacon Board always used **Malachi 3:10 (KJV)** during the service.

> Bring ye all the tithes into the storehouse, that there may be meat in mine house, and prove me now herewith, saith the LORD of hosts, if I will not open you the windows of heaven, and pour you out a blessing, that there shall not be room enough to receive it.

Then he asked rhetorical questions to the congregation by paraphrasing **Malachi 3:8 (KJV)**

> Will a man rob God? Yet ye have robbed me. But ye say, Wherein have we robbed thee? In tithes and offerings.

It was interesting watching him give the same two scriptures and use the same approach, to encourage giving every Sunday. I tried to adopt his technique, but sometimes thought it was funny when I would make my plea. I really didn't understand the context of the scripture. Specifically, how churches regardless of their denomination, rely on giving to maintain their places of worship. It took me ten years from those experiences, as a young adolescent, to realize the value of giving tithes and offerings and how *"sowing a seed of faith"* was a major part of developing a true relationship with God.

I wasn't a good prayer and always tried to write a speech to memorize, before I closed my eyes and spoke. I was going over my prayer notes during one service. Deacon McClendon told me to stop making speech notes before I prayed. He said *"Relax and tell God what's on your mind, and take your time young man!"* I appreciated his wisdom and from that moment on, I tried to create prayers from my heart and let God speak for me.

I was an active participant at Indiana Street Baptist Church, but wasn't very spiritual. I only read the Bible during Sunday school, and at the beginning of the morning worship service. I became more engaged in

God's words, after I became a Mason, but would always pick the wrong time to try to read the Bible for understanding.

I wanted to study the word of God more fervently because of Masonry, which was based on sound biblical lessons. Our lodge always encouraged diligent Bible study, but unfortunately I found the best time to read the scriptures was right after the responsive readings, and during the pastor's sermon. One time in church, I was sitting in the front row where the Deacons sit and decided to read my Bible, during the pastor's sermon. Deacon McClendon, also a Mason, tapped me on my shoulder and said *"Listen to the pastor now and read the Bible later!"* It's not that I wasn't interested in what the pastor was saying; it had more to do with the fact that I felt most inspired to read the Bible during the church service.

I listened and complied with Deacon McClendon's request, because I knew he was telling me something for my own good. I tried in the future to always pay more attention to the *Word* delivered by Pastor Solomon. One of my favorite parts of the worship service was the responsive readings. Because of repetition, I had unconsciously memorized the entire passage.

Blessed is the man that walketh not in the counsel of the ungodly, nor standeth in the seat of the scornful. But his delight is in the law of the LORD; and in his law doth he meditate day and night. And he shall be like a tree planted by the rivers of water, that bringeth forth his fruit in his season; its leaf also shall not wither; and whatsoever he doeth shall prosper. The ungodly are not so: but are like the chaff which the wind driveth away. Therefore, the ungodly shall not stand in the judgment, nor sinners in the congregation of the righteous. For the LORD knoweth the way of the righteous: but the way of the ungodly shall perish.

Psalm 1:1-6 (KJV)

During this *"Call and Answer"* worship period, I was one of a few people who could actually keep up with the pastor's reading pace. Indiana

Street Baptist Church was a great church to grow up in. My pastor was a true shepherd in the church and community. I respected his position and understood and embraced his philosophy, because he baptized me as an adolescent. The pastor's ministerial staff and first lady were also very inspirational. They mentored young men in the church to respect, honor, and hold on to a strong spiritual foundation, inside and outside our church walls. Our motto was *"Indiana Street Baptist, A Church Where Everybody is SOMEBODY In Christ."*

I reflected as I turned over in my bed and looked at the clock, frustrated because I had only thirty minutes to get to church on time. All of this ran through my mind, as I rushed out the door to attend Calvary Baptist Church, located on the outskirts of Dover. I sped down the highway, because by the time I showered and dressed, I only had fifteen minutes to get there. This would be my first time attending that church, so I didn't want to be late. Once I got there, I drove into the parking lot and from a distance thought the church was smaller than Indiana Street. But when I got inside, it was adorned with spiritual artwork and the multiple rows of pews made it seem much bigger.

The service was long, but the preaching was on target. The choir was inspirational, but I felt odd going to another church, even though Indiana Street Baptist's church's covenant said *"It is the responsibility of members to reconnect with a new church, if ever out of the range or jurisdiction of your home church!"* I really used my feelings of loyalty as an excuse not go to church as often as I should have. After service, I promised myself that I would be more involved with this church, but my intentions never quite matched my efforts. Slowly, I got away from my initial training in the church as a young adult, but God never let me forget several life changing scriptures.

Rejoice, O young man, in thy youth; and let thy heart cheer thee in the days of thy youth, and walk in the ways of thine heart, and in the sight of thine eyes: but know thou, that for all these things, God will bring thee into judgment.

Ecclesiastes 11:9 (KJV)

> Remember now thy Creator in the days of thy youth, while the evil days come not, nor the years draw nigh, when thou shalt say, I have no pleasure in them; And further, by these, my son, be admonished: of making many books there is no end; and much study is a weariness of the flesh. Let us hear the conclusion of the whole matter: Fear God, and keep his commandments: for this is the whole duty of man. For God shall bring every work into judgment, with every secret thing, whether it be good, or whether it be evil.
>
> **Ecclesiastes 12:1, 12:12-14 (KJV)**

I attended Calvary Baptist Church one or two more times, while I lived in Dover. I did attend other churches, but never supported my Christian faith, as much as I tried to as a youth in Arkansas. I felt like God would always be there for me, whenever I decided to embrace my faith again. I decided instead to concentrate more on my studies and everything else I wanted to do.

The rest of the semester I worked really hard in all of my classes and used my success, in those classes, to compensate for the frustration I was dealing with in the laboratory. The experiments were always hit or miss, but now the protocols and procedures complicated data collection and analysis. I talked with my advisor about the project and looked for some guidance, but he continued to press me to re-evaluate my technique and stay the course until something worked. Now, I was impatient because DSU was the middle step in my journey to pursue the doctorate degree. I didn't want anything to disrupt my plan.

T.S. and I were told that the DEVELOP program outlined two years of study at DSU for the Master's degree, and three to four years of study at the University of Vermont, to earn a Ph.D. We already knew in order to finish within the allotted time frame we would have to go to summer school and work in the laboratory. There were no more long summer breaks, as we were accustomed to in our undergraduate days, so my plan was to move out of the dormitory, at the end of the semester, and relocate to a new apartment.

I asked Mrs. Givens about the most cost-effective and best places to live in Dover. She said she would do what she could to help get me a place. I diligently looked for apartments near the campus. The problem for me was still money. My stipend wasn't big money, but it allowed me to eat and go out on a date from time to time. Most of the places I found were more expensive than I could pay.

I wanted a one-bedroom, so I could organize my things and lay out my plan to write a book. Unfortunately, all of the one-and two-bedroom apartments were hard to get. Most rental agencies also wanted a comprehensive rental history, which I didn't have. I finally found a place near Dover Air Force Base called *"General's Greens"* that was willing to work with me, my income, and lack of rental history. The only apartment type I could afford was one-bedroom efficiency. I was happy with that. The apartment complex needed a reference; Mrs. Givens gladly supported me through Dr. Reed's office, and my lease agreement was approved. I was so elated to finally get my own place and felt doubly blessed to have a car and new residential address.

I was more motivated in my classes and finished the semester strong with a 3.0 GPA. I took some time off, but didn't go home because I wanted to prepare to move. Lots of things were happening on DSU's campus, including the building and construction of a new science facility. The new building was adjacent to our old laboratory site, so we would have to help relocate our equipment and supplies during the summer. I was excited about the move and felt that a change in location would give my experiments a new "karma." We made our move quickly. It didn't take me long to be back in the laboratory working to isolate and characterize proteins and carbohydrates from electric eels.

Meanwhile, I put all of my things in storage to prepare to move into my apartment in June. I couldn't wait until that day. As much as I anticipated my independence, I was also thinking about my book project and began reminiscing more about $KK\Psi$ and the band. I watched that year's *Extravaganza* tape over and over again and thought about how I would build a monumental story.

I still owned the computer I used in Arkansas, so I decided to type notes on it every day and then compile the information later. My goal for the next couple of months was to at least outline the project, so when I could work on it, there would be nothing stopping me. This was no easy task because Microsoft® Office wasn't available, so I used the DOS operating system to input and format all of my information. The work I had to put in didn't matter. I wanted to publish this book because it gave me a sense of purpose and I was determined to accomplish my mission.

The day of my big move was here. T.S. helped me get organized and transport my things to my new place. I really didn't have much stuff, considering the fact that everything I owned was still in Arkansas. Once I got settled in, T.S. and I planned a road trip to Arkansas before the new school year. I was more familiar with the drive and could do it alone or with a co-pilot.

We both knew that the next six to eight months would be a pivotal time in our graduate careers, so the time for travel was now. We only enrolled in one pre-requisite class and thesis research during that summer, so we could maximize our time in the laboratory. We planned our trip and both of us went home for completely different reasons. T.S. wanted to reconnect with his family, just in case the time between his next visit was extensive. I was going home to gather more information for the book.

As soon as all of our in-class laboratory experiments were complete, we left for Arkansas. T.S. still owned a Jeep and told me he had driven it across the country, but I was so excited about my car, that I volunteered to use my vehicle instead. We left the same time Dr. Reed and I traveled and saved about an hour, using a few shortcuts. Once we got to Arkansas, I dropped him off at his family's residence and went straight to the UAPB band room to take pictures and gather more information. I talked a lot with *"Hud"* because he was the oldest member of the chapter and advised the fraternity for many years. I knew he would be a great resource. *"Hud"* loved passing on historical information related to UAPB's legacy and our fraternity's musical history.

"Hud" was the official historian of the fraternity because of his tenure, but I wanted to step into his role and saw this book project as an opportunity to do that. *"Hud"* and I would talk for hours, during his regular work day, while many of the younger fraternity and sorority members stopped by the band room, curious about our efforts. I didn't spend much time with my family during that visit to the Bluff, and they wondered why I so focused on something I couldn't name.

I did take some time to make sure my family was all right, but my passion grew for this book project and all of my energy was directed towards it. T.S. and I spent about a week in Arkansas, then returned to Dover. Once we got back, the next couple of weeks were business as usual. We prepared for the start of the new school year and our final three courses. We still had more laboratory bench research to do, but after this semester, we wouldn't have to worry about class lectures or exams.

Our advisor wanted more effort in the laboratory. He knew that our tenure was quickly coming to an end, so we really had to get moving with the experiments. T.S.'s experiments were working from time to time, and mine weren't working at all. My advisor could see my frustration building. Every time I asked him about the next step, he reminded me that *"Research is a process so stay the course."* I had never done research of this nature before, so I tried to do everything I could to prepare for writing and defending a thesis. I knew I could write, but needed to work on interpreting and presenting data, in a forum of my peers.

The time had come to organize a thesis committee of three faculty members and the Dean of the Graduate College, to oversee my work. I selected four people including Dr. Reed, to help me manage my remaining time at DSU and keep me on target to thesis completion. Once our committees were formed, our advisor was more proactive with his role in our research decisions and goals. Now, we would meet regularly with him and began presenting weekly updates on the progress of our individual projects, as well as our timetable for going to Vermont. We talked some about why the projects weren't working, but the majority of our meetings were planning sessions to try to keep us on track.

T.S. and I both got into a rhythm in the laboratory and were learning, but my problem was still the inconsistency of the experiments. I felt more pressure to try to get things moving, since I would now have to answer to my thesis committee, but more importantly to Dr. Reed. I had so much respect for Dr. Reed that I didn't want to let him down, and remembered how my relationship with Dr. Orr changed after my sophomore year at UAPB. I was ready to give it all I had, as the new semester was about to begin. I was so focused I forgot that band camp was about to start.

Feeling the Music but Walking Away

I knew I had given up band music, but really looked forward to seeing the *Approaching Storm* this year, as a true spectator. I still had a musical spirit, but I lived off campus and didn't have to worry about seeing the musicians, until the start of the football season. I still had them on my mind, but my time was filled with laboratory work. I worked days and nights to complete my research project. One evening, about a week before classes started, I stayed late in the laboratory to help T.S. setup a protein prep. By the time we left, it was late in the evening. I walked to my car that was parked several blocks from our building, because of construction on the campus. As soon as I passed the Fine Arts Building, the doors opened and I heard the bustle of band members preparing go to the practice field.

I told myself to stay composed and I picked up my walking pace to try to get to my car before someone I knew saw me or I heard the band play. I couldn't walk fast enough. The distance to my car seemed to increase, as I took each step. I finally decided not to run away from my true passion, which was music, so I slowed my gait and watched the band line up. By the time I reached my car, the drum major blew the whistle and their drum beats echoed across the campus. I stood by my car, with the door open, and watched them march to the field as they played another Earth Wind & Fire song. I closed the car door, put my keys in my pocket, and remembered what it was like to march with the *Approaching Storm.*

I could still hear them play, so I got out and sat on the hood and listened. I felt a strong sense of pride and accomplishment. I thought about music and Mr. J., but this time I was in control of my emotions and realized I could still play and perform, but just sat there and enjoyed the show. I guess I was addicted in a positive way to music and band, but smart enough to realize my marching days were over. I was FINE with that. I stayed in the parking lot, until I saw the last tuba player disappear from sight, and then headed home. I enjoyed that brief musical interlude and knew then that I could support the band the rest of the football season, without joining their ranks. I was proud of my maturity.

By the beginning of the 1995-1996 football seasons, I was ready to see the band in action. Because of my tenure with the *Approaching Storm*, two of the members from the *10 Augmented Surround Sounds* decided to transfer from UAPB and join the DSU band. Wash was gone, so many students wanted to look for other opportunities, in different HBCU bands. I was happy they were coming because it would give me an opportunity to fellowship with some familiar faces and stay connected to the band.

When they arrived on campus, it was like old times. I had an apartment off-campus, so they felt they had some support in a new area. I tried not to monopolize their time in Dover, because Mr. J. was still very strict about band conduct and academic achievement. What I did do was try to make myself available as much as possible, so they didn't feel the sense of "newness" I felt when joining the band. Both of them were percussionists and familiar with HBCU marching band styles, so it didn't take them long to get the routine.

When the marching season began, I wasn't as concerned about the day-to-day activities of the band, but still supported them. I was proud of my fraternity brothers and their role in the *Approaching Storm*, but my graduate work took priority. The only game I was really interested in seeing was the last game of the season against Howard University. I wanted an opportunity to see Wash again. Meanwhile, my fraternity brothers were settling in with the band. They kept me posted regarding the band's travel and performance schedule.

I was more comfortable living at *General's Greens* and felt pretty good about my new housing arrangement. I had an efficiency that was one big room with a kitchen, bathroom, and bed. This was a great place because it was adjacent to the Dover Air Force Base and DuPont Highway, and a quick ride to DSU.

Once I got my things spread out, I began gathering more information for the book. I had old notes and pamphlets from my days at UAPB and wanted to use every piece of information I could find. Some of my fraternity brothers helped me remember the history of the fraternity and sorority chapters and catalogue the actual and musical names of the members.

As I thought about my line's legacy and the book project, I wanted more than ever to make a line board so that members, who followed fall '91, could see who pledged on the largest line to date (17). This would be our gift to the fraternity. My passion turned into doing the project on my own. I didn't have much contact with my other line brothers, so I found documentation from our pledge period and used that information to come up with a writing concept.

The first Saturday, after the football season started, I went to the local flea market and found a guy who could cut and carve any design imaginable in wood. He made his money by making signs for doors and mailboxes. I asked him if he could cut a specific design based on our line name SΨS. He told me he would think about it and let me know, but needed to know what the design would be.

I told him I would get back with him the next week and I tried to brainstorm an idea that would match our signature name and experience. It didn't take me long to come up with a design that looked like a large Ψ (psi) with our real names and line names listed side by side. I went back to the flea market and described my design to him, which was based on other line board designs, but it had to be much bigger because we had so many members. The board also included our Dean of Pledges and Advisor. It took him about a week and he cut the board design for a reasonable price. When I went to pick it up, I was amazed at how skilled he was with woodworking. I paid him $50.00 for the wood and then started to make the board in honor of my line brothers.

I was spending more time trying to make the line board than do research, and felt I needed to try to balance my professional and personal aspirations, before they both got out of control. Unfortunately, the line board was my pet project and had my full attention. I wasn't interested in what was going on in the laboratory because my experiments weren't working. I also got nervous because I knew I had to complete a project, before the summer was over, to keep my tentative date in Vermont.

I asked my advisor about the work. He continued to tell me to work harder and be patient, but patience has never been one of my strongest qualities. I was looking for more guidance and maybe my advisor thought I was trying to get him to do it for me, but that wasn't the case. I really wanted to work hard and get the project completed on my own. T.S. was having more success than I was, but we were a package deal. I wanted to know that my advisor had the expertise to help me finish the job.

The laboratory atmosphere wasn't pleasant. Tempers and frustrations were evident. I tried to be patient and listen to my advisor, but sometimes I felt he wasn't in tune with my future goals. He allowed us to use state-of-the- art equipment and the best computers available, but I think I was missing Dr. Orr's mentoring and teaching style. I desperately wanted to learn and succeed in my advisor's laboratory, but after four weeks into the new semester, our work seemed to stall.

I was frustrated, T.S. was frustrated, and my advisor was frustrated because of his teaching load and mentoring duties. I felt trapped in a sense by the research because I knew that my enrollment at the University of Vermont was directly related to my success at DSU. I talked with my advisor again and we discussed some goals for the next couple of weeks. I decided to be more patient and follow his lead. T.S. and I also had classes to deal with, including *Population Biology*, *Advanced Genetics*, and *Proteins: Structure and Molecular Properties*, which was taught by our laboratory advisor.

These were fun classes, but research success was all I cared about. I talked with Dr. Reed about my research woes. He allowed me to use some research money allocated within the DEVELOP program, to support my project. T.S. and I were studying daily to keep up with the work and spending the rest of our time in the laboratory. After hours, we would turn the music up loud to motivate us to get the research completed. We both liked Michael Jackson and alternated between songs from his *Thriller* album and "*HIStory, Past, Present and Future Book 1.*"

Sometimes, we would have to come back to the laboratory to adjust the equipment or our protein extraction experiments would fail. We devised a plan to alternate those duties because he was still on campus and could get to the laboratory faster than I could. I didn't mind coming back to campus, because it gave me a reason to get out of my apartment late at night. Sometimes I stayed in the laboratory for hours studying and monitoring our protein prep. I was determined to make this project work. This was my ultimate goal. I focused on the job at hand and developed tunnel vision for success.

The next week I stopped by Dr. Reed's office and sat with Mrs. Givens. I brought her a gift for helping me get my first apartment. She was excited and that made me feel good. I really appreciated her help and knew the only way I was able to get the apartment was because of her recommendation. Dr. Reed was in a meeting, but told me to wait because he wanted to discuss something with me. One thing I could always say about Dr. Reed was that whatever he was doing or involved with, he would always make time for T.S. and I. We had the option to discuss whatever was on our minds. He was never too busy to try to help facilitate our personal and graduate school success, and always had a calm and professional way of handling business.

When Dr. Reed's meeting was over, he invited me into his office and asked me if I was still working out in the gym. I told him my schedule was so hectic that I forgot all about working out or lifting weights. He then asked if I wanted to walk with him in the mornings to stay in shape. My first question was "What time in the morning?" His response was "5 a.m.!" I paused for a moment and then said "Sure," because I didn't want him to think I couldn't walk with him or that I was indifferent in any way. He never told me how far he walked and I never asked. I just prepared myself to meet him every morning at 5 a.m. He did tell me that he walked in the morning, to prepare for his work day.

I wanted to get in shape, but spent so many late nights in the laboratory that getting up early in the morning wasn't something I wanted to do. Dr. Reed was my mentor and like a father to me, so I wanted to help him with his fitness program. He told me that he would ride his bicycle, from time to time, to try to stay in shape and asked if I owned one. I told him no, but had been thinking about getting one to ride around the apartment complex. Dr. Reed talked about his bicycle like it was his favorite truck and suggested I get one. I told him I would think about it and let him know if and when that happened. We shook hands and he told me to be at his house next week promptly at 5 a.m. I smiled nervously and said, "OK that will be FINE!"

When I left his office, I began looking for bicycles because I had this bright idea to ride to his house every morning. Once I got there, I would walk with him for whatever distance he wanted, to try to develop an intense morning workout. My funds were low. When the weekend came, I went to the local flea market to look at bicycles.

I found one vendor who specialized in bikes. He had an old *Schwinn*, which reminded me of my childhood. It was rusty, but I knew I could fix it up before the following week and then ride it to Dr. Reed's house. I asked the vendor how much he wanted for it and he told me $15.00, which was perfect for my budget. I bought the bicycle, put it in the back seat of my car and went home. I don't think I rode it that weekend and only oiled the chain and pumped up the front and back tires. It shifted well, when I test rode it around the parking lot of the flea market. I was satisfied with its performance, so in my mind additional maintenance wasn't necessary.

The weekend seemed to go by faster than usual. Early Monday morning, Dr. Reed called me to make sure I was coming to do his daily walk. He actually woke me up. I knew I had an appointment with him, but stayed up late the night before watching movies. I got out of bed, showered, and left my apartment complex with my bicycle on my shoulders. I jumped on the back of it and rode out to the street, which led to a two-lane highway. I watched for traffic and started peddling on the shoulder of the road. It felt like I was moving in quick sand. I stopped the bike and looked at the tires, to see if they were fully inflated, as trucks and cars zoomed by me. I got back on the bike and tried to peddle again, but felt the same, and knew it would be impossible for me to ride to Dr. Reed's house.

I learned that morning that riding on the highway was very different than riding on a flat enclosed surface, such as a parking lot. Without the rigors of band rehearsal, I wasn't in the best shape. I was frustrated because all I wanted to do was get across the city of Dover, on my bicycle, using a familiar route, but it wasn't possible. I went back to my apartment, angrily got into my car, and drove to Dr. Reed's house very disappointed, but still upbeat about the possibility of getting into shape. When I arrived, Dr. Reed was already stretching and ready to walk. We shook hands and then he told me to follow him.

We walked out of his complex and I still didn't know how far we were walking. He carried two hand weights and offered a couple of weights to me, but I declined. Since I didn't know how far we were going, the last thing I wanted to do was complicate this new workout regimen. We walked and walked and walked. Dr. Reed was an older gentleman and kept the pace very brisk. I struggled at times, but didn't want to let him know that I was nearly exhausted, by the time we reached the half-way point. Before we turned around to go back, I moved as best I could. By the time we made it back to his house, I was winded but felt good that I at least made it the first day.

Dr. Reed was right about working out in the morning. I was tired but energized for the rest of my day. We shook hands again and I thanked him for the opportunity. We walked for the rest of the week and then took the weekend off, as I started to regain some of my post-band stamina. Now when we walked, I knew where we were going and how much energy I needed to use to make the journey successful. After about three weeks of daily walking, I was almost in top form. Then, I made a crucial mistake.

Youth Challenges Experience

One morning I decided to try to lead the walk and moved much faster than I had before. I had a competitive spirit in everything I did and now I tried to challenge Dr. Reed and push him to his limits. What happened next was comical. Dr. Reed saw me inch up past him as sweat glistened off my forehead. I turned my motor into overdrive. He immediately adjusted his walking stride and rhythm to match my efforts. I felt I was younger and stronger and wanted to let him know that I was fitter than he was. This was my big mistake. I respected Dr. Reed, but wanted to beat him at his own game. Normally we would talk during our walks, because they were casual, about my work, my goals, and the best way to succeed in graduate school. That morning no one said a word. All we both heard was the sound of our shoes digging into the rocky asphalt pavement and our breathing, which was short and stressed.

When I walked faster, Dr. Reed walked faster. When I picked up the pace, Dr. Reed picked up the pace and before we knew it, we were both trying to beat each other to the finish line. I didn't care because I wanted to win. I wish I could have recorded those events of that morning. We both were so driven and walked at such as pace, that by the time we got to the end of our walk, we were exhausted.

I was tired and knew Dr. Reed was tired, but neither one of us would give in. To me it was like a *right of passage* as a younger man, who challenged an older man. What was real for me was the fact that I still didn't win the unspoken contest. Dr. Reed finished the walk before I did, even after all of my effort. I was still proud of my attempt. The rest of the morning I felt great and was energized in the laboratory. I told T.S. about our walks because he played pool with Dr. Reed in the evenings. They always joked about my pool skills, which was a game I had difficulty grasping.

T.S. and Dr. Reed were arch rivals, when it came to eight and nine-ball games of pool, so walking with Dr. Reed gave me an opportunity to compete on another level. Besides, T.S. did his own workouts and decided not to join us in the early mornings. I felt pretty good that evening, but the next morning I woke up and was sore all over my body. I knew it was because I tried to beat Dr. Reed, at his own fitness program, not realizing that he had been walking that route for over four years. When my alarm clock went off, I lay in bed and contemplated cancelling because I was in no shape to try to walk, but my pride wouldn't allow me to pick up the phone. I called Dr. Reed and told him I was on my way. When I got there that morning, Dr. Reed was ready to walk, but this time he had his water bottle and heavier hand weights. I was ready to try to out walk him again, but for some reason I felt this would be one of those days.

We started our normal walk and I noticed that he established a more rigorous pace. I had difficulty keeping up with him, even though he was carrying weights and I wasn't. He never seemed to slow down and because my body was so sore, it was difficult for me to match his intensity. I tried to keep up, but I used all of my energy the morning before, not realizing that we were walking together every day.

Dr. Reed wouldn't slow his pace, and by the time we got back to the house, I was more tired than I had been in about six months. I did eventually keep up but realized that Dr. Reed had more experience that I did and he let me know that. I was young and strong, but not as experienced as he was in things he did for longer periods of time. I learned a valuable lesson that morning. In a subtle way, he was showing me how much farther I had to go. The other lesson was to always respect those who had traveled where I was trying to go. I got that lesson!

The next couple of weeks I cancelled walking from time to time, to allow my body to heal. Every time I called to cancel, I was reminded of lessons taught by my father figure and professional mentor. Eventually, I only walked with Dr. Reed two times a week and finally let him know that because of my laboratory schedule and the late nights I worked; it would be too difficult for me to continue walking with him.

I know he was disappointed because we did keep good company. But he showed me that a competitive spirit is good, but I had to learn when to bring it out. Dr. Reed kept telling me that my graduate work and life were about challenges. I needed to understand that the person I was then, wouldn't be the same person I would be years later. He made it clear that I must be more patient and humble in order to achieve my greatest successes.

As soon as I stopped walking with Dr. Reed, I felt better because I didn't want to challenge him anymore. *It was more important for me to get wisdom than try to be or know more than he did.* Dr. Reed and I laughed about that morning, once I realized he was trying to teach me a lesson and demonstrate how to make it in life. I really understood how blessed I was to have him take the time to plant a seed of knowledge that would stay with me for the rest of my life. Dr. Reed continued to walk alone the rest of my time in Dover. I was happy to be able to sleep late, before going to the laboratory each day.

I was still on target to finish my course work by the end of the semester, but my research stalled. I formed my thesis committee, with people in the biology department, and tried to keep them updated on my progress. My problem was I didn't have any data from my protein isolation studies to present, which made me very nervous. My advisor was still trying to place the blame on my shoulders and I became more frustrated. One day during a laboratory meeting I lost my cool. I was trying to tell my advisor about my research problems and felt he was discounting what I was saying. When he referred me to the laboratory manual to redo the experiment, I harshly told him, *"You do the experiment!"*

I never thought about it at the time, because I was so frustrated my experiments weren't working that I lost all tact and didn't care what I said to him. I knew when those words came out of my mouth that Dr. Reed wouldn't support my actions. I should have understood before coming to DSU, that research is a patience builder and could be difficult if things didn't work out as planned. After the advisor meeting, there was more tension in the laboratory.

My advisor and I didn't speak very often after that. T.S. told me that he had talked to him about what I said and asked if he should pursue it further with me. T.S. defended me and let him know that I was frustrated and wanted to work hard and finish the thesis project. My advisor never asked me about that meeting. After that, we still could work together, but our relationship changed.

Later in the semester, I realized I was wrong for saying what I said, not thinking that my advisor was the same person, who had to sign off on my thesis, in order for me to earn the Master's degree. This was one of many classic examples of being "green" that Dr. Reed and my father alluded to.

From that moment on, I tried to be more focused on my research and spent every day and night in the laboratory. I really looked forward to the spring, because all my classes would be finished and I could work without academic pressure. In the spirit of my work schedule, I listened to Michael Jackson's "*Off the Wall*" album and really grooved to "*Working Day and Night.*"

So many things were going on that I decided to put my dream of writing a book on hold, because I had to finish my work at DSU. T.S. and I both knew we would be in the laboratory working, during the summer months, and may miss the deadline for spring graduation. Our coursework would be done by the end of the semester, but our experiments didn't produce enough data to survive a thesis committee defense. I was frustrated but persevered. Even though I wasn't writing notes for my book, I did decide to try to finish my line board before the *Extravaganza*.

There wasn't much more to do to the board. I wanted to give it some glamour and class so it would stand out among all of the other pledge boards. Because I loved Science Fiction (Sci-Fi), I got most of my materials for the board from a specialty store that sold models of planets and other space memorabilia. I used fluorescent paint and glow in the dark stars to decorate the board.

When the lights were turned off in the band room, our board would still glow. This wasn't the most original idea for a line board, but it came close. When I finally put all the names on it, I was the proudest member of the EX chapter of Kappa Kappa Psi. The board was ready for the *Extravaganza* and I hung it in my house until spring.

The next week I got a call from Vermont. Dr. Mossman was interested in our progress and offered T.S. and I two slots, on the *Environmental Pathology Training Grant*. This was an exciting opportunity because it meant we could come into graduate school with funding and be able to choose who we wanted to work with. I talked with T.S. about the grant and we both agreed it would be a good idea to accept. After our discussion, I was more motivated to try to finish strong, get my degree, leave DSU, and complete my life-long dream. I spent so much time in the laboratory that my days and nights seemed to run together, but the experiments weren't cooperating. T.S. and I were both really frustrated with the research process.

We still worked hard but decided to focus more on our classes. By the end of the semester, we were burnt out. T.S.' protein isolation experiments were working for him, but mine were still inconclusive. I was so busy in the laboratory that I almost forgot about the last home game of the season against Howard University. I talked with my fraternity brothers that were still in the band and they told me that the *Howard University "Showtime" Marching Band* was coming and the *Approaching Storm* would present a special end of the year appreciation show. I was excited to see Wash again because things at DSU had not progressed like I envisioned.

I worked hard in the laboratory the entire week until Friday. I took some time off to rest before the game the next day. I thought I was close to making a breakthrough with my experiments, but the gels I analyzed didn't reveal great results. The morning of the game I was so pumped, because I had only attended one other home game the entire season. I wanted to see and hear the *Approaching Storm* as well as Howard University's band. I got to the game early and walked through the parking lot, as the band buses lined up. I randomly chose one bus and walked towards it. The first person who got off was Wash. He looked up and saw me, with a surprised look, and shook my hand.

As a point of historical reference; most people who have either marched or supported Black College Marching Bands have a special camaraderie with their band directors most people don't understand. Just like the fans of college football coaching legends, such as the late *"Eddie Robinson,"* from Grambling State University, who holds the most wins of any head coach in Division I-AA; *Joe Paterno*, legendary coach at Pennsylvania State University that has amassed 394 wins, and *Bobby Bowden*, an inductee in the College Football Hall of Fame, who has mentored young men at Florida State University to become successful NFL players.

The loyalty and respect for these coaches' impact on players and fans, is the same for many Black College band directors. Our band directors were like our fathers, who instilled discipline and knowledge, but also gave us opportunities to be the best we could be in music and in education. Seeing Wash was important for me. I will never forget how he taught and helped me.

Wash and I walked and talked. He told me about his life in Washington, D.C. I told him about the graduate school process and my ups and downs. He offered me the same advice he had given me years ago. *"Be patient. Things will work out for you in time. Take your time."* It felt good to hear a friendly word, from someone I knew always looked out for my best interests.

I needed someone more experienced in life to remind me of the big picture. As we talked, the Howard University band members unloaded their bus and warmed up. I told Wash I would catch up with him after the game. I shook his hand and went into the stadium early, so I could see both bands march in. As a former band member, I knew what the *Approaching Storm* was capable of musically but wasn't as familiar with the musical trademarks of the *Showtime* band. I was looking for Wash's musical style and attention to detail within their field work and musical selections. I thought he was the Director of Bands, as he had been in Arkansas, but was surprised to learn that he was the Assistant Band Director. He was now responsible for arranging the music, charting the field shows and directing bands and ensembles during concert seasons.

I heard the *Approaching Storm* come into the stadium first and they rocked as usual. Mr. J. was leading and making sure everyone was ready to entertain and inspire the home crowd. As soon as they sat down, the *Showtime* band marched to their seats. Howard University's band was larger than our band. It was fun to see two band directors trained by Dr. Greggs go at it.

Because it was the last game of the year and neither team was going to the playoffs, the bands played wide open during the entire game. *Showtime* played a song, then Mr. J fired his band right back at them. I could see Wash on the other side of the field passionately directing his band students. Wash was always more focused on the tuba section and today was no exception. I sat near our band and celebrated with them. The game was uneventful. My concern was the half-time festivities. Both bands performed well during their showcases. They used similar songs that were arranged differently.

The second half on the football game was just as boring as the first. Most people stayed to see the battle the bands, during the Fifth Quarter. I don't remember what the score was, but I do remember it was cold and rainy. By the end of the game, only the die-hard music fans were left. Both bands battled back and forth for what seemed to be an hour. I sat there watching to see who would finally win or quit. When I looked up, Wash had left the visitor's side and was walking toward our side of the stadium, with slow measured steps.

By the time he reached where our band was, he motioned to Mr. J. and they shook hands. He saw me in the stands, called my name, and then gave me the KKΨ salute. That was the first time I had ever seen an opposing band director walk to the other side of the field, during the Fifth Quarter. Afterwards, my fraternity brothers and I met up with Wash to fellowship. We talked about old times in the Bluff. We all were glad to see him and let him know how important his tutelage was in our musical and personal success. We also let him know that our band experiences, since leaving UAPB, were very different. We fellowshipped for about an hour, as his students loaded up their buses to return to Washington, D.C. Wash gave me his number and told me to keep in touch.

The next week I was ready to get back to research. The semester was almost over, so I started slowing down a little bit. I was still frustrated about my experiments. On Tuesday of that week, my advisor walked into the laboratory and told me he needed to talk with me. I thought this would be his usual *"How's the experiment going?"* talk, but was shocked and surprised when he told me I had to change the scope and hypothesis of my research project.

When he broke the news, I instantly thought back in my mind to when I told him my experiments needed a better approach, so I could graduate on time. I stood there and listened to him tell me why I needed to change direction six months before my graduation date. Nothing he said could stifle the frustration already built inside me. The next time we met with Dr. Reed, to update him on our progress, T.S. raised the issue. Dr. Reed was surprised too. He declined to comment on the issue, until I met with my advisor and gathered more information. I didn't want to tell Dr. Reed until I had a specific plan of action, but T.S. brought it up because he knew I needed his support. I gave Dr. Reed a historical perspective of my work, progress, and the frustration I experienced during the last eighteen months.

I appreciated my advisor's guidance and the opportunity to work in his laboratory, but my goal was to get to Vermont. This new plan would significantly disrupt my timetable. Dr. Reed told me I had to *"Make it happen"* with the research, my thesis committee, and writing. I promised him I would come up with succinct plan to finish, but this time I wanted to do everything on my own. The next couple of days in the laboratory were very contentious. None of us really spoke. I didn't dislike my advisor.

I just didn't understand why it took him so long to figure out my experiments weren't working, when I gave him the same assessment every week. Now, I understand why my experiments were minimally successful, after seven years of dissertation research, three years of post-doctoral work, and two years of training under *No Child Left Behind Legislation*. What I learned was that things sometimes happen in the opposite direction of your most thought out plans. But at the time, I still suffered from a "green" and "idealistic" mentality and just knew things would always go as planned and my way. I also never thought about how God may have been giving me pause, before I took my next journey, to make sure I was ready.

The next week, we finished our classes and our grades were submitted to the registrar. I knew we wouldn't be participating in the graduation ceremony, but still wanted to go to see how graduate students received their degrees and how their gowns looked. Dr. Reed kept telling me about being "hooded," at the end of my studies at DSU and I was curious about this special ritual.

I felt honored the first time I put on my graduation gown, at UAPB, and wanted to experience those feelings again. I was still disappointed that T.S. and I weren't going to graduate during that ceremony, but Dr. Reed made it clear that we had to focus on next semester and the summer, so we could finish our work. Dr. Reed also told me that at the end of the day, the degree is what matters the most. *"It is your pass to open more doors and experience other opportunities."*

I decided to go home during the Christmas holiday with Dr. Reed. We didn't stay long this time, because we both had pressing matters to attend to. I enjoyed the ride and we talked about the future. I tried to be angry about what happened in my advisor's laboratory, but Dr. Reed never let me feel that way. He told me it was time for me to focus and concentrate to get the job done.

I appreciated his sentiments because *"misery always loves company,"* but Dr. Reed made it abundantly clear that when things happen unexpectedly, you have to adjust, get better, and succeed. I expected a more sympathetic ear, but what I got was a pep talk that placed the burden and responsible right back on me, which is where it should have been all the time.

When we got back to Dover, I scheduled a meeting with my thesis committee to update them on my progress and let them know that the scope and hypothesis of my research had changed. They wanted to know my plan of action. I told them that over the break I had come up with a new research plan. If I worked diligently in the laboratory, I could finish my thesis work and defend it by the middle of the summer.

They all were skeptical about this plan, but my advisor believed that I could get the work done. I was more determined than ever to make my work in the laboratory productive and develop independence in the process. Since all of my classes were done, my daily routine was simple; Come to the laboratory in the mornings and stay there until midnight. I worked so hard the first couple of months that no one ever saw me. If they lucked up and found me, I was either going to or leaving the laboratory. T.S. and I both spent major time troubleshooting and working out the glitches of our equipment and research hypotheses.

I was making progress. My advisor allowed me to use his computer when he wasn't in his office. He owned the largest computer screen I had ever seen. I laughed when he bragged about his mouse pad, which responded to touch. There were no buttons on the mouse, so users could move the cursor with their fingers. I appreciated the fact that he allowed me access to his office, which also contained a life size poster of Marilyn Monroe.

In a cautious way, I was happy doing a new project, because the work I had done for the last eighteen months wasn't very interesting. I was less angry and more motivated to succeed. I utilized all the resources I had at that time, including members of my thesis committee. I began meeting bimonthly with them individually, to keep them posted on my progress. They were just as informed as my advisor. We were all on the same page. I learned so much, during the first months of the spring semester, that I felt my graduate studies would still provide a fruitful learning experience. By the middle of the spring, I prepared to go to the *Extravaganza* and present our line board to the fraternity.

I decided to fly to the event this year because I didn't want to be in Arkansas very long. I shipped the line board home. I was nervous about doing that because I didn't want the board broken or misplaced, but the shipper assured me that if I packed it correctly, it would arrive FINE. I arrived in Arkansas on Thursday of that week to make sure I was there, before the board arrived. When the box came, I opened it and found that it was broken. I was so upset that I called the company and angrily scolded them about my shipment, until I realized that there were only small damages that could be fixed with strong glue and patience.

I apologized to the customer service representative for my attitude and then patch-fixed the board to its original specifications. It looked good. I was so excited that I carried it over Keith's house to show him and Moe Bass. When I finally presented it to the fraternity and placed it on the wall, in our historic band room, it became a culmination of my band and fraternity experiences at UAPB.

I spent one more day at home to finish up some business and let my parents know not to expect to see me anytime soon. I enjoyed the *Extravaganza*, saw how the fraternity had progressed in my absence, but was ready to return to Dover. The visit was quick but necessary because I have always prided myself on *"doing what I said I was going to do."* Presenting our line board to the fraternity brought one of my major life goals to completion.

I flew back on Sunday and was back in the laboratory on Monday. Once my jet lag cleared, I got back into my schedule of working day and night. I made good progress, as my technical writing skills improved. My advisor was proofreading my thesis and offered me pointers to help it read better.

I tried to get Dr. Reed to read it, but he was so busy with new graduate school initiatives, that I decided not to bother him. I did get many of my thesis committee members to read and critique my work as I wrote, so when it was finally ready to submit, I would only have to make small changes. T.S. was further along than I was, because his data was more consistent and reproducible.

The semester was winding down and I had accomplished a great deal, but still needed two more months of solid research to complete the project. I was running out of time. Dr. Reed advised to me call another thesis committee meeting to try to get them to sign off on the work I had already done, so I could prepare to defend. Dr. Reed knew I had worked hard on my project, but for whatever reason the original concept wasn't reproducible. He was unbiased, but wanted to make sure my committee knew where I was and where I was going.

I scheduled the meeting as he had instructed. My committee questioned me about every aspect of my project. It was almost like a run-through of the actual thesis defense; intense from the beginning until the end. The entire committee came to a consensus about my work and agreed that I had done enough to defend a thesis.

I was so ecstatic when I felt the committee had offered me a chance to defend in the coming months, I just kept talking and trying to engage them in their individual discussions. In the corner of my eye, I saw Dr. Reed motioning me to be quiet, but I didn't understand what he was trying to convey to me. When I stopped by his house later to debrief, he told me that I had done a good job, but needed to learn when to *"Shut Up!"*

I understood what he was trying to say. I did try to enrich my experience, as they engaged each other during the meeting. Dr. Reed helped me understand that different situations call for different responses. He explained *"What you should have done was let them hash out the details among themselves, then be ready to respond if they had questions."* I never forgot his words of wisdom and by the middle of May, 1995 I had finished my experiments and was writing my thesis full-time. It was fun writing all day instead of doing bench work.

Graduation and Dr. Benjamin Carson

Graduation was the next week, and I made it a point to attend the ceremony because *Dr. Benjamin Carson* was the keynote speaker. I knew Dr. Carson lived and worked in Baltimore, Maryland, but never thought I would actually get a chance to see him in person. By the time graduation arrived, the city of Dover was filled with people from all over the country. The Class of 1996 was one of the largest classes to graduate in a number of years, so the crowds of people seemed to swell at gas stations, grocery stores, and local malls. I knew if I wanted to hear Dr. Carson speak, I would have to arrive early. I got a good seat near the 50-yard line of the stadium.

This was the first time I had been to an outdoor graduation and wondered if the weather would cooperate. During my undergraduate years, the Pine Bluff Convention Center[51] was always booked for graduations, so people never really worried about rain or bad weather. This year the Sun was shining brightly. Everyone was out for this event. I saw Dr. Reed and the candidates for the Master's degrees, from various academic departments

---

51 Pine Bluff Convention Center- is located in Pine Bluff, Arkansas and is an 8-500 seat multi-purpose arena where concerts, basketball games, and rodeos are held each year. The convention center is used by people in Pine Bluff and throughout the state of Arkansas for weddings, graduations, and community festivals.

Four Tubas, a Guitar, and a Gallery of Cheerleaders

and schools, line up on the field. They wore traditional graduation gowns, but had colorful hoods with DSU colors draped across their forearms.

I thought they would be dressed differently from the undergraduates. They were awarded their degrees first, which was really cool. I was more interested in Dr. Carson's speech because of his trailblazing and innovative work in medicine, as an African-American. After the initial introductions by the President of DSU, Dr. William Delauder, and recognition of academic deans and departments, Dr. Carson was introduced as our keynote speaker to a standing ovation.

The first thing I noticed about him was how calm he was. When he spoke, he talked with a very light but measured tone. He talked about his education triumphs, setbacks, and the many obstacles he had to overcome. He also discussed his life and battle with uncontrollable anger, which he had to address and overcome, in order to become a successful neurosurgeon. Dr. Carson mentioned his mother and what she meant to him and how she stressed education all of his life. She didn't allow him to believe that he couldn't achieve because of his circumstances or economic status.

I was so impressed with him and his story that it really motivated me to want to become a medical doctor again. He spoke proficiently and timely, but the most important thing I will always remember about that speech was what he said about the *"Power of Education."* Near the end of his address, Dr. Carson said, *"If I lost everything tomorrow, I have enough education to get it all back!"* His words moved me and resonated with others in the crowd. Dr. Carson finished his commemorative graduation speech to a standing ovation, from an immense crowd of students and alumni. I was truly inspired that day. As the degrees were awarded, I thought about my thesis defense date and what it would feel like to achieve a graduate degree.

The next couple of weeks were very hectic. T.S. and I set a tentative date for our defenses. Based on department policy, we were required to invite the entire campus community to watch. I couldn't renew my lease at General's Greens, so I prepared to move out and sub-lease the basement of one of my classmates. She was sub-leasing a home for the summer and wanted to save some money, so I moved in with her.

My goal was to be out of General's Greens, by the end of May, so I could prepare to defend my thesis near the end of June. I was fortunate and blessed to be able to live in her basement, because I still had all of my things with me. I didn't have time to put them in storage. My move into the house was smooth. I just had to get used to living in tight quarters. The rent was cheap and the company was friendly. I didn't have any complaints.

My plan was to defend my thesis at the end of June, so I could have some time to go home before leaving for Vermont. By the end of May, I finished writing and was preparing my thesis defense seminar, as well as corresponding with the University of Vermont regarding my potential arrival date. T.S. wasn't as certain about Vermont as I was. He kept his options open because he had family and other ties in Arkansas that could potentially complicate his move farther north. I respected T.S.

He always put his family first, regardless of what was going on with him. We talked about our immediate future. I told him Dr. Reed advised me that if I wanted a Ph.D., I needed to get to Vermont. T.S. was thinking about his family and wanted to wait until after the defense, so he could determine the best course of action.

Meanwhile, I made projection slides of my laboratory results and put my talk together for the defense at the end of the month. I went over every aspect of my talk and decided to ask my advisor to listen to my presentation and give me some constructive criticism, which he loved to do. He was very helpful and offered great suggestions to make the presentation better.

We seemed to have grown from our strife, from some months back. I began to get nervous, as each day passed, because this was new territory for me and I wanted to do well. I knew Dr. Reed wanted me to finish strong and I wanted to have a good defense, in the midst of everything that happened. Each week I rehearsed more and more, until my talk was like a rhythm in my mind.

T.S. and I tried to polish as many rough edges as possible. I set up a slide projector in the basement of my new home, so I could review thoroughly. We knew we would be defending on the same day, right after each other, so we flipped a coin to determine who would go first. I chose "heads" and he chose "tails." When the coin stopped spinning, heads it was. We agreed that I would go first because my project was so new. The days felt like they were zooming by. Before I knew it, there was only a week to go before the defense.

As the time approached, I was a nervous wreck and found it difficult to think about anything but my defense. Even the women in my life were put on hold, until the defense was over. I felt burnt out, so I took a day off and just rested, still running the presentation through my mind. This was so helpful, because the rest reset my internal clock and I felt fresh and revitalized. Now with one day left, I tried not to focus too much on the talk, but wanted to be ready. T.S. and I went over our speeches one last time and made our final slides a day before our big event.

When I went to sleep, I prayed for success the next day. I closed my eyes for what seemed to be a couple of minutes, when my alarm clock went off, reading 8:30 a.m. This gave me about an hour and a half to get ready for the defense. Everything I did that day had purpose. The suit I chose was the same suit I wore when I graduated from UAPB. It had been dry cleaned and pressed so many times, it shined. I have never been superstitious, but wanted to bask in the moment, using things that were familiar to the successes in my life.

Defending My Thesis

The morning of the defense I showered slowly and contemplated the future. When I got dressed I was nervous, but focused on the job at hand. I called my parents the night before and let them know what would happen that day. When I left the basement and got into my car, I felt ready to step into the next stage of my life. When I arrived at DSU, I took my slides directly to the thesis defense room, where my advisor and T.S. were already waiting. We decided to go over a few slides one last time and my advisor reminded me that my talk should be no more than thirty minutes long. I rehearsed to speak for that length of time, so I sat down while they checked the status of the audio and visual equipment.

My stomach was in a ball, as people began to file into the room. I tried to steer clear of any conversation, because my life would truly change in the next thirty minutes. As 10:00 a.m. approached, I found personal peace and comfort and then noticed that President Delauder walked into the room. I was honored to have him sit in the audience, while T.S. and I presented, and I wanted to do a good job. By 10:05 a.m., both our thesis committees were in the room.

My advisor stood before the audience to explain how the defense would proceed. He told the audience that we would present our work for no longer than an hour, and then the audience could ask questions. Once the audience was finished, they would be asked to leave. The candidates would then go into a closed-door session with their individual thesis committees, until such time as the committee was satisfied with their defense. He also stated that after the candidate was finished with the closed door session, they would be asked to leave, as the committee deliberates their fate amongst themselves. Once the committee was finished, they would notify the candidate if their work was sufficient to earn a graduate degree. I was pretty calm, until I heard all those stipulations and closed-door sessions, but felt good. Dr. Reed asked if T.S. and I were ready. We both said "Yes!" and he smiled.

All the introductions were finished. My advisor introduced me to the audience. I stood up, took a laser pointer, and began one of the most amazing experiences in my life. I started my talk very slowly and remembered to stay calm, by focusing on the information on the screen. I did notice that I kept buttoning and unbuttoning my coat jacket, but this was due to nervousness. I remembered to take the loose change and keys out of my pocket, as advised by Mrs. Mattie Glover years ago. My goal was to stay on pace. I knew if I messed up to keep going, so I wouldn't lose any momentum. During the first couple of slides, I was so nervous that my voice was short, choppy and trembled. By the fourth slide, I calmed down, felt safe and confident, and then got into my speaking rhythm.

I was amazed at how the information flowed from me and when I paused I was able to quickly get back on track. By the middle of the talk, I knew I had gotten past the most difficult part, which was data interpretation. Soon, I would speak about my conclusions and what should be my future research steps. Near the end of my talk, I was really relaxed and tried not to get overly confident. I realized I would only have to do this presentation once, which was emphasized by my advisor. By the time I got to my conclusion slide, I stretched out the discussion because I felt more comfortable. When the next click of the slide project remote was the Acknowledgements, I let out a sigh of relief. I had done it.

When I finished, the crowd applauded and the floor was opened for questions. Most of the crowd was composed of students, so they didn't ask me anything, but I did receive some tough questions from a few faculty members. The most intense moment for me was when one of my thesis committee members started off his question by saying, *"I don't believe anything you have just said,"* and told me he would address his concerns within the closed-door meeting. I knew he would probably be my toughest critic, as a Harvard graduate and former DuPont Corporation researcher. We disagreed respectfully before, in his Molecular Biology classes, so I knew he was thorough. He asked the last question from the audience and my advisor stood up and asked if there were any more questions.

I got nervous again, but knew that my advisor was there to help defend my work, if the other members of the committee felt unsure about my results or conclusions. No one said a word, so he asked the audience to leave. As people walked out the door, many stopped to shake my hand and congratulate me on my thesis. There were so many people that converged on me at one time. I tried to shake everyone's hand and mistakenly reached out for Dr. Reed's hand.

He quickly pulled his hand away and said *"Don't shake my hand, you are not done!"* I understood what he meant by that gesture, because I still had to endure the true defense process among my committee members. Once everyone was out of the room, they began grilling me about the research.

I remembered what Dr. Reed told me about talking too much, but I tried to answer questions as honestly and respectfully as I could. Dr. Reed also told me to always say when I didn't know something, instead of trying to reach for an answer. The first question was from the guy from Harvard and I was ready. To my surprise he told me that he said what he said so that when I came into this closed-door session, I would be confident my answers were sufficient to support the defense. I was flustered by his sense of humor, during a tumultuous period of my life, but appreciated what he was trying to teach me. My committee was helpful but critical and wanted to know why I changed my research. Before I searched for a politically correct answer, my advisor stepped in and defended me.

The rest of the members asked their questions until it was Dr. Reed's turn. He paused before he spoke and focused more on the future aspects of my research and how my graduate school experience could have been improved. I answered the best way I could and let him know that my laboratory and personal accomplishments were still a work in progress. He was satisfied with my answers. The chairperson of the committee asked if there were any more questions for the candidate. No one said a word, so my advisor asked me to leave the room while they deliberated. I stepped outside. To my surprise, President Delauder was waiting outside to congratulate me on my defense. I was elated he waited to see me and we made small talk.

He talked about being an analytical chemist by training, but decided not to continue in bench research, opting for administration instead. I was honored he came to my defense and really excited that he congratulated me personally, while my thesis committee determined my fate. I shook his hand and he left, as I waited to hear their verdict. My committee deliberated for about thirty minutes. Dr. Reed opened the door and invited me back into the meeting. My advisor spoke and was the first to congratulate me on successfully defending my thesis. The other members stood up and congratulated me. I was finally able to shake Dr. Reed's hand.

He told me he was proud of me. I remember that feeling of accomplishment. I still had to make several grammatical corrections to the thesis and address each reviewer's comments, but it didn't matter. Dr. Reed told me to try to smooth out the sentences, thereby reducing the number of times I used "the" in the manuscript. Before I left the room, the chairperson of the biology department offered me one the most memorable comments I received that day.

She told me that when I was speaking, she thought it was a tape recording, because it was so smooth and I was so calm. I thanked her for her gracious words and continued to enjoy the moment. T.S. defended his thesis right after me. His closed-door session was next. I waited outside to see what his verdict would be, but knew his work was much stronger than mine. When he came out of his session, I knew he had done well and we both celebrated. He didn't have to make as many corrections as I did. We were glad this process was over.

By the time I left the building, I was exhausted. I went to my basement home, got in the bed, and slept for five straight hours. When I woke up it was 7:00 p.m. and as Dr. Reed liked to say, *"Hungry as a newborn wolf!"* I still couldn't believe how my day went. I was so focused on the defense that I didn't realize it was Friday night. I had comments and the rest of the weekend to make the corrections to the manuscript. T.S.' committee asked him to do one more experiment, which took a day to complete.

My biggest challenge was trying to remove all the excessive "the's" and addressing each committee member's concerns. Dr. Reed was very serious about complete and accurate thesis. There were rumors that he once denied a thesis because the presenter defended well, but didn't format the manuscript correctly for library archiving. I made sure all of the parameters outlined in the thesis manual were addressed. I wanted to start work on it right then, but decided to party the rest of the weekend and enjoy the moment.

On Monday, T.S., and I came to the laboratory to clean up and use the computers to make the final changes to both our documents. I thought this would be an easy process, but it took me almost a week to finish the corrections. I still forgot to address Dr. Reed's most pressing concerns (the excessive use of "the"), but took a chance he would accept it. We both worked really hard on formatting and word placement.

I had another issue to deal with: I needed to go to Arkansas to get the rest of my things, because my next stop was Vermont. My plan was to rent a U-Haul, with a trailer hitch, and drive to Vermont with my car on the back. When I told my father my plans, he was concerned because I did plenty of driving with Dr. Reed, but never drove that far north, while transporting a vehicle. I talked with the U-Haul company the next week and was confident I could drive from Dover, Delaware to Burlington, Vermont without breaking a sweat. I reserved a twenty- four foot Household Mover and trailer, for July 6, 1996. I needed to carry all of my things to Vermont, including my bed. I wanted to save my car's mileage by securing it completely off the road.

I was excited about going to Vermont and all the new things I would see. The ride from Dover would take me through New Jersey, New York State, and then into Vermont. At that time, I had AAA[52] and they would give travelers a step-by-step map (Triptik) from destination to destination, as a courtesy of membership. I asked them to map out several routes from Dover to Pine Bluff, then from Dover, to Burlington. I studied those maps as if I was preparing for another thesis defense, because I wanted to be ready to travel north.

Meanwhile, I finished my corrections, and tried to address all the issues Dr. Reed had presented to me. When I went to his office, he read the thesis and told me that I still needed to get rid of some of the "the's," but signed off on it, with the hope that this wouldn't be a problem in the future. He told me I really needed to address that style of writing, but in his opinion the other comments from my thesis committee members were addressed sufficiently.

I thanked him and went to the library to print out the final copies to prepare for formatting and binding. Before I left his office, I asked Dr. Reed if he wanted to go out to Arkansas with me, because I hadn't been home in the last six months. He told me he would like to, but he had some work to do in Dover, so he couldn't make the trip. I asked T.S., but he was busy as well, so I decided to take the ride by myself. The goal was to see my family and get more road knowledge from my father. My mother still

---

52   AAA- is the American Automotive Association, an automotive group with over 50 million members. AAA provides emergency road side services to its members and works as a service organization to people who travel the nation's highways.

missed me and I knew I was going further north, so trips home would be few and far between.

Once I got all of my signatures from the other committee members, Dr. Reed and Mrs. Givens planned a party to celebrate the first successful graduates of the DEVELOP program. They ordered cake and invited faculty from all over the campus to attend. Dr. Reed made it a big event and waited until the event, to sign our theses signature pages, so we could get some publicity and make DSU history. He formally signed our theses, using special pens like the President of the United States. It was fun being honored, but I didn't have time to feel nostalgic. I was focused on getting home and returning to Dover, so I could get to Vermont. After the party, I talked with T.S. about Vermont. e was still up in the air and I knew I was probably going there alone. I had to deal with that in my own way.

We were so close. He was like an older brother to me. I really valued his wisdom and experience. He never said he wouldn't come to Vermont. He did say he had some things to take care of back home, so he wasn't going to go there right now. I still tried to convince him to come. He said he would think about it. The next week I loaded up my car and took the long drive to Arkansas. Dr. Reed really taught me how to manage the road.

I was patient and made good time, arriving in Arkansas seventeen hours later. I was glad to see my parents and took a couple of days to rest before my next journey. I didn't see PBH or my other fraternity brothers during this visit. I was busy packing and making sure I had everything I needed for Vermont. I spent the majority of my time reading and analyzing maps, while my father critiqued my driving plan. We discussed best-and worst-case scenarios.

I asked him questions about the highways and exits, which were the most important to me. I didn't want to get lost in a huge truck towing a car. I had never driven that far north before, so every day me and my father went over different driving scenarios and options. By the end of the week, I was ready to drive back to Dover. I packed my Cavalier with as much stuff as I could carry. My father and I went over the maps one more time. I said my goodbyes and headed back to Dover.

The drive up north was as smooth as the drive down. My car was road ready and seemed to respond much better on the highway, than it did in the city. I was glad to have a dependable car, which is why I wanted to make sure it got to Vermont safely. My drive back was uneventful and I arrived in Dover seventeen hours later. I had already packed most of my things and put them in storage, but decided to hang around Delaware until after the Fourth of July.

I was in no big rush to get to Vermont, but knew that it was where my next journey through life would begin. I caught up with T.S. and let him know how to contact me, if he decided to come to Vermont and we said our goodbyes. I rested and thought about my journey. To pass the time, I watched fireworks on the Fourth of July, in Wilmington, Delaware, and then picked up the U-Haul on July 5, 1996. I rented the truck for a one-way trip to Burlington, Vermont and it cost me $500.00, including the trailer.

Before the trip, I got a free tutorial about the truck from the service manager. He taught me how to control the truck, if I was going down steep roadways or hills. He also told me to always downshift to *L1, L2, or L3*, which would slow the engine down and keep the truck from moving too fast down declines. I thought the technique was interesting. I felt the lower gears were used to help stabilize the vehicle and give more pulling traction going up hills. The service manager helped me understand that pulling and traction were similar concepts, just reversed. By the end of our conversation, I learned how to properly hitch and position my car on the trailer.

Now, I was all packed and ready to ride. I stayed in Dover one more day, so I could make sure all my items were in the truck. I rested on July 5, did my final checklist, and left on July 6, 1996 at 2 p.m. I headed north toward Burlington, which based on AAA estimates would take me ten hours to get there. I carried a cell phone, gum, food, and a will and desire to get to Vermont. Dr. Reed was the last person I talked to in Dover before I left. He wished me well.

I thanked him again for all of his help and tutelage. He told me to always view him as a personal and professional resource. I knew our paths would cross again, because he was still coordinating the DEVELOP program and would be traveling to Vermont on a regular basis to monitor the status of the program and its students. I was now on my way to get *"Northern Exposure."*

Chapter 6.
Burlington, Vermont

> By faith Abraham, when he was called to go out into a place, which he should after receive for an inheritance, obeyed; and he went out, not knowing whither he went. By faith, he sojourned in the land of promise, as in a strange country, dwelling in tabernacles with Isaac and Jacob, the heirs with him of the same promise: For he looked for a city, which hath foundations, whose builder and maker is God.
>
> **Hebrews 11:8-10 (KJV)**

Today was a good day. I had achieved what I came to Delaware State University to do. My mind was still blown by how it all transpired, but I knew that this was only the first step in a more rewarding journey. I wanted the Ph.D. and needed to finally achieve what I had always heard about from my family and peers. I also wanted to know what it felt like to be called Dr. Rice, since my desire to go to medical school was gone.

As I drove cautiously through the suburbs of Dover, with my car perched on the back of the trailer, my compass pointed north toward Philadelphia, New Jersey, and New York. I drove on I-295 North for a brief moment, which eventually turned into U.S. 40 East, and then crossed the Delaware Memorial Bridge towards the New Jersey Turnpike. I wanted to reflect on life in Vermont, but was too busy concentrating on driving the truck and monitoring the status of my car, that seemed to sway in my side and rear view mirrors.

I followed the instructions of the U-haul representative, but was still nervous. Not because I thought I couldn't handle towing a vehicle, I just didn't want something to happen to cause the car to come off the trailer, onto the drivers behind me. I was extremely cautious, but had good reason to be. The New Jersey Turnpike was no joke, and this was all very new driving territory for me.

The drive to Vermont normally takes about eight hours, but because I was new to the route, I gave myself a very liberal driving time of ten hours. This would put me in Burlington at or near midnight. I don't remember what my rationale was for leaving that late in the afternoon, but it was probably because I procrastinated the night before. It would have made more sense to leave in the morning and get there in the late afternoon, instead of trying to navigate a place I had never seen before, in the darkness of night. I still think I made the best decision, due to my route through New York City. I heard the traffic there was mind boggling.

I finally got on the New Jersey Turnpike. When the lanes cleared, I picked up speed. I monitored the rear view and side mirrors constantly because I worried about my car and the hitch connected to the towing bar. Eventually, I felt my driving pace and attention to detail would make sure me and my car got to Vermont safely. Once I crossed into New Jersey, the traffic became more intense. Other drivers were flowing with the cars, in the slow and passing lanes. I stepped on my gas pedal to match their speed, as the U-haul truck swayed from the rapid acceleration. All was well in the back and I relaxed and prepared to drive, as I had done so many other times with Dr. Reed. I thought about him a lot during the drive and felt nostalgic that if he could see how far I had come, he would be proud. I had my gum, Blues, and caffeine, but the excitement and attention to the map made me more alert.

The truck was considered oversized and regulated like larger trucks by the New Jersey state troopers and highway patrolman. I had to stay in the right lanes the entire drive, so that other cars could pass me at will. The turnpike, at that time, didn't allow large trucks on it. Trucks had to take an alternate route as required by state law. My vehicle didn't have tremendous power, but my driving experiences helped me keep the speed steady. I was nervous because there weren't many vehicles on the turnpike that looked like mine and I didn't want any problems with the police. We were all required to drive very carefully. I took my responsibilities seriously, by keeping a steady pace and speed.

I was just about to settle down and listen to some good music and review my map, when a sign ahead read *"Toll 1 mile."* I heard about the numerous tolls on the turnpike, but was surprised I was already paying a fee. I had to go through the oversized vehicle lane and instead of paying one dollar, which was normal for a 2-axle vehicle; I had to pay three dollars because of the size of my truck and the trailer. I made my first stop and was ready to continue driving and thanked God that AAA already informed me about potential construction and each toll stop on my journey.

I passed one hurdle as I pulled away from the toll booth, but was still concerned that I didn't see any other vehicles like mine on the turnpike. I was focused and just followed my map and drove the speed designated for safe vehicle maneuvering, which was five miles/hour less than the normal speed limit. Other cars were averaging 70 MPH, but I was only going 65 MPH and never left the right lane. The trip from Dover to Burlington, Vermont was about 480 miles and didn't seem that long considering the fact that I was used to driving seventeen hours to Arkansas, with Dr. Reed.

I learned that day that the turnpike is one of the busiest and most heavily traveled highways in the United States. I drove with confidence, as cars in the slow and fast lanes whizzed by me. I'm sure some motorists were annoyed, but I was prepared to maintain my present speed and stay the course.

I noticed that the lanes were much bigger than I had seen on I-40 or I-66. Sometimes it appeared as if there were six lanes on each side of the highway packed with cars. Further up the turnpike, the highway split into outer lanes, which all vehicles could use, and inner lanes for cars only. The turnpike merged with part of the Garden State Parkway. Unfortunately, I was caught in the inner lanes, from not paying attention. This lapse caused me to stay there for most of the ride. Soon after I got my bearing, another toll stop was ahead. It seemed like I had to pay every couple of miles. Now, I understand why New Jersey had some of best highways in the country, because the patrons who drove on it paid for it.

I did enjoy seeing the green scenery and was sometimes overwhelmed by how beautiful the state was. I always thought of New Jersey as an industrial state, with steel mills, blue collar workers, and heavy traffic, but my drive made me more appreciative of its culture and agriculture. Everywhere I looked was *"green"* and I thought about how my father and Dr. Reed talked about me being *"green."* It was ironic and interesting that *"green"* was the shade I saw the most on my drive to Vermont, and the fact that Vermont's motto is *"The Green Mountain State."*

I stopped at two more tolls, before the turnpike changed into I-95 North. The last toll I stopped at, the attendant asked me "They didn't tell you that trucks aren't allowed on the turnpike?" I said "No!" He smirked, then asked me for three dollars and my journey on the turnpike had come to an end. I was glad none of the highway police stopped me and asked me to get off and use an alternative route, because I would have gotten lost. God was looking out for me that day.

My car was still stowed securely behind the truck and I took the next exit onto I-287 for the next 70 miles. This part of my journey led me closer to New York City. As I drove, I could see the landscapes of the *"Big Apple"* on the horizon. The next exit I took was I-87 North heading toward Albany, New York. I took a quick glance at my Triptik and my navigation markers indicated that I was about 200 miles from the great state of Vermont. I still averaged about 60 MPH to be extra careful. I figured at this rate, it would take me about four hours to get off the major highways and onto the two lane access roads. This part of the drive was much more serene, even though I still had to deal with tolls. Driving was also much easier, because I didn't have to stop every five miles to pay. The New York Thruway used a system of long-distance tickets that had to be paid when vehicles exited.

I picked up speed as day turned to dusk and night. The lights were beautiful on both sides of the highway and the silhouette of New York City illuminated in the distance. I planned my trip so that I would miss the major traffic going into and out of the city. It was the weekend, so traffic wasn't as heavy as usual, but it still became bumper to bumper and slowed to a crawl periodically. I was glad I gassed up in New Jersey, at one of their many rest stops, and found it interesting that it was against the law for drivers to put gas in their own cars.

Everywhere I looked there were attendants waiting by each pump and when I drove up with my car attached, the attendant asked me how much gas I needed. This was really convenient, but unusual. It was important for me to use the thruway rest stops because they had larger lanes. One of my major concerns was getting into a situation, where I would have to backup the truck and trailer. I didn't have a problem backing the truck, but the car's trailer moved separately. This was a skill that most truck drivers have to master before they are offered a commercial driver's license (CDL). I didn't have enough time to learn this technique, so I made sure whenever I entered or parked in an area, I had enough room to maneuver in it.

At this point, I had driven about 100 miles on the thruway and decided to gas up one last time, which would last me until I got to Burlington. It was now 9 p.m. and darkness covered the road. The interior lights inside the truck matched the glow from the headlights of cars in front and back of me. The next sign read 50 miles to the *RT-17 N/Albany exit*, which meant I was close to Vermont. I turned on the radio and started chewing more gum, not because I was tired but because I was ready to get to Vermont. I had been in the truck for more than seven hours and wanted to stretch my legs.

I got bored so I sped up, but made sure not to weave in and out of traffic. I drove for another hour and finally saw my exit. I turned off I-87 and slowed my speed for residential driving. The AAA Triptik gave turn by turn instructions and by the time I reached the city, I knew I was almost there. My father called me and asked where I was. I told him about seventy miles outside of Burlington and I would keep him posted. As the quaint city I passed disappeared in the background, the well lit streets seemed to vanish suddenly and it became dark on the two lane roads.

I noticed that the landscape of the roads changed. Instead of driving on flat surfaces, I saw and felt rolling hills and inclines. The roads curved more often than I had seen in several hours. Instead of gradual curves and inclines, the changes were more sudden. I sat up in the truck seat, as darkness from the road made me focus more on driving. I thought about my experiences through the Smoky Mountains. Even though the roads weren't foggy, they were still quite difficult to navigate. My car was secure on the back of the truck, but I worried about keeping the truck under

Four Tubas, a Guitar, and a Gallery of Cheerleaders

control as the road became steeper. I remembered to use the lower gears and was amazed at how it actually slowed the truck down hills and helped me stabilize the vehicle.

I felt like I was driving through a small country town in Arkansas and could see outlines of houses and farms. I went up and down hills for the next thirty miles and eventually got used to the road. The U-haul I rented was almost new (40,000 miles), so it performed well. I took my time on hills, while the roads became one lane passages, where no vehicle was allowed to pass. I know the cars that were stuck behind me were upset because I drove about 45 MPH. There was no room to go around. I had never been here before, so I was more careful with my life. By the time I got to my next major direction change, the road flattened some, but I could see in the distance several silhouettes of mountains and my ears began to pop. I knew then that I was close because of the change in elevation.

I drove on *RT-9N* for about seventeen miles, then took *RT-903*, which eventually became *VT-17*. I probably drove the best at this time, than I had all day, because the roads narrowed and my truck seemed to hug the center line. There was no major traffic because it was Sunday evening, which actually made the drive harder. I would have liked to have seen a few cars or houses spaced closer together, but that wasn't the case. I kept my pace steady. Because there was no traffic, I decided to increase my speed. I turned on the interior lights and saw that my next turn was coming up, in about five miles. By the time I reached the turn, my AAA Triptik indicated that I had less than thirty miles to go before reaching Burlington.

I made a sharp left turn on *VT-22A* and drove for about thirty minutes. I dropped the Triptik because now it was a straight shot to Burlington. I looked in the rear view mirror to check on my car, then gave the truck more gas and was comfortable with my progress. I probably was going too fast for the truck, but had held my speed at bay all day and night. I didn't go overboard, but I did pick up the pace. It was now close to 11:00 p.m. and I had another 30 miles to go. I wanted to arrive in Burlington at midnight. It was a personal goal for me to set out hours, with a succinct plan, and arrive at the time estimated.

I knew Dr. Reed would be proud of my advanced driving skills, so I relaxed and prepared for the last couple of miles into Burlington. I didn't expect to go through any more towns before I got there, but was surprised to travel through a place called *Vergennes*. I would have almost missed the town, if I didn't go through it. I was speeding based on residential zoning signs. It was interesting coming into a town that I didn't remember seeing on my map. I'm sure it was there, because AAA was very thorough, but I didn't expect to see people. The area lacked well-lit homes or stores. Once I knew I was in Vergennes, I slowed down and looked to my left and saw they were celebrating the Fourth of July, with a big fireworks show.

That was really cool to see because it was almost as if they were welcoming me into the great state of Vermont, but in actuality they were celebrating the nation's Independence Day, after July 4, which is a tradition of many Vermonters. With sparks in the distant horizon, I drove aggressively through Vergennes and only slowed some because of one stop light and curvy hills. I found out later that Vergennes wasn't a place that I should have been speeding through at night, but God was on my side. I wasn't stopped and there was one more turn before heading into Burlington.

Vergennes quickly disappeared in my rear view mirror, and the sparks from the fireworks faded as I approached *U.S. 7*. Time was on my side. It was 11:30 p.m. and after my left turn, the highway sign read "Burlington 20 miles." I was so psyched because I would finally get there, after a long day's journey, and start a brand new life. As I drove the final minutes of my trip, I thought about Vermont and the fact that this was a state that lacked a number of things I was used to, including African-Americans.

I tried not to have my own stereotypes regarding the state, but since I was traveling alone and prepared to go to school there without the support of people in my past, I prepared for everything. I knew from my multiple trips to Vermont that there were many opportunities for me. I wanted to take advantage of all of them. I hoped T.S. decided to come as well, so I would at least have one familiar person to work with in the doctoral program.

I turned on the radio to listen to a couple of stations. All I heard was Country music and immediately scanned the rest of the stations, to see what else was playing. The reception was spotty, so I cut the radio off and kept driving. What was interesting about this part of the drive was that I experienced the most hills and inclines coming into Burlington. I wondered where all these curves and hills came from, ten miles outside of the city.

I knew I was in the mountains, but didn't know how much work it would be to get me and my car there. I began to see lights and my eyes opened wider. I could see businesses and stores and was somewhat familiar with the area, but not enough to know exactly where I was going. When I saw the sign that read "Burlington, Vermont," I rejoiced because in the last week, I had driven from Delaware to Arkansas and back. Today, I had driven through Delaware into New Jersey through New York State, saw New York City, and now was in Vermont. That was an awesome feeling.

As I came into Burlington, I looked for Main Street, because I knew the University of Vermont was adjacent to it. If I could get there, I could drive until I saw the part of the campus I was familiar with. I drove for another fifteen minutes and thought I was lost. When I stopped at a gas station to ask for directions, they told me I had just missed the campus, and to go up the next hill and it would be on my left. I followed the attendant's directions and when I came over the crest of the hill, I could see familiar landmarks.

I knew what part of the campus I was looking for, but also knew I couldn't park my truck there. The lanes were too tight. I knew if I went in there, I probably couldn't get out. I drove around the building and found a large parking lot, where I could park the truck horizontally. It was now 12:05 a.m. There were no cars there, so I had plenty of room to maneuver.

Once I stopped the truck, I jumped out of the driver's seat and took a big breath of fresh Vermont air, as I stretched like a bear awakening from hibernation. I closed the door and the first thing I did was go to the back of the truck, and get on the trailer where my car was stationed. I removed the wheel locks and pulled out the ramps, so I could take it off.

I started the engine and slowly rolled off the back of the truck, until I hit the pavement. I got out of the car, left it running, and repositioned the truck vertically, so the trailer was behind the truck. I decided to leave the truck there overnight, until I found a U-haul distribution center. I locked it and jumped back in my car and drove in circles around the campus.

I don't know what got into me, but I found the first roadway I could use and drove through it. I saw signs that read "Do Not Enter," but I didn't care because I was in Vermont and it felt good to get my bearings in a brand new place. Driving like that wasn't very smart. These paths were routes for the Campus Area Transportation Systems or (CATS)[53]. I drove on the CATS routes for about ten minutes and then found the dormitory, where I would be living. T.S. and I had stayed there before, which is why

---

53 CATS-is a system of buses and bus routes that shuffle students around the entire UVM campus. The CATS also operates off-campus shuttles to help students go downtown and to the waterfront.

I was more familiar with this location. These dormitories were known for having some of the smallest rooms on campus, but I didn't care.

Settling in Vermont

I parked my car and knocked on the door of Chittenden Buckingham Wills (CBW). Shortly after, a very friendly resident assistant let me in. I told her who I was and she said she was expecting me, and then gave me keys to my room. I was glad to finally get off the road and happy I made it there safely. I called my parents and let them know I was in Vermont. My father was most proud of my journey, because of how I navigated at night through unfamiliar states, not really knowing where I was going. I placed some of the credit on the AAA Triptik maps and the approach my father and I took, by studying them and going over best-case worst-case scenarios for the highway. The real credit goes to God, because without his favor, I would have had a much more dangerous and difficult drive.

When I opened the room door, it was just as I remembered; two desks and bunk beds. My brother and I slept in twin bunk beds for years. He always got the top bunk and I slept in the bottom. I just felt more secure in the bottom bunk and knew that some nights, after eating too late, I could be very active, in my sleep, and probably would have fallen from the top.

Now, I had the whole room to myself. I don't think I got undressed. I just settled down and went to sleep. I didn't have any sheets on the bed or a pillow. I used my jacket and pants to support my head. The next day was Sunday, so I assumed the truck would be FINE where I left it. As I closed my eyes, I dreamt of my day and thought about things to come, as a graduate student at the Universitas Viridis Monits (UVM), which translates to mean "University of the Green Mountains." I loved their motto *Studiis Et Rebus Honestis*, which is Latin and means *"For Things and Studies That Are Honest."* I purposely slept until noon and was so tired that when I woke, I had to get the U-haul to a local drop-off center.

On my way into Burlington, I saw several U-haul stores, where I could leave the truck, but was already over the mile limit for the rental contract. I didn't want to go back onto U.S. 7, so I remembered where I got directions the night before. There was a U-haul store there. The problem was unloading the truck, dropping the truck off, and then getting back to campus. The first challenge was "Where would I put my stuff?" I jumped into my car and drove around Burlington, until I found a storage facility on U.S. 7 that was reasonable, and not too far from the campus. I was blessed to get a spot, with no prior notice. They really tried to work with me and my budget. I signed some papers and gave them a down payment for the first month's rent.

Unloading the truck was easier than loading it. I was able to stack and store all of my things in about an hour, because I had consolidated and thrown away so much in Delaware. Everything I brought with me was valuable. I got the basic essentials for my room (sheets, towels, music CDs) and left the rest for later. My next issue was to drop off the U-haul. I drove to the U-haul depot near UVM and asked if they could take the truck. I also asked if one of the attendants could give me a ride back to campus. Once I told them my situation and let them know the truck and trailer were almost new, they were willing to help me.

The depot was teaming with trucks that had license plate tags from all over the country; some as far away as California. I'm sure most of their trucks came from other one-way trips, which is why they barely had room for mine. The manager wasn't bothered by the confusion in the parking lot, because he wanted as many vehicles as possible to rent to others.

After they checked the truck, I paid the difference for extra miles and they gave me my final receipt, before taking me back to the dormitory. When I got back to the room, I relaxed and slept. I was glad it was Sunday and needed the rest to prepare for the exciting activities next week. Monday was the day I would reconnect with Dr. Brooke Mossman and begin my graduate school orientation process.

My living arrangements in CBW were only temporary. I had already established a lease contract with an apartment complex adjacent to the campus. I negotiated with them, for about two months, and was finally able to pay the first month's rent and security deposit. I couldn't move in until August 8, so living in CBW was a great opportunity. I was worried about the lease because the rent was $700.00/month. My fear was that my stipend wouldn't be enough to cover the rent, utilities, and prior debts from Delaware. I knew I would have a roommate, but had no idea who he or she would be. I focused my mind for Monday and wanted to make sure I was ready to learn.

The next day, I went to meet the Dean of the Graduate School. I told him of my adventures on the highway and he helped me schedule an itinerary for the week. He thought T.S. came with me, but I explained to him that I came to Vermont alone. My next stop was to meet Dr.

Mossman. When I got to her office, she greeted me and we discussed the Environmental Pathology programs and then introduced me to her laboratory staff.

I found out during this meeting that *"rotations,"* are a requirement for all new graduate students. A rotation is a six-month to a year commitment in a laboratory that is designed to determine if the research focus was interesting enough to pursue in the doctoral program. I didn't want to rotate for that long, because I knew I wanted to work with someone who did cancer research.

I was familiar with the campus from other visits, which made it easier to navigate the various research departments, and decide where I wanted to work. I had no plans to rotate for more than a month, because I felt it was time I could spend working in one laboratory. I knew I had to comply with at least the initial interview process in several laboratories, but wanted to find where I would be for the duration of my studies as soon as possible.

Once my tours were over, I set a tentative schedule to stop by three or four laboratories, before the end of the week. I was determined to keep my time line. I had a plan and my advisor at DSU gave me some of the best advice I had ever been given regarding working with research scientists. He told me to *"Choose someone who is fairly young and didn't have a full laboratory, because he or she would be the most interested in helping me earn the Ph.D."* He also felt that research scientists, who have large laboratories, numerous research staff, and several post-doctoral fellows, wouldn't have time to be an effective mentor.

"Professional Mentor and Trailblazing Scientist"
Dr. Brooke Mossman

Wisdom Inspired By God

"In terms of your difficulties in Biochemistry, I think it would be important that you get additional tutoring to help you pass the course. Don't worry about the cost, because I will find the money to make it happen. In this game of science, students and professionals need to understand that it takes more than good research skills, a good attitude, and a dream to be successful. Politics is involved in every aspect of research and higher education. One has to be connected to the right people and use every "angle" they can to achieve their goals. I am one of a few women, who have been able to successfully navigate a once male dominated culture and have been involved in science at the highest level. I can tell you Sederick that opening up doors for women and other underrepresented groups has not been easy, but I do it because it needs to be done.

We didn't have the best relationship, but I was glad he offered me some pertinent advice I could use. After meeting with the pathology department faculty members, my day was over. I took some time to go back to CBW to rest and set my goals and objectives for the week. The next couple of days would be spent talking with research scientists about their laboratory projects. That afternoon, I drove around Burlington and became more familiar with the area and learned that downtown was a good place to be on summer nights.

Burlington was a quaint little town with interesting people. My concern was that I wouldn't see anybody who looked like me. I had my own stereotypes about the city and knew before I arrived, that it lacked diversity in a lot of areas. I tried to put that in the back of mind because Vermont was my new home, and I had to make it work. It was difficult to come from a place where everyone I saw looked like me, but now everyone I saw looked like SOMEBODY else. I never had a problem with being unique, but this environment would be my greatest challenge.

The first thing I noticed, when I traveled around the city, was that people seemed to stare at me. Maybe I was paranoid and looked for anything to concentrate on to take my mind off the fact that I was farther away from home, than I had ever been in my life. I didn't feel like I was in a zoo, but I did feel like I was alone in the city. I had my own expectations about UVM and Burlington and already missed Dover. I hoped those feelings would subside soon.

That evening, I settled into my room, and the resident assistant of CBW helped me feel more welcome by introducing me to other residents. There were several students from various colleges and universities living in CBW. Many of them were there to take summer courses at the medical school. I was more social in CBW and eventually made some new friends, who shared similar experiences. The only problem was that they were only there for the summer. When they left, I felt more isolated.

The next day I rotated through another laboratory. The people I met were friendly and helpful. Dr. Mossman told me the format and schedule for the fall semester and setup my graduate stipend through the training grant. I was glad, because I was out of money and my DEVELOP stipend ended, before I arrived in Vermont. I didn't have a steady source of income, so I used credit cards to buy food and gas. Vermont was much more expensive than Delaware, and I soon felt how living in a sales tax-free state was a truly a blessing. I got into a routine of viewing laboratories and talking with faculty around the campus. I still had in my mind to only be in Vermont for three years, but my former advisor made sure he told me it was impossible to earn a Ph.D., in that time frame. I didn't believe him and only focused on the information in the DEVELOP brochure, which I probably misread in haste.

I liked living in the CBW dormitories, which were convenient to the laboratory rotations, but was still anxious to live in my own apartment. I saved some money from the last check of the DEVELOP stipend, and used cash advances to get the first month's rent and security deposit. $1400.00 was no joke. Now, all of my resources were gone. For the rest of the summer, I tried not to buy anything.

I had enough money to get in the apartment, but not enough to get the utilities (gas, electricity) turned on. I hoped UVM would start my training grant stipend soon, but based on the current fiscal year, my first check wouldn't be ready until September. The problem was my move in date was in August. This was my second big hurdle in Vermont, so I planned every night and used the remaining summer days to come up with a new financial plan.

My routine was the same everyday. I woke up, visited different laboratories, and talked with other scientists and their staff. Most were friendly, but they all talked about six month rotations. I was definitely not interested in rotating for that long and never let the graduate school or Dr. Mossman know how I felt. Whether I realized it or not, I was exhausted from Delaware.

I never took any time off to reset. Instead, I tried to do what I could to quickly adjust to a new and more rigorous environment. By the end of the first week, I was tired but had one more meeting with a physician scientist, who was highly recommended by Dr. Mossman. I wanted to know more about the last person I would talk to. She told me he was a physician and young faculty member that did cancer research, in the UVM College of Medicine.

On Friday morning of that week, I stopped at his office to speak with him. I read his biography and tried to understand the scope of his work the night before. I was excited to talk with him. Up until that point, I hadn't found a laboratory that really sparked my interests. I think I was holding out until the right opportunity presented itself, and hoped that this would be the one. I was also a little distracted because I worried about money to pay my bills.

I arrived a few minutes before our scheduled appointment at 10:00 a.m. When I walked into the laboratory, it was smaller than my former workstation in Delaware or Arkansas. The workbenches were clear and I didn't see any major equipment. Over in the corner, was an office that appeared too small for one person to work in. I heard someone talking on the phone. I knocked on the door and his voice became louder and more distinct, as he peered into the other room. He asked me to hold on for a moment.

I stepped back from the door and looked around his dimly lit laboratory. As I waited I met Heather, his laboratory technician, who walked in and introduced herself. She sat at her desk and asked me who I was. I told her my reason for being there and she responded with genuine small-talk. I was about to strike up a deeper conversation with her, when I heard the voice on the other side of the door say " *Mr. Rice*," and I said "*Dr. Finette.*" He immediately corrected me and asked that I call him "*Barry.*"

"Physician, Scientist, and Papa"
Barry

Wisdom Inspired by God

"You know Sed, the Aborigine people of Australia have a custom called the "walkabout," when a boy has to go out into the Australian outback for six months with only a knife and instructions from his father, as a tribal test of manhood. If he returns after 180 days, he is considered a Man and his father rejoices because he did his job. If he does not return, his father realizes he did not teach him enough to prevent his son from failing the test of manhood and survive. Innocence turns into experience for the young boy during this "walkabout" and there is a dramatic transition into the harsh real world. It's time for you to walkabout and get this Ph.D.! You know, when things get tough around here sometimes I wouldn't mind being a high school teacher."

I stopped my attempts at icebreaking conversation with Heather and shook Barry's hand. The first time I saw him, he reminded me of my former advisor, because of his height and facial expression. Barry welcomed me to UVM and immediately talked about his research. He was wearing a white laboratory coat, with a stethoscope in the pocket. We sat at one of the work-benches, as he described his research and mission to help children with cancer. I was interested in his research, because it was so different from any of the other laboratories I visited. Barry's focus was Leukemia and he told me he also worked in the hospital as an on-call physician.

I had a hundred questions, but Barry changed the subject and asked me about graduate school funding. I assured him that funding wasn't a problem, due to my status on the training grant. He knew Dr. Mossman very well and I reminded him that she was the one who sparked my interest in his work. We talked for about an hour.

I made sure to let him know that if he was interested, another student may want to join his laboratory. Barry seemed genuinely interested in taking on one student, but was skeptical about two. I told him that the other student and I could be a great package deal and we worked well together. He asked where the other student was. I told him that he may come up later, but was still deciding on the possibilities of graduate work in Vermont.

I made my decision about where I wanted to work, after our conversation, and then let Barry know that I really wanted to join his laboratory. He asked me about the rotations. I told him about my experiences in Arkansas and Delaware. We talked about my goal to do cancer research. I was excited because Barry had an M.D. and Ph.D. When I was in Chicago, I learned a lot about *"Physician Scientists,"* who had achieved both degrees, and could work in a hospital treating patients, or in the laboratory developing cures.

One of their mottos was *"Working from Bench to Bedside."* Barry and I talked a little while longer, as I became more resolved about my decision. I got a good vibe from him during our first meeting. I didn't know what was to come, but was certain that he was who I wanted to work with and learn from. I left his laboratory feeling renewed and confident. I felt I made a good decision to come to Vermont.

Nothing else was scheduled for me that day, so I went back to the dormitories to rest. Next week would be even busier. I was scheduled to meet the Dean of the Graduate School, to finish my paperwork, get my student ID, and learn more about the Cell and Molecular Biology (CMB) program.

Before I got to Vermont, the CMB program sent a brochure and logistical details to DSU, as an introduction to new graduate students. I briefly read the details, but didn't focus on the fine print. This experience was so new to me, that I just focused on the classes I would have to take to satisfy my degree requirements. As I browsed through the pages, I realized the first class I would have to take was *"General Biochemistry."* When I saw "Biochemistry," I paused a moment and reflected on Dr. Orr's words, from so many years ago. I also read a paragraph about *Cumulative Exams*, but the monotony of the wording diminished my interests. My enthusiasm only peeked, when I read about the graduation timeline.

I should have studied the manual more thoroughly, before the start of classes, but it never dawned on me to pay more attention to the requirements of the CMB program. My goal was to take classes and then do research in my new mentor's laboratory. I felt privileged to be at UVM and was excited about future opportunities. Later that day, I went back to CBW to rest and spent the majority of my time in the TV room trying to stay connected with my favorite television shows. I really liked football and golf. When the room wasn't occupied, I relaxed by flipping through the channels. I made more friends and chatted often with the summer medical students, but didn't go out much, to save money.

The weekend seemed to go by fast and before I knew it, Sunday night was upon me. Everyone in the dormitory was out in Burlington, but I stayed in. One thing I had to get used to was how UVM focused their resources on security. Our dormitories were always locked. As a matter of courtesy, visitors were let in the building by an intercom system, which became a big annoyance.

People in the dormitories would invite friends or relatives to visit, but wouldn't give them their room numbers to call them upon their arrival. They would beat on the outside doors until someone answered. That night, I was up late watching television because the lounge was free. I heard someone banging on the front door. Normally, I would wait for SOMEBODY, from upstairs, to come down and greet their visitors. This time, I was so tired of the noise I went to open the door myself.

As I approached the door to stop the incessant banging, to my surprise it was T.S. I opened the door and asked him what he was doing here. He told me he decided to come check Vermont out and then make his decision about graduate school. I was glad to see him and felt better about being in Vermont. I was hoping we could work together like we did in Delaware. His presence helped me with being, in my perception, *"The only Black Man in Burlington."* This was a wide generalization, but my interactions with other African-Americans were limited to people, who were only there for the summer.

T.S. told me he had been driving all day and remembered where we had stayed, so this was his first stop. The resident assistant on duty checked him into CBW and he became my roommate again. When he got to the room, he commented about how small it was. He had packed his Jeep with all of his things from Delaware and asked me to help him unload it.

By the time we finished, the already small room was packed with his stuff and mine. I never slept in a place that was too small for one person, but normally used to house two people. I was sleeping on the bottom bunk by habit, so when he started putting his things on the top bunk, we flipped a coin and I lost. I didn't mind because I had more support on the bottom and wouldn't run the risk of falling out of bed.

We discussed the plan for tomorrow and our tentative meet-and-greet schedule. He had already missed a week, but really didn't lose a lot of information from the sessions. We still planned to work in the same laboratory, especially in this new and culturally unique environment. We both had difficulties with our advisor in Delaware, so this time we had a plan to hit the ground running and not get behind in classes or our laboratory work.

The next day we went to the graduate school office to let the dean know that T.S. arrived and was still interested in UVM. The dean was glad to see him and worked on his paperwork to setup his graduate stipend. Dr. Mossman was also glad to see T.S. and reminded us of our busy week. That week was different because we both were spending the entire time in one laboratory. The program slated for both of us to work in three different laboratories, over the next three weeks. This week, we worked in an Immunology laboratory and learned interesting concepts related to the treatment and potential cures for Lyme disease[54].

We also got a chance to work with mice, and learned how they were used to support clinical research. This was an interesting but rigorous

---

[54] Lyme Disease- is a common tick-born disease in North America which is transmitted to humans from the bite of an infected tick. People affected by this disease usually experience fever, headache, fatigue, and depression. If left untreated, Lyme disease can affect the heart, joints, and central nervous system.

training assignment. We had to monitor mice everyday and make sure they were bred correctly. We worked primarily in the basement of the building, during this rotation, so every afternoon we cherished seeing the Sun. The next week we worked in the pathology department with Dr. Mossman and learned about *Asbestos*[55] and its role in lung cancer. Her laboratory was state of the art.

Dr. Mossman gave us several key pointers regarding graduate work and encouraged us to consider her laboratory, because she had two open slots. By the end of that week, I wasn't as tired as I was the first week, so I decided to venture out into Burlington. T.S. wanted to start weight training again to catch up on his former baseball glory days, but I wasn't interesting in any type of physical exercise. I was only concerned about my next apartment. The walls of my dormitory room, in CBW, were closing in on me. I did start walking downtown, which was about a mile each way up and down a steep hill.

It was fun going down the hill, but difficult coming back. This was my daily exercise routine. T.S. wanted to run downtown, but I was more comfortable leisurely walking up and down *Pearl Street*. By the time the weekend came, I was energized and used the gas I saved during the week, to ride around the city. T.S. interacted more with the medical school students. I had my days of shyness and instead looked for a low-cost movie theatre. Both of us were out of summer money and my credit cards were almost maxed out. Eating everyday with a credit card was no financial joke. I eventually cooked in the dormitory kitchen to save money.

T.S. and I decided to let UVM know that we didn't have a stipend any more and needed some funds to make it through the summer. We discussed our issues with the dean, but he thought we were still being paid from the DEVELOP program. We tried to convince him that we weren't, but there was some confusion with our transition from DSU and no one took responsibility. This didn't make us very happy about Burlington or UVM. T.S. was a family man with ties in Arkansas and Texas. I noticed he began contemplating his future in Vermont. He wanted and needed to be closer to his family, which was understandable, but he also felt he could provide more if he stayed in Vermont and finished the Ph.D.

We both thought about the next three years and tried to create a best-

---

55 Asbestos- is a naturally occurring silicate mineral composed of long fibrous crystals, which was used primarily to insulate homes and buildings throughout the 19th century. Asbestos is toxic and can cause lung cancer, mesothelioma, and asbestosis in animals and humans.

case worst-case scenario of the future. I could see that everyday in Vermont, T.S. weighed the pros and cons of staying. Meanwhile, we continued to do our rotations, but felt tremendous pressure living in a more expensive city and state. The final week of our rotations was in a familiar laboratory in the biochemistry department. We visited this laboratory before and spent time working on several chemistry projects. T.S. liked chemistry, but my passion and love was biology. We both chose this rotation to give us an idea of other departments inside the College of Medicine.

To our surprise, this rotation wasn't as rigorous as the other laboratories and our potential advisor was preparing to retire in a couple of years. We calculated that if we worked with him, we would need to progress very quickly. After our week's tasks we both agreed that this wasn't what we wanted to do. My interests were still with Barry, but when I followed up with him, he was busy writing grants to buy equipment and negotiating with UVM for more laboratory space. I pondered my future at UVM and tried be optimistic.

T.S. and I were glad our major rotations were over for the summer and looked forward to relaxing near the end of July. We still lived in CBW and I prepared to move into my new apartment on *August 9, 1996*. I still worried about my graduate stipend, because by that time, I worked enough hours to submit a timesheet but because of my pay schedule, the first month's rent payment would be late. I employed the old trick of *"Robbing Peter to Pay Paul"* and used the remaining room on my credit cards to get enough cash to cover me.

Unfortunately, I was out of money going into August. Meanwhile, T.S. thought more about his future and weighed his options. We both talked with Dr. Reed to keep him updated on our progress. T.S. wanted to discuss other educational options besides Vermont, but Dr. Reed was adamant, for both of us to stay the course and earn the Ph.D. I felt T.S. wouldn't be happy in Vermont, but held out until he made his final decision. The next week we took some time off and met with a few more CMB faculty members. The summer medical school students finished their classes and left the campus and city, during the first week of August.

I checked with my apartment complex and discovered that my roommate had already moved in. I was upset at first because the rental company didn't warn me before hand. I quickly realized I didn't have the money to get the water, electricity, or phone turned on, so it really was a blessing in disguise. T.S. was quiet about his plans for the future, so I just waited to see what he was going to do.

My birthday was coming up, as we both prepared to move out of CBW. When we left, first year students began moving in. I was just excited to get out of those cramped dormitory rooms. Our paperwork was finally complete in the graduate office and the first stipend check would be ready on *September 15, 1996*. There was nothing we could do about it. This was good news, but we still had to wait to get paid.

T.S. packed up his Jeep as I put the rest of my things in storage. We decided to party for my birthday, as we gathered our final things from CBW. We celebrated my birthday like my KKΨ fraternity parties in the Bluff. The only thing missing was a room full of beautiful African-American (Black) women. I had a good time that night and felt good about my future. The women in Burlington weren't that bad, but I missed seeing women of color.

The next day, T.S. helped me move into my apartment, but was still vague about his future plans. By the time we finished loading and unloading boxes into my new place, he let me know that Vermont wasn't where he wanted to live for an extended period of time. He wanted to be closer to his family and didn't want to miss valuable time with his children. I respected his decision, but was sad because I knew it would be difficult living in Vermont, making new friends, and adjusting to the rigors of graduate work in an unfamiliar place.

I tried to convince him to stay, but his decision was final. We shook hands and I told him to keep in touch. He jumped in his Jeep and that was the last time I saw him. I didn't have time to feel nostalgic because of my new "*lease on life*" and concern that my second rent payment would be late. I shook off the emotions of the last hour, walked upstairs to meet my new roommate, and began my education in the "*Green Mountain State.*"

Summer/Fall 1996

My roommate was cool with me for no other reason than he turned on the phone and other utilities in the apartment. I was happy with my new living arrangements. It was a two bedroom duplex, with two sets of stairs. The rooms were big and the living room had a balcony that faced the rest of the complex. I tried to organize my things from storage, but my roommate had already brought a microwave and other household supplies and said he didn't watch TV. That was perfect for me, because I brought my television from Delaware and was happy to put it in the common area.

We seemed to get along FINE. He was a first year undergraduate student from Seattle and seemed disinterested in going to school in Vermont.

There was one more week to go before classes began, so I had some down time to do my own thing. I lived fairly close to campus, so getting back and forth to class wouldn't be a problem. The pressing issue was there were no parking spaces on campus. It was cool because my apartment was right next to the CATS bus stop. There were dormitories right across the street from our building, so when the bus came, it was always full. I had to time it correctly to get on. I didn't care about a seat, I just wanted to get on the bus and ride the route to my classes. I rehearsed my morning routine, during the end of the summer, to make sure the routes would get me to class on time. I settled down some, but still felt intense isolation and loneliness. I missed everything I had always taken for granted in Delaware and Arkansas.

As much as I complained about Vermont, UVM was a very classy university and really welcomed new students to the area and school. That Saturday, a graduate student mixer was planned in the historic *Billings Student Center* to welcome students, from around the country, to UVM. I dressed down that day and decided to try to meet new people. I arrived early, but when I got there, the event was already crowded. I didn't feel out of place, but did feel like I was living in a fishbowl. I couldn't shake the feeling that I was missing culture and everything I once knew. Once I got my bearings and tried to have a good time, I didn't feel so bad.

The meeting was long but informative. Afterwards, a luncheon was organized on the terrace. I met a few people, but wasn't networking like I should have. After about 20 minutes of watching other people talk, I decided to leave and walk back to my apartment. Other people were leaving too, so my exit didn't seem out of place. As I walked up the street, I heard someone yell in my direction. I stopped and turned around and saw what appeared to be an African-American (Black) man running towards me. I was puzzled because I didn't see him in the mixer, but as he got closer, I could see the enthusiasm on his face. As he approached, he greeted me and said *"What's up Black Man! My name is Cleo!"*

I was glad to meet him. After introducing himself, he told me he was glad to see another *"Brother"* in Vermont, and wanted to know why I was here. I told him I was a new graduate student in the CMB program and would be working on my Ph.D. Cleo mentioned that I was the first Black person he had seen at UVM, and he wanted to make sure we stayed in

Four Tubas, a Guitar, and a Gallery of Cheerleaders

touch. It was kind of funny that we were the only visible Black people at the gathering.

Cleo was really cool. The first thing I noticed about him was his huge Afro. It reminded me of the hairdos from the *Black Panther* eras, with an almost militant persona. He talked really fast and with so much energy and enthusiasm, it was hard to keep up. Cleo told me he was born and raised in Toledo, Ohio and went to school at the University of Dayton, before coming to Vermont.

He was an education major and recruited by UVM to complete his Master of Education degree, as part of the Phillips Academy, Andover[56]. Once I found out who he was and knew he would be at UVM for at least the next year, we immediately bonded as friends and kept in touch regularly after that. I still felt isolated, but not as much as before and realized that there was at least one other person at this school, who looked like me.

> A man that hath friends must shew himself friendly: and there is a friend that sticketh closer than a brother.
>
> **Proverbs 18:24 (KJV)**

---

56 Phillips Academy, Andover- is an exclusive education program designed to train new teachers of color to work in urban high schools.

"Cleo"

Meeting Cleo was good for my morale, but there were still so many things I was used to that seemed to be missing in Vermont. I missed the hustle and bustle of urban radio stations and their incessant advertisement of SOMEBODY'S birthday party, as well as the camaraderie of the local barber shop. One thing I knew would make me feel better would be a clean haircut. I guess it's a Black man's elixir. When I was growing up and things seemed chaotic in my life, the best thing I could do was get a good haircut, and an invigorating *hot towel* shave.

As I pondered where to get a haircut in Vermont, I really didn't know where to start. I wanted a Black barber that knew how to cut Black hair, but thought to myself "where in the world would I find that in this area?" I drove around for a while and tried to find where barber shops and salons were usually located, but the culture of this city was different from anything familiar to me.

I knew a barber shop was there somewhere, but when I asked anyone about a location, they often referred me to Supercuts or Paul Mason, in the downtown shopping area. I finally browsed through the yellow pages and decided to take a ride into Winooski, Vermont, which was a small suburb outside Burlington. Winooski citizens felt separate from Burlington, but it was so close that by the time you realized you were in another city, it really didn't matter.

I found a listing for *"Horizon Salon,"* which was one business not located in downtown Burlington. I had already seen the downtown grooming places and knew they didn't service Black hair, so I decided to try to find Horizon Salon. I drove into Winooski and made a right at one of the few lights in the city and saw the address.

My first impression was that SOMEBODY must be *"doing hair"* in someone's house, because when I drove up, all I saw was a duplex apartment with a flag draped across the front steps. I double-checked my address from the phone book and went inside. I really wanted to get more information about other potential barbershops in the area and hoped that SOMEBODY would be able to at least point me in the right direction.

I walked in the door and couldn't see anyone, so I thought no one was there. The room smelled like French vanilla candles and was decorated with African and Caribbean Art. A candy dish, at the reception desk, was filled with caramel cubes and peppermints. Before I could grab a piece, I heard "Hello, How are you?" I turned where the voice came from and when I focused my eyes, I saw a woman pressing out a young woman's hair, in the reflection from a mirror next to the back wall. Every time she combined through the young lady's hair, her head moved in the direction of the comb and she seemed annoyed and disinterested in being there. I walked closer and met the woman *"Behind the Chair"* and she introduced herself. She said, *"Hi, I'm Josie."* I responded, *"Nice to meet you Josie, I'm Sederick." I stopped by to get a haircut."*

"Confidant, Cheerleader, Dynamic Entrepreneur"
"Josie"

Wisdom Inspired by God

"Sed, now you know I'm the cheapest therapist in town. Most times people come into my salon to de-tox from whatever was wrong with them before they got here. They make dramatic changes to their hair, which lets me know that some aspect of their life is in disarray. They sit in my chair, immediately relax, and then start confiding in me. I try to listen, counsel, and console, just from my own experiences. One thing I have noticed about you is how you always put others' needs before your own. If you like, I love it, but you may co-dependent. You have a big heart and I know this makes you treat people a certain way and live life the way you do. I respect you because you follow rules. Most people can't say that. My dream is to write three bestsellers and sip French vanilla bean coffee and decorate chateaus part-time in Paris, France. It's not about the end of the journey that's the most important; it's about the journey itself."

Josie asked if I was new to Burlington and I said "Yes!" She replied, "Welcome to Vermont, this is my salon." I looked near the mirror and saw hair clippers, before asking if she cuts hair. She said "Yes!" and asked if I wanted a haircut. I delayed my answer to ponder a major life question, as I gazed upon the first African-American (Black) woman I had seen in several weeks. I answered "That's FINE," which is this case meant Freaked-out, Insecure, Neurotic, and Emotional, as I sat in an empty chair, until she finished her current appointment.

Josie didn't say much while I waited. I really admired her salon and all the current edition magazines she placed around the room. On previous occasions, I would go into barbershops in Delaware and down south and read about people, places, and things that happened ten years before I was born. Barbershops were notorious for keeping magazines like Ebony and Jet years after the featured articles came out.

I read quietly as Josie finished her patron and waited in the main part of the salon until she settled with the girl's mother. While I sat, I noticed that Josie was very talkative and friendly; almost in a bubbly kind of way. She came back into the room and stood behind her salon chair and asked me if I was ready. I moved slowly out of my seat and sat in her barber's chair. She immediately asked me *"Has a woman ever cut your hair before?"* I said "No!" with subtle confidence and obvious nervousness. My other response was *"All the barbershops I have ever been in were run by men."* In the back of my mind, I always thought that men should cut men's hair, and women should only style women's hair.

It was an interesting experience sitting in her chair for the first time. She asked me if I was nervous and I said "No!" Josie spoke softly and asked me how I wanted my hair cut. In a moment of humor, I flashed back to a scene from the movie *"Coming to America,"* when Eddie Murphy's character sat in a barbershop chair and was asked how he wanted his hair cut. His response and mine were the same *"Just make it nice and neat!"*

Josie smiled and laughed, which did ease my tension, as the buzz from the clippers reminded me that she was about to cut my hair. I wasn't complaining because this was the closest contact I had with a Black woman, since I got to Vermont. I wanted this feeling to last. The first time she cut my hair, she took her time, and did a great job tapering and boxing my fade. After the haircut, she showed me the mirror and asked me how it looked. I said it was FINE, but what she said next astonished me.

Josie asked me *"Do you want me to wash your hair?"* I said *"Do What Now!"* She repeated *"Do you want me to wash your hair?"* The first thing that came to my mind was *"Is she serious?"* I was used to going to an overcrowded barbershop that employed overbooked barbers that didn't believe in special treatment. Once your haircut was done, money exchanged hands, sometimes a brotherly embrace took place, but then the barber would yell *"Next"* or *"Does somebody need some help?"* and you left. I gave her a puzzled look. Then she said she would wash my scalp to get rid of the loose hairs, from the haircut. Now, I understood what her motives were and was excited to find out what it felt like to get my hair washed by a Black woman, in the middle of Vermont.

I felt like I was in an upscale salon, as seen on television, because Josie was attentive and made me feel relaxed and comfortable. As she washed my hair, she spoke softly and asked me questions about my background and why I came to Vermont. She wasn't intrusive and very skilled at making conversation from any answer I gave her. Josie did most of the talking, while I thought about being in a salon, and how a very attractive older woman had just cut my hair and was now washing it. This was probably as close to true contentment as I had felt in months.

When she finished, she dried my scalp and moisturized it with olive oil and some of her famous Dudley[57] hair care products. When I sat up in the chair, I knew this would be a place I would come to often. I asked her how much for the haircut and she told me $10.00. I just laughed because $10.00 in Delaware or Arkansas would only get you a buzz cut and you better not ask for a tapered fade, or any kind of special treatment.

For $10.00, I would be lucky to leave the barber's chair without excessive nicks and cuts and hair still in my ears and on my clothes. I truly enjoyed meeting Josie. My haircut experience was amazing. I paid her and told her I would definitely be back. She gave me her card and asked me to spread the word about her business. We shook hands and I went back to my apartment.

As soon I stepped outside her salon, I felt better about myself and Vermont; primarily because of my new haircut. I also felt encouraged because I knew that any time I wanted to get some Black culture, I could go to Josie's salon and get a "Cut, Wash, and Style" for only $10.00 and good conversation, which was free. I really liked Josie's spirit and outlook on life, from our brief conversations. She reminded of people from Arkansas by her mannerisms and demeanor. She acted like a woman with southern

---

57   Dudley Hair Products- was founded in 1967 by Joe Dudley and wife Eunice to break into the Black hair care market and has served as a model of Black business ownership. Dudley currently manufactures and sells over 400 beauty products.

roots, but I didn't know her long enough to inquire about where she was born and raised. Josie's friendly and nurturing spirit would eventually become vital to my survival and success in Vermont.

> Be careful for nothing, but in everything by prayer and supplication, with thanksgiving, let your requests be made known to God. And the peace of God, which surpasses all understanding, will guard your hearts and minds through Christ Jesus.
>
> **Philippians 4:6-7 (KJV)**

When I got back to my apartment, I rejoiced because I finally found a place where I didn't feel like a stranger. I knew the way Josie pampered and made me feel at home would be motivation for me to get a haircut as often as possible. I spoke briefly to my roommate and decided to read more about the UVM Graduate School and CMB program. I still only focused on the course work and the number of credits needed to graduate. Classes would start in a couple of days and I wanted to make sure I knew where to go. I enrolled in *General Biochemistry* and a *Cell Biology* course, as part of my first credit electives.

At the beginning of the week, I prepared myself for classes and let Barry know I wanted to work in his laboratory exclusively. He seemed FINE with that and I got to know Heather a little better. Barry already had a graduate student in his laboratory, who was working on his dissertation. I found out later that he accepted and mentored him because the student had difficulties in other departments around campus.

Barry only spoke briefly about him, but I learned that he was from Japan. I also took time to finish my paperwork, before the close of business everyday, and was ready to start receiving my stipend from the training grant. The rest of the week went by fast. I concentrated so much on organizing my things, and contemplating how I would pay my rent each month that I didn't pay attention to the time.

That weekend I tried to get out, but the city was packed with parents and students loading and unloading their things around the campus. I had never seen so many people with trucks and beds and other household items double-parked on the grass, in the street, or wherever they could find. The dormitory across the street from my apartment was buzzing with activity.

I saw firsthand how *"UVM Move-In Day"* differed from my experiences in Arkansas and Delaware. All the greens around the campus were filled with merchants that arrived specifically to sell and market their products. Special lots were designated for local and box businesses like Wal-Mart, Best Buy, Circuit City, and Sears. They sold everything from beds to refrigerators and TVs. I watched from a distance and was glad I moved in early. I did get a chance to go downtown, which was just as packed as the campus, and tried to make the most of my time on Burlington's famous *Church Street*.

Fall 1996

I waited anxiously for Monday to arrive. By Sunday night, my nervousness turned to calm, but my anticipation was high. When the alarm clock went off, I dressed and headed for the bus stop. My first class started at 10:00 a.m., so I tried to arrive early to make sure I could ride on the CATS. By the time I arrived at the bus stop, there was a line of people. Thankfully the CATS' buses were on a new schedule and made a loop around the campus every nine minutes. I couldn't get on the first or second buses, so I waited and finally was able to get on and ride toward the main campus.

When I finally arrived, my class was about to start. *General Biochemistry* met in the mornings and *Cell Biology* met in the afternoons, three days a week. I found the classroom and when I went inside, most of the seats were already filled. The instructor was at the board writing his name. I immediately felt uneasy, because no one in the classroom looked like me. I inched my way through a few rows of seats and sat in the back of the room.

Once class started, I felt better and relaxed enough to understand the introductory lesson. The first day, the instructor lectured for eighty minutes and I tried to take good notes. By the end of the class, I was confident I could do well in *General Biochemistry* and was ready to learn new things in *Cell Biology*. After class, I went to the laboratory to talk with Barry. He was in the hospital performing clinical rounds, so I made myself more comfortable and found a place to sit and work.

I finally met Makoto, Barry's Japanese graduate student, and we talked about my background and his, before my next class. I enjoyed meeting

Four Tubas, a Guitar, and a Gallery of Cheerleaders

and conversing with him, but couldn't stay or else I would've been late. I walked across the green to the biology building and when I entered the classroom, I felt the same way I did in *General Biochemistry*. No one in the class looked like me. I tried to remember what Dr. Reed told me about improving my networking skills in any situation. *Cell Biology* seemed interesting.

After that first day, I was confident I could do well at UVM. I felt more prepared for graduate work, because I had already earned a Master's degree from DSU; the primary mission of the DEVELOP program. I still waited to receive my degree in the mail. Dr. Reed promised me that T.S. and I would be listed with the DSU Graduating Class of 1996. Most graduate students, in the CMB doctoral program, came right out of college, but I was unique. DSU and DEVELOP gave me an opportunity to experience graduate work, so I would be ready for doctoral level training.

Later that afternoon, I went back to the laboratory. Barry was still gone so I talked briefly with Heather and went home. That evening, I studied my class notes thoroughly and prepared to learn more about Barry's research. His schedule was hectic due to his extended work in the hospital. That month, he was on-call a lot, so I used the down time to study and rest. The next couple of days were the same and I had a good idea of what my schedule would be like over the next couple of months. By the end of the week, I was bored and really wanted go back to Josie's shop, just for the conversation, but decided to wait another week so my hair would grow enough to be cut.

Instead, I slept in my room and drove around Burlington to find other hang out spots. My real mission was to find people who looked like me. I guess at that point in my life, I was starving for culture and Burlington wasn't a cultural paradise for me. I learned from research, that in Burlington and all over Vermont, African-Americans made up less than one percent of the total population.

I thought I would see one or two *Brothers* or *Sisters* somewhere downtown. Unfortunately I didn't, so I spent more time at home and scanned through old VHS tapes and photo albums. This way my way of staying connected to African-American culture. Even on campus, I didn't see any African-American (Black) faculty, so my mission to achieve a Ph.D. was complicated, because I felt totally alone. My goal was still clear, and that was to *"Get the Ph.D."*

The next couple of weeks I attended classes as usual and prepared for my first sets of tests. I had an exam in *Biochemistry* early in the week on

Wednesday and a test on Friday, in *Cell Biology*. I didn't have a chance to stop by Josie's before that time, because I really prepared and studied for the exams. Based on the syllabus, there were only <u>four</u> exams in each course, so every point was critical.

There were no cumulative finals or extra credit points, so I knew if I didn't do well on one exam, I wouldn't do well in the class. This caused me great anxiety leading up to test day, but I studied as thoroughly as I knew how and prepared for the challenge. My courses were also team-taught, which meant that before each testing session, specialists, in a field of study, gave instruction during the class. I wasn't familiar with this teaching style. All of my classes in Arkansas and Delaware were taught by the same person the entire semester. I wondered how consistent instruction would be and hoped that by the time I learned their styles and grading tendencies, I would be able to adjust to someone new.

Test day was finally here and I got to class early. I studied up until an hour before the exam because I wanted to cover everything. When the clock struck 10:00 a.m., the instructor asked us to clear our desks and he passed out the exam. During my previous exams, I usually read all the questions from beginning to end, and then answered the questions I knew first. That day, I looked at the essay style exam questions and immediately panicked because I wasn't familiar with what was being asked. I was frustrated because I studied so hard, but seemed to study the wrong things. I went through the rest of the exam, but because I couldn't readily answer the first question, my confidence was shook for the rest of the test.

I sat in my chair, at the back of the room, and stared into space for a moment, while I desperately tried to re-focus. I looked at the clock, adjusted my collar, scratched my head, and did everything but open that test booklet again. After about fifteen minutes, I opened the booklet and tried to answer more questions. My eyes darted from the clock to the desk, as each question seemed to take forever to answer the way I felt was correct. My time was running out. The test was smudged with pencil and erase marks because I had re-written my answers so many times.

I felt better about fifteen minutes before the exam was over and reconciled in my mind that if I didn't do well on this exam, I could always do better on the next one. With five minutes to go before the exam ended, I rushed to answer the final questions and dusted the eraser resins off the pages, right before I gave my exam to the instructor. I had an unusual smile on my face because I felt I had just endured intense exam anxiety, but recovered and survived. I knew the exam wasn't my best effort, but hoped to understand how the instructor graded, when the scores came back. Later that week, I had the same experience in my *Cell Biology* class, but thought nothing of it because this was only my first exam. I knew it would take me some time to adjust to a new grading system.

That weekend, I went back to Josie's to get another haircut and have conversation. I was tired and felt that something was always going on in her salon. I also checked to see if she would wash my hair again. Sometimes salons and barbershops use gimmicks to try to get customers to return for follow-up visits. I felt Josie was sincere in her actions, but did want to experience that kind of hair pampering again. I scheduled an appointment early in the week. When I arrived on Saturday, I didn't have to wait. We talked a little more this visit and she told why she moved from Florida to Vermont. Josie was a student of the *Dudley School of Cosmetology* and decided to open up a business in Vermont, because there were no Black salons in the state at that time. She and her husband moved to Burlington in 1995 and decided to follow a dream and bring some culture to the "Green Mountain State." I was glad she was in Vermont. My haircuts provided more than a style for me; they provided Black culture in a state that lacked it. We talked a lot more during this visit and both of us decided to confide in each other.

Josie told me she was a proud member of *Delta Sigma Theta Sorority, Inc.* I have family members who are Deltas and they always represented African-American women and Black culture with style and class. Josie was cool to talk to. Her words were so calming that the time I spent in the salon was therapeutic. Our time together was my only cultural outlet, so I made sure I let her know how much her business and presence meant to me. I liked Josie because she was wise. Everything I decided to talk about, she could discuss with quick wit and intelligence. I always wanted an older sister like her. When we conversed, I felt like I was learning from a woman with a *"seasoned"* passion and experience for life.

I admired her dream and vision to move to Vermont, but thought it would be nearly impossible to operate totally by Faith in an unfamiliar place, until I realized I did the same thing. Josie had an entrepreneurial spirit and knew how to make real money. She consistently talked about *"Multiple Streams of Income."* I was so comfortable in her salon that sometimes I didn't want to leave, but I did respect her space and our business relationship. Before she finished my haircut, I mentioned my initial experiences at UVM and first exams. I told her about my testing anxiety and how I wanted to do well. I didn't want to have to struggle to finish this degree, like I did in Arkansas and in Delaware. Josie listened and offered warm words of advice, as if she had known me for years.

Josie told me *"Today is today and tomorrow is tomorrow, so make sure I get ready to do better the next time."* Her words were kind and compassionate and really made me feel better. She finished my haircut and on queue asked me if I wanted my hair washed. I said sure and from that moment on, I knew I wanted to develop a lasting friendship with her. I didn't get a chance to meet her husband, but she briefly told me about his struggles and triumphs with *Biochemistry* in Florida The conversation with Josie helped me not feel so bad about my exam performance. She knew how to make people feel better, even if it meant sharing personal aspects of her life, to provide the best example.

After she finished my haircut, we talked a little more and I left her salon feeling renewed and energized. I thought about our conversation and the time spent there and decided to do something to show my appreciation. Later that evening, I drove to Sear's to look for a gift or small token to thank her for her kind words and attentive ear. I didn't know what she liked, so I browsed the aisles until I found something to fit my budget.

I looked all over the store, but couldn't decide on one specific gift, until I saw a crystal elephant sitting on a display table, in front of the jewelry department. I knew she was a Delta and understood their tradition of collecting elephants. I thought it would be a nice gesture to show my appreciation for the haircuts and conversation. I bought the elephant and saved it until the next time I got a haircut, hoping she would accept and like it. In her shop, she had beautiful Caribbean and African artwork. My goal was for her to put the elephant in her display case, so when I visited, I could see something I contributed to her business.

The next week was back to business in classes and in the laboratory. Barry was still on call, so I used that time to study and learn more about cancer research. I talked with Makoto a lot and he gave me some very good advice about graduate work and what Barry expected from his graduate students. I hoped to interact more with Barry, but was thankful that my time could be spent focusing on classes. I still had a three-year timetable in my head for completing the Ph.D., even though my former mentor in Delaware facetiously told me *"No one can get a Ph.D. in three years."* I felt his words were just banter. I had my own vision for success. My former advisor also gave me that advice when we were distant in the laboratory, so I know I discounted what he was saying. I knew what I was doing and believed that I could get a Ph.D. in three years.

Meanwhile, we changed instructors in the *Biochemistry* and *Cell Biology* classes and our new professors taught new content. I wanted to know what I made on the first *Biochemistry* exam. By Wednesday of that week, I got the news. Our former instructor stopped by after class, to distribute the scores. I was nervous because I knew I didn't do great, but felt I didn't do that bad. The instructor passed out the tests from the highest to the lowest grades. As he called names, mine never came up. He had gone through sixteen exams before he read my name and I knew my scores were terrible. I opened the exam booklet and was highly disappointed. I couldn't understand why my score was so low.

I felt like I shouldn't have studied and could have gotten the same grade. I sat in the classroom, while everyone filed out, and pondered my I didn't to better. I kept telling myself that I had studied enough, but still questioned the grade. There were red marks all over my exam and each page was more depressing that the previous. I left the classroom in a somber mood and searched for answers. I knew I was smart and had been successful other places, but wondered why my graduate career started like this.

I went home, thought about my big plans, and immediately read the *Biochemistry* course syllabus and grading scale. By my calculations, I needed to score perfectly on the next three exams to earn a "B" in the class. I knew a "C" wasn't an option, so I tried to cheer myself up and hope for the best. I spent two days thinking about that exam and decided to change my strategy and study even harder. I was determined to do much better in this class. Now, passing *Biochemistry* was my personal mission. Everything else would have to take a back seat.

Later that week, I got my grade from the *Cell Biology* exam. The results weren't as bad, but still the same. I had a pretty good idea I studied the wrong materials in *Biochemistry*, but *Cell Biology* should have been my *"Bread & Butter."* I had two missions. Improve my study skills, and score well on the rest of the exams. Both classes used an essay question format, which has always been one of my academic weaknesses, every since I studied in Dr. Fitzpatrick's *Botany* and *Microbiology* courses at UAPB. I never like essay questions because they were always so subjective. I preferred short answer and fill-in-the blank options for tests.

This was a new system for me, so I kept quiet about my first exam and concentrated on working harder the next couple of weeks. I felt uneasy because I was in a new location and didn't "fit in." To top it all off, my first set of grades were unacceptable. To give me a boost, I spent more time in the laboratory and learned more about my role and expectations as a graduate student. Barry presented a seminar during our weekly update meeting, and outlined each staff member's research project. Makoto's project was almost complete. All he had to do over the next two years was complete his experiments and defend his dissertation. My assignment was to learn more about cancer research in children.

Barry wanted me to use the skills I learned in Dr. Orr's laboratory to begin working on the *"HPRT T-cell cloning assay."* I was excited to get some hands on experience. Barry wanted me to shadow Heather and the other laboratory technicians to polish my skills. There were other scientists associated with Barry's research that worked in the *Genetic Toxicology Laboratory*, which was located near the main part of the campus.

Instead of going directly to Barry's laboratory after class, I walked to the Genetic Toxicology Laboratory and trained. I didn't spend lots of time there because my mind was on *Biochemistry*. I did learn how the cloning assay was done and hoped to have an opportunity to do it first hand. The next time Barry and I talked, he asked me how classes were going. I told him "FINE," but wanted to be more honest, so I let him know that I did have some difficulty in *Biochemistry*. Barry seemed to understand and told me to keep him posted on my progress. I expected him to ask more questions, but he took some notes and left the room.

The next week I was more focused and attentive in class. I took more notes and studied them daily. I was glad to learn new things, but needed to be able to grasp the material and score well on the next exam. I read my book, wrote better notes, and felt more confident this time around. I thought I had recovered from my first bout of exam anxiety, so each day I reminded myself of scores from the last test. During those next couple of weeks, all I did was read and write notes. By the time the next exam came, I was ready and tried to remember my previous errors.

Test day was here again. The instructor distributed the exams and I opened mine with anticipation. After reading the first page, I felt the same way I did during the first exam. For whatever reason, I couldn't answer the first question, which always frustrated me to the point that it hampered my ability to focus on the rest of the exam.

I flipped through the rest of the test and felt pressure building in my chest, neck, back, and head. I just knew I hadn't got myself into this situation again, but it was staring me in the face. I paused and tried to refocus, but every question on the exam was something I either studied lightly or not at all. None of my major study points were on this test.

This time I didn't look for an out and tried to answer questions to the best of my ability. Halfway through the exam, my motivation was gone and I lost all confidence in the answers I submitted. I finished the exam and turned in my paper. I left the classroom feeling low because I knew I would get the same or lower score, as the first exam. I tried not to think about it until I got home; right before I got in bed, and tried to sleep.

All I heard in my subconscious was Dr. Orr's words' begging me to take an *Introductory Biochemistry* course. His words stressed me, as I tossed and turned in bed. I kept waking up thinking about Dr. Orr and his prophetic speech. What was most frustrating was that I couldn't go back in time and get the background to compete with other doctoral students. I tried to get the exam out of my mind, but knew the cause of my troubles happened years before I came to Vermont. Maybe I was in denial, but I dreaded seeing my second exam results.

When the weekend came, I needed to feel better so I got in my car and headed to see Josie. I had an appointment, but got there an hour early just so I could be in a place that made me feel comfortable. I watched Josie start and finish two appointments before me. She was lively as usual and made sure to include me in any conversation she had. By the time I got in her chair, she asked me if something was wrong. She could see it on my face.

I told her the troubles I faced at UVM. I talked and she listened. I was in a barber's chair getting life counseling. Every phrase she spoke was filled with wisdom and experience. I probably wouldn't have confided as much if she were a man, because my pride wouldn't have let me share my pain. Josie offered me some advice, which was to keep pushing and *"People who earn Ph.D.s do so because they want them, not because they are easy to get."* I felt like a weight was lifted from me. The burden of *Biochemistry*, at least for the rest of that weekend, was gone. When she finished my haircut, I brought the elephant into the salon and gave it to her. She smiled and was thankful. She asked me why I bought it for her. I told her because she was really helping me adjust in Burlington. I also let her know that her place of business was a cultural Mecca for me and I was so glad she decided to come to Vermont.

Josie told me she would display the elephant in her shop and thanked me again. I felt good about the elephant and hoped it would help build a stronger friendship with her. Later that evening, just so she wouldn't be outdone, she called me and stopped by my apartment to give me two sweet potato pies, as a goodwill gesture. I asked her why she brought me the pies. She said *"I just did this to let you know that you can't outdo me in giving!"* I laughed and accepted the pies, which took me almost two weeks to eat because of my low tolerance for sweets. I knew then that she was special and every time I got a haircut, I felt like I was learning from her experiences. Josie always teased me about being so young and trying to get a Ph.D., but it was cool, because she supported me like one else had in Vermont. I knew her husband was a lucky man and I looked forward to meeting him.

The next week I got my exam scores and just as I predicted, they were extremely low. I was now on a fast track to failing *Biochemistry*. I didn't know what to do because it was bad enough to get a "C" in a graduate school course, but to get an "F" would be devastating. I avoided talking with Barry about my scores and decided to confide in Dr. Mossman, to determine my options. There was such a build up about DEVELOP students coming to Vermont, that I felt additional pressure to succeed. During the meeting with Dr. Mossman, I honestly let her know what was going on. She was compassionate and understanding, as I became more stressed, disappointed, and depressed. I felt *Biochemistry* would define me at UVM, and literally kicked myself for not listening to Dr. Orr and taking the course sooner.

One option Dr. Mossman gave me was to withdraw from the class, focus on *Cell Biology*, and take the class later. I quickly accepted her advice and filled out the paperwork to withdraw. I let Barry know what was going on and he seemed to understand, but told me not to keep him in the dark about my progress. I withdrew from the class, but continued to go so I could learn the background concepts. Dr. Mossman's goal was to give me a break, so I could take the second part of the course in the Winter/Spring semester. I appreciated the option and continued attending the class.

My work in *Cell Biology* wasn't much better. Each essay I wrote apparently wasn't good enough to warrant passing scores. I was frustrated all the way around and before I knew it, I had to write a mock grant proposal and got a notice to take a cumulative subject exam the next week. I should have paid more attention to the CMB guidebook, but had enough on my plate than to worry about another exam.

I felt overwhelmed and my time in the laboratory diminished. I had never been one to stay in the laboratory all day, but understood that I had to do more work and keep Barry posted on my class progress. The next week, I took the cumulative exam not really knowing what to expect. I found out, four weeks prior to each exam, key words are distributed and it is the job of the pre-doctoral fellow to research each key word and be prepared to answer questions related to them.

I was so busy worrying about *Biochemistry* and my other class that I totally forgot about it. When the time came for the exam, I asked another graduate student for advice. She told me that cumulative exams were a new system for assessing graduate students' bid to earn their Ph.D.s. I wanted her to tell me it was ok to skip the exam, but she encouraged me to at least take it and try to score something on it.

I was completely overwhelmed with life. In the last month, I had withdrawn from a major class needed to finish the Ph.D., had to take a cumulative exam I didn't study for, and couldn't find time to work in the laboratory. My rent was also due and my graduate stipend wasn't enough to pay it, leaving me $200.00 in the hole. I heard that *"pressure makes diamonds,"* but I was about to crack.

I settled down and tried to approach one challenge at a time. I took the cumulative exam and answered the questions to the best of my ability. I felt good because at least I didn't skip it. My next move was to talk to Barry about my troubles and keep him informed, so my absence in the laboratory wouldn't be considered insubordination.

I still had money problems and knew that *"Robbing Peter to Pay Paul,"* wouldn't sustain me much longer. I needed to find another job, but heard that most graduate programs strictly forbid pre-doctoral fellows from working outside the university. I thought this was a stupid rule and didn't understand why we had to live only off the stipends they gave us.

I had to use my entire check on the first of the month and half of my check on the fifteenth, just to pay the rent, which didn't include electricity, phone, or cable. I honestly thought about the graduate school's reasoning behind their decisions, which were designed to make sure doctoral candidates focused primarily on their work, but I didn't agree with their policy. The bottom line was I needed to find a job fast. Withdrawing from *Biochemistry* bought me some time to find additional work. I went to find a part-time job and kept it quiet.

Kappa Kappa Psi (EX) and Tau Beta Sigma (ΔΠ) Pledge Boards.

Kappa Kappa Psi Pledge Boards

Kappa Kappa Psi Pledge Boards

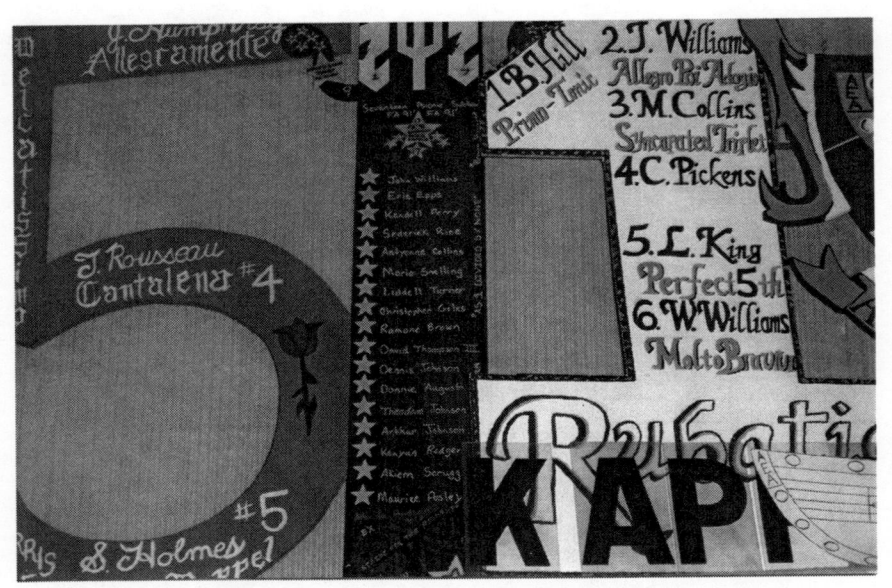

Kappa Kappa Psi (EX) and Tau Beta Sigma (ΔΠ) Pledge Boards.

Mr. Harold Strong and Mr. Odie Burrus.

Kappa Kappa Psi (EX) pledge boards

Kappa Kappa Psi (EX) memorial rocks

Tau Beta Sigma (ΔΠ) chapter members

Kappa Kappa Psi (EX) chapter members.

Epsilon Chi (EX) Pledge Line Root Board

Dynamic Dozen Pledge Board

Gerome Hudson "Hud"

Caption: Root Board II

Arthur Johnson (Fall 91') Drum major

The lovely ladies of Tau Beta Sigma.

My first KKΨ fraternity jacket illustrating my musical line name, Prince Serpentes "Bass" #4.

My Grandfather, Victor Charles Rice sitting at the "*Shop*"

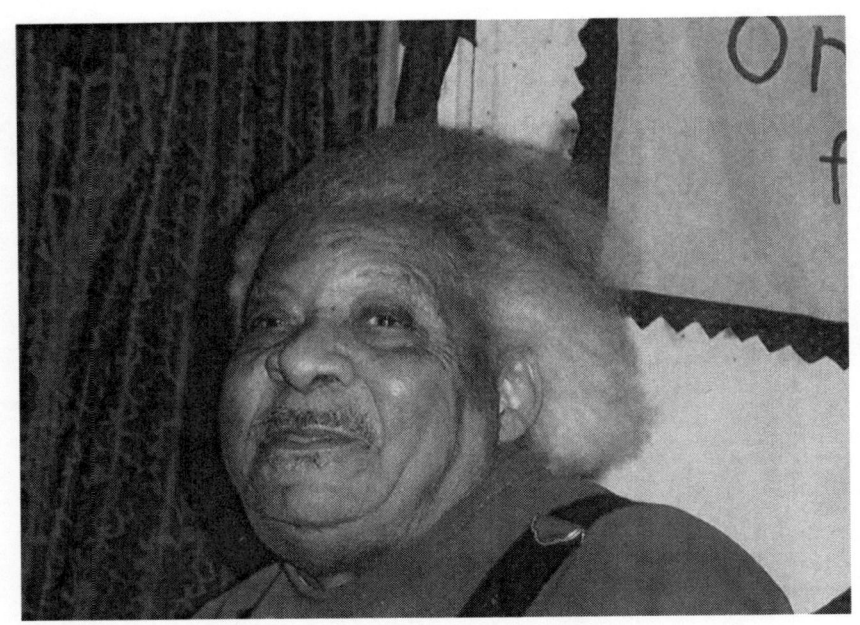

My Grandfather "Paw-Paw," Reverend Joseph Spears, Sr.

Master's Thesis Defense at Delaware State University (1996)

Delaware State University Biology Department
Thesis Committee (1996)

Thesis signing ceremony.

T.S., Mrs. Givens, and the author.

A tuba and a guitar.

The author meets Dr. William P. Foster.

The author and student trainee in Barry's laboratory.

Thesis signing ceremony.

Kappa Kappa Psi and Tau Beta Sigma Pledge Boards

Indiana Street Missionary Baptist Church

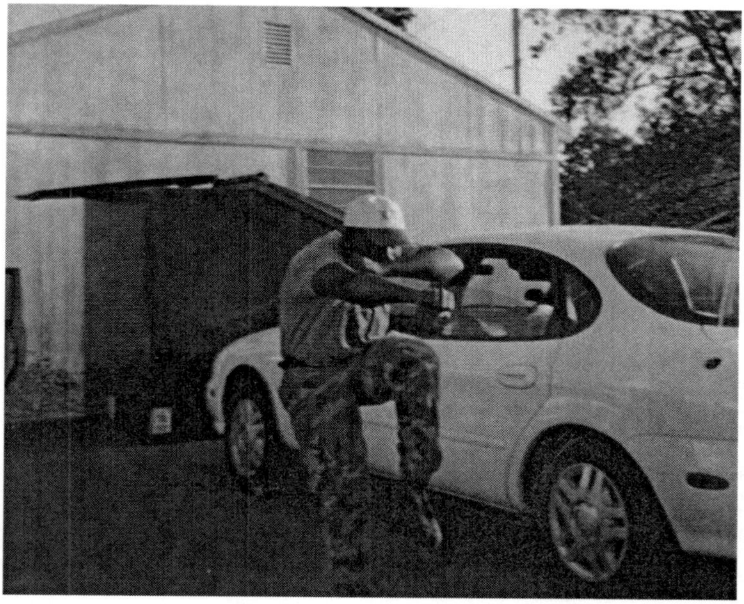

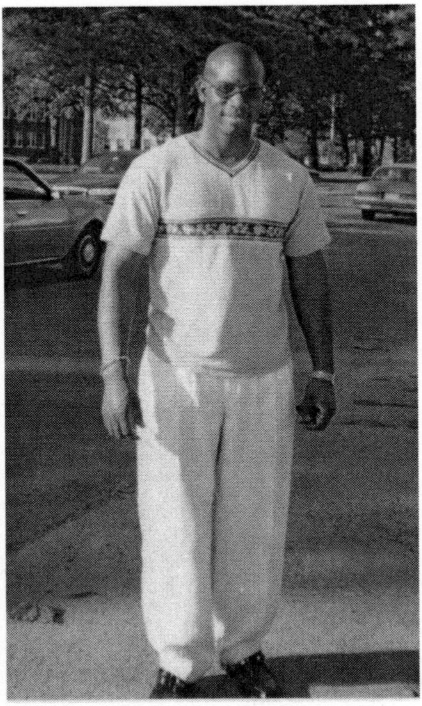

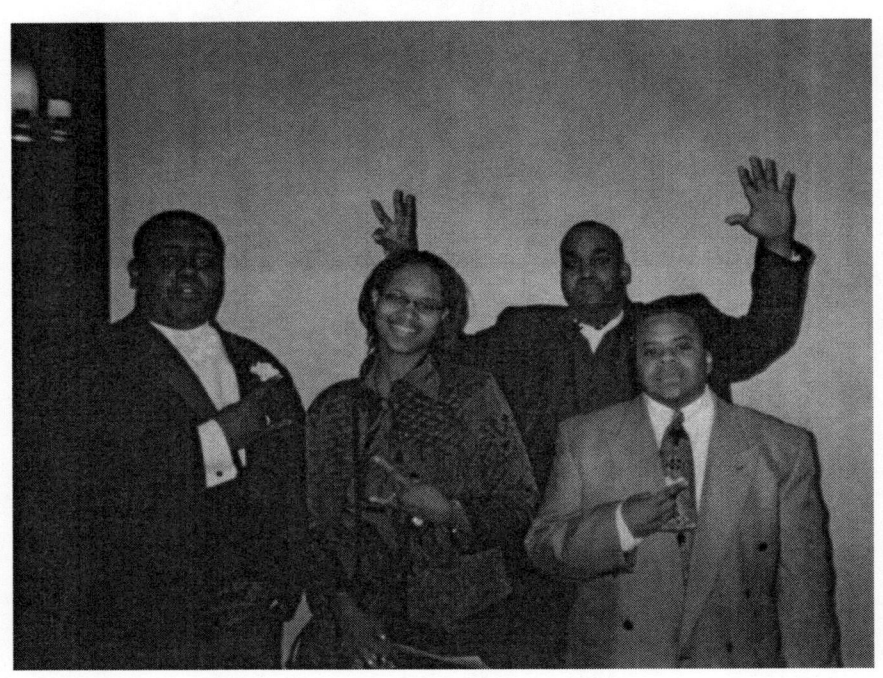

Brother Stephen Collins "Chico."

Dr. Joseph "Doc" Miller and the author.

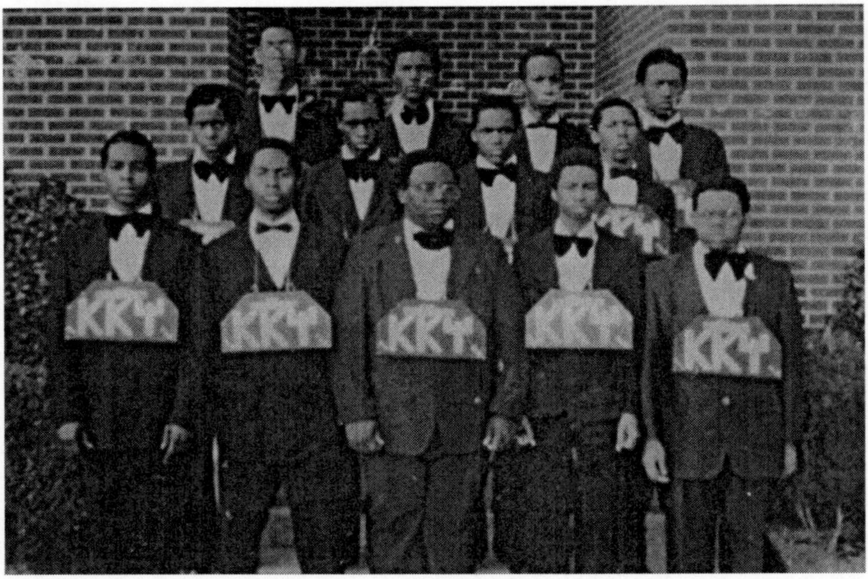
KKY
KKY
KKY
KKY
KKY

Four Tubas, a Guitar, and a Gallery of Cheerleaders

Delivering Pizzas to Pay the Rent

My goal was to find a job that would fit my schedule. I needed to work in the evenings or at night. Unfortunately, most of the available jobs were day shifts. I drove around Burlington one evening and happened to stop at my favorite pizza place *"Little Caesar's."* When I opened the door, I saw a sign that read *"Drivers Needed!"* I always wanted to know what it took to make a pizza and this seemed to be my best opportunity to learn. I ordered a pepperoni pizza and asked about driving for the company.

The manager gave me the scoop about pizza delivery and the company's expectations. My only concern was I wasn't that familiar with the area and would probably get lost. She told me that drivers were paid $1.00/pizza delivered and $3.25/hour. I didn't realize the company always gets the better deal on pizza delivery, because of the wear and tear on your vehicle. She gave me an application and I told her I would think about working for Little Caesar's. That night, I reflected on my money troubles and the solution became clear. I had to deliver pizza part-time.

I waited about a week before I started delivering. I watched my co-workers make pizzas with dough, marinara sauce, and an assortment of meats, vegetables, and cheese. It probably cost about $3.00 to make a pizza, but they always sold for $15.00 or higher. I enjoyed learning the inner workings of the pizza industry. My first night, I drove like a taxi-driver in downtown New York City. I was nervous because if the pizza wasn't delivered in thirty minutes, it was free. This meant I would lose $1.00 for every late pizza, not to mention the penalty of burning more gas, with no monetary reward.

I understood the rules and during my first night shift, I delivered seven pizzas without a problem. Becoming a delivery driver really helped me learn the area more quickly, but I was really tired after the shift. The first week I made $50.00, so I calculated that if I worked harder on the weekends, I could potentially gross $300-$400 each month. This new plan of action worked for me in the short term, while I tried to be more focused in the laboratory.

My schedule was from the laboratory, to Little Caesar's, and then back home. I kept Barry updated on my progress in *Biochemistry*, but because I withdrew, I could only update him on what I learned, while sitting in on the class. I did feel that some of the pressure was off me, but was frustrated that I had gotten myself into academic trouble the first semester at UVM. I went to class diligently, but wasn't allowed to sit in on the tests. Meanwhile, I learned tissue culture techniques and finally completed my first experiment. The results were positive, so the first thing I did was show Barry.

In my mind, I thought he would be proud of my initial successes, as I gallantly walked into his office with a smile on my face. Barry, with a stern demeanor, looked at my laboratory results and without pause told me *"Don't ever show me any data, unless you have analyzed it!"* My exuberance quickly turned to concern. I felt like a child in a room of adults. I guess it felt good to achieve something, even if it was small. What I learned in those briefs moments was that it would take more than a smile to earn the Ph.D. I never forgot that day and realized my tenure in the laboratory and at UVM would depend on my work ethic, and the strength of my learning curve. I went back to the laboratory and regrouped; feeling as if I had one of those "green" moments.

The next week was the *Annual Graduate Student Research Forum*, hosted by the pathology department. This was a venue where new students presented their research to faculty and staff in the CMB program. I geared up for this meeting because I needed something to help build my spirits. Barry and I worked on a presentation and I knew I would be one of the best presenters. The forum was similar to my thesis defense at DSU. Research scientists and their staff came quickly filling the small room.

Graduate students were introduced to the audience, before they presented their work. I waited anxiously for my turn. The opportunity came to present our laboratory's work. I was so "*full of myself*" the entire presentation. I had worked in the laboratory less than a year, but felt superior to the other graduate students because of my master's degree. I thought I spoke well and was confident others felt the same way I did.

After I finished, I returned to sit in the audience and asked Barry "How did I do?" Barry told me I did FINE then I said "I did the best!" I didn't think about what I said at that moment, and didn't realize other people heard me. I just tried to relish in the moment and latch onto something to give me more confidence. As I sat by Barry, he told me that I shouldn't have said what I said, because my words could be perceived as "arrogant" and "disrespectful," especially from a first year graduate student, in a room full of tenured professors. I took his words to heart and we discussed my presentation, when we got back to his office.

I honestly was proud of my presentation, but that wasn't the point. The point was that I had so much more to learn. Making statements like that could create anger and hostility from faculty members, who would be responsible for my success at UVM. When I thought about that day, I felt bad, but tried not dwell on it too much and was able to move on. I vowed to do better next time. This was another one of those "green" moments that now seemed to be happening more often. After my experience in the forum, I was more mindful of my mouth and how it could affect me and other people.

> My brethren, be not many masters, knowing that we shall receive the greater condemnation. For in many things we offend all. If any man offend not in word, the same is a perfect man, and able also to bridle the whole body. Behold, we put bits in the horses' mouths, that they may obey us; and we turn about their whole body. Behold also the ships, which though they be so great, and are driven of fierce winds, yet are they turned about with a very small helm, whithersoever the governor listeth. Even so the tongue is a little member, and boasteth great things. Behold, how great a matter a little fire kindleth! And the tongue is a fire, a world of iniquity: so is the tongue among our members, that it defileth the whole body, and setteth on fire the course of nature; and it is set on fire of hell.
>
> **James 3:1-6 (KJV)**

No other major events happened after that. The rest of the semester seemed to fly by. I was still in *Cell Biology*, trying to rebound from errors made on the first exam. I worked really hard because I wanted to build some momentum going into the spring semester. I thought my work ethic and new concentration on studying would help improve my test-taking abilities.

Unfortunately, my scores never changed. I tried to keep a good attitude, but every exam score was the same and I didn't understand why. I became so frustrated and spoke to the professor on numerous occasions. She didn't offer what I wanted, which were keys to being a successful graduate student at UVM. I thought about Mr. Woods and his "knowledge box" analogy and recognized that some things had to be experienced instead of talked about, in order to make sense. By the end of my first term, I improved some, but ended up earning a "C-".

An "F" in any class is disastrous, but a C is just as bad. This concerned me the most about *Biochemistry*. Based on the grading scale, anything below a "C" was marked as an "F." I had lots of explaining to do and my mood changed. I was working nights to pay the rent and during the day, I was in the laboratory trying to learn as much as I could. My grades distracted me and I felt isolated and alone even though Cleo and I would spend time playing pool, video games, and cards. Cleo's personality and outlook on life helped me cope. He was supportive, even though he had issues of his own. He was a great friend.

Eventually, delivering pizzas wasn't all it was cracked up to be and I found myself trying to reconcile why I was in a doctoral program and delivering pizzas every night for a "$1.00 a pie." Near the end of the semester, the weather changed dramatically. Icy conditions and snow forced me to resign from Little Caesar's. It became too dangerous to drive.

I finally realized my car was more valuable to my living arrangements in Burlington, than driving around the city delivering pizzas. I talked to Barry near the end of the semester and we discussed a comprehensive plan for the next year. I was disappointed with my progress in the laboratory and in classes, and really wanted to move back to Arkansas. Barry saw some frustration on my part and concerned I wouldn't return. I never said one way or the other and probably left my decision up in the air, because I wasn't happy. The fighter in me didn't want to quit, before I gave it a chance.

I was scheduled to leave Vermont, right before Christmas, and decided to stay nearly a month due to the university's winter break. I never told Barry how long I would stay home and he never asked. I just assumed this would be ok because I yearned for some culture. Before I left, I went to Josie's for a haircut and finally met her husband. He was an interesting person. I was glad we met.

She was like the older sister I never had. I listened intently to her wisdom and knowledge every visit, which recharged my spirit. Her husband was friendly, but we couldn't talk long due to his busy schedule. He did let me know he was thinking of enrolling in graduate school at UVM and gave me some incite into his experiences with *Biochemistry* in

Four Tubas, a Guitar, and a Gallery of Cheerleaders

Florida. I appreciated his words and he promised to give me the real deal about *Biochemistry*, the next time we talked.

Josie smiled when I saw her and was more talkative and enthusiastic than before. She shared her entrepreneurial philosophy and goal setting concepts for making money. She did it with such flare and animation, it was funny and I kept laughing. Josie had a passion for life and a spirit that could lift anyone, when they were down. Her personality was what kept me coming back to see her. Whatever was going on with her I never knew, but if I opened my mouth to vent about UVM, Burlington, or being Black in Vermont, she could offer sound and timely advice. We talked a great deal about the rigors of college life and she kept saying that I was *"Young in the Game,"* and cautioned me to be patient. Patience has never been my strong suit, especially during difficult times.

> Knowing this, that the trying of your faith worketh patience. But let patience have her perfect work, that ye may be perfect and entire, wanting nothing.
>
> **James 1:3-4 (KJV)**

I was in a season of frustration and difficulty. The first thing I wanted to do was have everything I ever wanted right then. It never dawned on me that life is a process. Josie helped me realize that by sharing her mantra *"The end is not what is important. It is the steps you take to get there!"* I heard her, but never full embraced her words of wisdom. She just kept telling me the same thing, whenever I was depressed. I shared a lot about me that day and wanted to know more about her. Today would be the day I asked more personal questions, with caution, because I didn't want to be intrusive. My question topics began slowly, until I realized she was willing to share her life story with me in detail.

Josie told me she was born in Orlando, Florida, but "claimed" Winter Park, Florida as her true home. She spoke briefly about her travels and life in Okinawa, Japan and Montreal Canada. What intrigued me was why she decided to settle in Vermont. She had already mentioned her dream of establishing a business to serve African-American people, in a region of the country where quality ethnic hair care was lacking. Then, she gave me an abbreviated version of her entrepreneurial story.

She and her husband decided to move to either, Burlington, Vermont, Seattle, Washington, or Juneau, Alaska, when they were living in Florida. The final decision was based on their bank account and how far the money they saved would get them. Based on the cost of gas and their resources, she told me they could only get to Vermont. Josie and her husband left in August of 1994, in a U-Haul and 88' Toyota Corolla.

They were new parents and brought their four-month-old baby and everything they owned, tightly packed in the trunk and interior of their car. Vermont was a *"prime target"* in Josie's opinion, because there was a population and clientele yearning for hair care services she could provide. She told me funny stories about her clients, who religiously drove to Montreal, Canada or New York City to get a haircut or *"Press & Curl,"* before she arrived. I laughed with her and thought about my struggles to find anyone in the city with skills to cut my hair like I was accustomed to.

Josie told me some interesting things about her, including the fact that she was a female "junior." When she first described herself a *"female junior,"* I didn't understand what she meant. All the "juniors" I knew, including people in my family, were men. She explained that she and her mother had the same first name, so she was considered a female junior. I thought her first name was Josie, because that's what people called her. I found out it was short for Josephine.

She was graceful, strong, and had a pioneering spirit, which reminded me of Josephine Baker[58]. Josie was also a former high school cheerleader. I could tell because she always knew how to cheer me up and motivate her clients to pursue their dreams. She described herself as a true Gemini, born on the seventh day of June, the same birth date of the musical artist *Prince*[59].

She warned me that she can have two different personalities, which I later understood. She was a loyal wife and mother, who respected and

---

58 Josephine Baker- was the first African-American to star in a major motion picture. She was deeply involved in the Civil Rights Movement in the United States, and the French Resistance during World War II.

59 Prince- (Prince Rogers Nelson) is an American songwriter known famously as an unpronounceable symbol, The Artist Formerly Known as Prince (TAFKAP), and The Artist. His creative music has influenced a generation of musicians. Since 1978, Prince has composed 33 albums and established a fan base around the world.

honored God, her mother, and one of her biggest influences, *Shelley Kolin*, a trailblazing entrepreneur, and executive in Interior Design. Josie supported Kolin because she managed plumbers, electricians, carpenters, and contractors, and built a corporate business with innovative ideas.

According to Josie, after opening up her own business, her next greatest achievement was joining Delta Sigma Theta Sorority, Inc. From my perspective, she was one of the most patient, organized, talkative, and hardest working people I had ever met. She had interesting ways of seeing the world and even approached her hair salon with a different level of class.

I noticed that Josie always referred to her customers as *"clients,"* which intrigued me. I asked her why she didn't describe them as appointments. She responded by sharing her experiences in salons in Florida, and while working part-time as an insurance agent. Her view was that patrons of her salon were special and deserved the best, so she recognized them as "clients," rather than appointments, to be more official.

I never heard anyone else use the term client in the barbershops or beauty salons I went to. It was nice to learn more about the professional side of the hair care business and Josie was a great teacher. I could have stayed there all day. Many times, I would fall asleep in the chair and wake up when my haircut was finished. I believe it was the French vanilla candles that helped me doze off. Once I heard the buzz of the hair clippers, and the aroma filled my nose, I was out like a light.

I had fun that day and learned a little more about someone I wanted to develop a stronger friendship with in the future. Josie was true to her words and placed the crystal elephant I bought her in the cabinet adorned with African silk tapestries and other cultural fabrics. Before leaving, I paid her $10.00 and really thought I was getting a deal. She never asked me for more money.

Josie was an easy person to do things for and she told me that most of her clients had given her gifts and she had given them gifts, to develop stronger business and personal relationships. She mentioned that she took a business class once and wrote down some goals she would like to achieve in the next ten years. At that point, she had achieved about half of them.

Josie wanted her business to be exclusive, so she would only have to service a small number of high profile clients each year. In the meantime, she wanted to travel to Paris, France and decorate chateaus on the French Riviera. I was always under the impression that all hair stylists and barbers made excellent money, but Josie schooled me to the fact that the first seven years of any business are the most critical and financially damaging.

She felt that the hair business is one of the most cutthroat conglomerates, in the world's supply and demand structure. This was years before the documentary/movie *Good Hair*, starring Chris Rock, described the ins and outs of the global hair business. Seven is a biblical number of completions. She wanted to be in business at least seven years, to really reap the benefits of birthing a business from scratch.

Josie was also very political and passionate about the fact that some immigrant groups could come to the United States and go seven years, without paying business taxes. She wasn't able to benefit from that provision, as an African-American woman, in such a competitive industry. This caused her to work longer and harder to achieve her successes. Josie's opinion was that *"Every new small business has to do whatever it takes to develop, in order to compete with more established companies and their competition policies."*

She never told me what her initial strategy was and I never asked. When we talked about this concept, she just smiled. I didn't care what she had to do to be in business, I was just glad that she was. One of her signature phrases was *"It takes a lighted candle to light another, so if our flames are extinguished then someone who cares and is near, can help us re-light our dreams."* Josie enjoyed helping others prosper.

The time had come for my shampoo. I had been to her salon enough times to expect a "good washing." She surprised me that day because not only did she wash my hair, she also added olive oil to the Dudley shampoo mixes. I never used olive oil for anything, even though I knew people who used it to cook. I grew up on shortening, margarine, and grease. When she rubbed it in my hair, it was a weird feeling. She told me that olive oil helps build the body of hair and strengthens my "ends." I didn't know I had "ends." My hair, after she cut it, was faded and almost bald. I learned that men's hair needed to be taken care of just like women's.

Josie knew the way she treated her clients could determine the fate of her business, so she would always go all out. Her clients would reward her by coming back and recommending her to their friends and co-workers. The *"lighted candle effect,"* began to work. I thought she was so amazing, because while all of this was going on, she was caring for her younger daughter. She ran a business and day care everyday. When I asked her if it was difficult to do both, she told me *"It's more difficult to pay high babysitting fees!"* She had a quick wit and sharp tongue and if she said it,

Four Tubas, a Guitar, and a Gallery of Cheerleaders

she meant it. I knew she had vision and her pre-meditated approach made me re-think how I approached my short and long-term goals.

All of Josie's clients were loyal and cared about her well-being. I wanted to be apart of her hair care network and got a good dose of African-American culture, knowledge, and laughter that day. When I went home to pack for the airport, I didn't feel totally alone. Cleo and Josie made up my inner circle of friends. I knew I had at least two friends in Vermont, even if I had to schedule an appointment to have a conversation with one of them.

The next day, I flew into Little Rock, Arkansas and was glad to be home. My father picked me up and I called Dr. Reed to see if he was coming home for the Christmas holiday. We talked briefly and he asked me how things were going. I told him FINE and he said *"really,"* as I quickly changed the subject to try to determine his travel plans. Dr. Reed told me he was only going to be in Arkansas, for a couple of days, and would like to try to catch up with me. Our schedules never matched this visit, so we didn't get a chance to chat face to face. I spent the majority of my time, with my family.

When I got back to the Bluff, things were a little different. Most of my friends had come home for the holidays. Kevin was back from Florida, Ralph was back from northern Arkansas, and Sedrick had come home from Illinois. Greg and Keith were still in the city, so we tried to get together as often as we could. I did get a chance to briefly visit UAPB.

I caught up with *Hud* and he updated me on the condition of the fraternity. I was glad he was still actively advising KKΨ and it made me feel good to go to the band room and see the SΨS pledge board. I turned off the lights, just to see if the fluorescent paints I used still worked, and they did. I stopped by Dr. Orr's office, but he was out, so I used the rest of my time to think about the next semester at UVM. I really had fun at home the first couple of weeks, but dreaded going back to Vermont. My undergraduate breaks had never lasted this long. I relished in the fact that I was home. I never thought I had responsibilities in Vermont, particularly in the laboratory, but my days of undergraduate leisure, during breaks was over.

After about three weeks, I got bored because I had seen and done everything on my things to do list. I was resting one day and got a call from a Vermont telephone number. It was Barry. I was surprised to hear from him and he asked me, if I was coming back to Vermont, with concern in his voice. I told him "yes" and that I had one more week to go, before flying back into Burlington.

Barry said he was just checking on me because he hadn't seen me in a number of weeks. I knew then that my vacation home was too long and I became anxious to get back to Vermont. The next couple of days in the Bluff were rough because I obviously shouldn't have stayed as long as I did. I wanted to get as much culture and home life as possible, to help me cope when I returned. I never knew Barry would take my absence so seriously. Dr. Reed tried to teach me that "Home is where the heart is!" I never realized the power of his words, until that day, and understood that if I wanted a Ph.D., I would have to make Vermont my home away from home.

Winter/Spring 1997

The weather changed in my absence. The streets of Burlington were now filled with powdery snow. The temperature was cold but not unbearable. The snow capped buildings and sidewalks made Burlington a serene and surreal place. When I stepped off the plane, the landscape had changed so dramatically, I felt like I was living in a new city. I knew Vermont was famous for its snow, but didn't expect to see so much so soon. I enjoyed changing seasons. The snow was a nice diversion from what was pressing most on my mind. I went right to the laboratory to let Barry know I was back. I felt bad about keeping Barry in the dark, but was glad to be back in Vermont, so I could try to do better. The first question he asked me was "How was home?" I told him FINE! He told me he really wondered where I was because I should have been working in the laboratory.

The first couple of weeks after my return, I became indifferent and felt bad for leaving Arkansas, where my family and friends lived. I tried to cope and reconcile that Vermont held the key to my life's dream. I didn't know what to expect over the next couple of months, but felt I had to really work hard, so Barry would support me. The daily weather forecasts were always for snow. Many of the undergraduate students on campus headed to the local ski resorts every weekend. I wanted to ski, but was afraid of getting hurt and jeopardizing my graduate work. I just wanted to get back on track with my studies and finances.

Barry and I talked about my future at UVM. After counsel from Dr. Mossman, I decided not to take the second part of *Biochemistry*. I wanted a break from what would be my greatest challenge, but also needed to stay

Four Tubas, a Guitar, and a Gallery of Cheerleaders

focused on courses that would help support my dissertation research. I was still funded by the training grant, so I had an option of taking specialty classes, which would help improve my GPA. I was glad Dr. Mossman and Barry supported me, but still worried day and night about *Biochemistry*.

When the semester began, I decided to work on my goal of writing a book. It had been more than two years since I last felt a passion for writing. Since my efforts and expectations at UVM were different, I knew writing would give me connection to the people and places I missed the most. While I was Arkansas, I gathered the remaining information to highlight all the pledge lines of KKΨ and TBΣ and was ready to outline the rest of my work. It was difficult to get back into writing, because most of my belongings were in storage; including all of my notes and important papers. I envisioned the project, but never really got a chance to organize it completely. It was still fun to try to bring together the history of the fraternity and sorority.

My main motivation to write came from Stephen Collins, known as "*Chico*," who was an older brother in KKΨ, during my time at UAPB. We had a misunderstanding, before a step show in 1992, about singing the fraternity song, which escalated into a shouting match. After the show, he took the opportunity to demonstrate to me how much of our chapter's history I didn't know. Writing this book would give me an opportunity to show him that I was listening and understood.

Back in the laboratory, things were picking up. Barry was off clinical duty, so he spent more time engaging his staff. He wrote a number of grants that were funded and requested more laboratory workspace, so he could hire additional personnel. Makoto was working hard to finish his experiments and Barry was pushing all of us to do more work.

I was still learning the experiment protocols. As the graduate trainee, I continued to shadow more experienced staff. I liked the work we were doing because it reminded me of Dr. Orr's laboratory. This was the main reason I chose Barry to be my dissertation advisor. It's always nice to discover new things, but sometimes researchers lose their connection with how their work can help others. Barry operated with a "*big picture*" attitude. His laboratory philosophy was designed to achieve great things, while helping children with cancer.

With all of the new changes occurring, my time was divided between classes and working in the Genetic Toxicology Laboratory. There, I learned how to do the *HPRT* T-cell cloning assay, which was the most important analysis tool in our research. As I shadowed more experienced professionals, I learned the importance of careful planning in each part of the experiment. I talked with Barry about my goals and objectives, which I thought were the same thing, but he helped me realize they were fundamentally different. Barry believed that *"Goals are plans for the future, but Objectives encompass the critical steps to achieving those goals."*

I enjoyed hearing Barry's philosophies, as they related to life and research, but was anxious to do more experiments. I watched the technicians do the cloning assay and wanted my chance to prove I could perform it successfully. Barry was hesitant to give me full reign over the experimental setup, for a number of reasons. The main reason was that he wanted all of the setups, for each experiment, to be consistent and use the most proficient person each time. I was still learning, but he agreed to allow me to perform the cloning assay under careful supervision of his senior laboratory technician.

In some ways, I was trying to compete with Makoto. I always watched how meticulous he was when he set up his experiments and envied his approach. Makoto would make you think he was preparing for surgery, because he was so detailed in every part of the experiment. I learned that Makoto rehearsed the same way he performed and thought carefully about every step in the experiment. I guess I wanted more responsibility and knew that to be more active in the research required me to be able to work independently. Barry finally granted me a chance to prove myself.

The next week, Barry called me into his office and told me I was scheduled to perform the cloning assay with his laboratory technician. I was excited because it would be the first time I led the experiment. I wanted to do a good job. When I got to the laboratory, I setup everything as I had seen it done before and started the experiment. The senior laboratory technician allowed me to control every step of the process.

I was on a roll and things seemed to be working FINE, until she asked about one of the steps in the protocol. I looked at my notes, but they didn't match what I was seeing in front of me. I had missed a step in the experiment because one of my test tubes was empty, but it should have been full. The technician and I immediately started reviewing what we had done, to try to determine if and when an error was made.

When we got to the step I was reviewing, that's where we discovered the mistake. I sat on the bench puzzled because I followed all of the steps to the best of my knowledge, but somehow still made a critical error. My mistake was major because that part of the experiment was unsalvageable.

The bigger issue was that we worked with chronological human samples, in a longitudinal study, that couldn't be replaced.

The technician called Barry and let him know what happened. I cleaned up the test tubes and Petri dishes and wondered how this would affect my tenure in the laboratory. The technician tried to console me, but I knew there would be some repercussions from Barry. When I got back to the main campus, I met with Barry and we talked about the experiment. He didn't seem that unnerved by my performance, but did express concern over my *"Lack of Attention to Detail."* He actually mentioned the error first. When he spoke about the incident, he was conciliatory and understanding. In one of my "green" moments, I got defensive and instead of listening and thanking God I wasn't asked to leave the laboratory, I tried to validate my efforts by saying *"I know I made a mistake, but people make mistakes all the time."*

It was my attitude that was the kicker. I had just made a major error, but was offering nonchalant explanations, to try to do damage control. I don't know why I was sitting in his office trying to tell him the obvious, but that's exactly what I did. Barry paused and asked me to *"listen to him"* for a second.

For whatever reason, I couldn't realize I was in error and his job was to try to help me learn, to prevent more mistakes. I left his office with a strange sense of empowerment, but didn't realize my actions demonstrated how "green" I really was. It was a long time before I was able to work on the cloning assay. In my mind, my role in the laboratory was just FINE.

So then, my beloved brethren, let every man be swift to hear, slow to speak, slow to wrath. For the wrath of man worketh not the righteousness of God.

James 1:19-20 (KJV)

Meanwhile, I was still having difficulty paying the rent and my credit cards were past due. I contemplated getting another job, but was afraid to because I had to rebound in my classes. The winter months were tough for me. Everyday I went to the laboratory, then back home, and tried to use the weekend to work on my book project. I did spend some time with

Cleo playing pool, but he was busy preparing to move to Boston to teach. The snow and culture was wearing on me. I was used to snow coming and leaving on the same day in Arkansas, but never lasting more than a week.

In Vermont, the snow never left and the ethnic dynamics of the city weren't changing fast enough for me. I was still going to Josie's, but I couldn't stay at her salon, for long periods of time, after my haircut. We were able to laugh and talk, but I needed to learn to adjust to Burlington, or my time in Vermont would be very difficult.

I really missed seeing African-American (Black) women and feeling connected with African-American culture. I used my own stereotypical views, as an excuse, to engage less with my classmates and people in the city. I also reconciled in my mind that I was supposed to be *isolated*, *reserved*, and *lonely*, in order to be successful. I don't know where those assumptions originated from, but they probably were in response to my unrealistic expectations of graduate school in Vermont.

I wanted and needed to be connected to things that were core to my being, but learned to substitute real things, for memories and fantasies of days past. One of the things I did was start surrounding myself with cultural markers, to try to stay connected with my so-called *"Blackness."* In my apartment, I had posters and pictures of Black people everywhere. Whatever I could find to stimulate my mind and remind me of my roots, I used. The walls were adorned with pictures of famous African-American movie actors, and *"Beauty of the Month"* cutouts from Jet Magazine. Most of my VHS movies had African-American themes. I loved watching movies like *Shaft*, *Enter the Dragon*, and *Cooley High*, because they reminded me of growing up.

I had cable television, with over three hundred channels, but really only watched Black Entertainment Television (BET). I tried to create a place I could go to at the end of the day and feel better about me, and support what I was doing in this place. I began calling my apartment the *"Fortress of Solitude,"* in honor of my favorite superhero, Superman. Based on cartoon lore, Superman used his fortress of solitude to think and recharge from fighting evil villains and crime. This is why I thought this title would be appropriate for me as well. I wasn't fighting crime and didn't have superhuman strength, but did feel challenged to live up to a standard I set for myself many years ago. I thought I would needced the fictional strength of Superman to bring me through, but eventually realized it would take God's favor, to keep it all together.

Four Tubas, a Guitar, and a Gallery of Cheerleaders

The one thing I was missing was my collection of *Ebony*[60] magazines. I loved reading Ebony, every since I was kid. If you were Black and living in the south, a copy of the latest edition was always on your coffee table. I always wondered what it would be like to get into *Ebony*. All of the features I read highlighted actors, athletes, educators, and business leaders. *Ebony* was a cultural icon for many African-Americans and I wanted to find copies of them to decorate my room. The problem was finding a business in Burlington who sold them. I should have gotten a subscription, but that would have meant waiting another six-eight weeks. I couldn't wait that long. Every bookstore I went to didn't subscribe to *Ebony* magazine. They subscribed to everything else, which increased my frustration. Even Josie didn't have current or old editions, so I knew finding them would be a challenge.

Ebony Magazines to the Rescue

One evening I was studying in the Bailey-Howe Library, and saw a student reading a popular cultural magazine and asked her where she got it from. She told me the circulation desk on the second floor had a list of current subscriptions, so I should check there. I never thought the UVM library would carry popular magazines like *Ebony*, but was surprised to find them and other cultural periodicals stored in their archives. I asked the clerk where the *Ebony* magazines were located. When I found them, I felt a sense of relief. I sat at a table and read each one of them from cover to cover.

As I turned each page and saw the images and feature articles, I thought about the way things used to be in my life. I stayed there for three hours reading and looking at the pictures, until I realized it was late and the library was about to close. I had to leave but didn't want to give the magazines back to the periodical desk clerk, so they could be restacked. Then, I had this brilliant idea I would take the magazines with me, read them again, and bring them back to the library later. This made a lot of sense to me because I couldn't check them out and really felt no one else wanted to read them like I did.

I stuffed all <u>nine</u> magazines into my satchel and walked toward

---

60 Ebony Magazine- is one of the oldest African-American magazines in the United States and founded by John H. Johnson in 1945. Ebony highlights African-American culture in areas of entertainment, politics, and fashion.

the entrance. I knew what I was doing was wrong, but I wanted those magazines and reasoned that no one else, on the entire campus, would want to read them. My conscious was bothering me, but I made up my mind that they were coming home with me. I knew that books in the library were tagged, so they could be checked out, but felt there was no reason for the magazines to be tagged, *"since they were never supposed to leave the library."*

As I walked toward the entrance desk, I dropped off a book as a small diversion, and then proceeded through the security checkpoint. Halfway through the walkway, the alarm sounded. The attendant asked me to walk through again because they had been having some problems with the sensitivity of the detector. I complied. The alarm went off again and then he asked me to open my bag. When I walked to the table for my preliminary search, I opened my bag and the magazines were the first thing he saw. I said "Oh, My Bad!" "I'm So Sorry!" All <u>nine</u> magazines were neatly tucked underneath my notebooks and manuals and it appeared as though I tried to hide them from plain view. I tried to play it off by saying I forgot I put them there, but he already knew I was trying to take them from the library.

I took the magazines out, handed them to him, and was embarrassed for two reasons. The first reason was because I tried to take them in the first place and got caught. The second reason was the fact that I never in my wildest dreams thought the library would electronically tag the magazines. My own actions proved why the deterrent was necessary.

I thought this ordeal was over, but then he asked me for my student ID and said my name would be put on a list. He never told me what the list was, but I'm sure it had something to do with people trying to take materials out of the library, without checking them out. I complied with the rest of his requests and he told me to have a good night. I walked outside the library literally kicking myself because my brightest idea, which I thought made a lot of sense, was monumentally unsound. That experience taught me that there were no shortcuts to becoming more comfortable in Burlington. I would have to do more legitimate things to be able to cope in Vermont and stop being so "green."

A Botched Grant Proposal

I found out the next week that I had to take another cumulative exam and write a mock grant. I was stunned I didn't pay more attention to the bulletins and notices, but my mind was so scattered. I had only three days to write the grant, so I did what I could, knowing that it would be critiqued by College of Medicine faculty members. I panicked and felt the pressure of my circumstances. I wanted to do what was required, but was too busy worrying about my cultural happiness. I cut and pasted some information and tried to establish a clear hypothesis, statement of work and plan, but knew what I was submitting was bad.

I asked Dr. Mossman for help and she allowed me to work with her secretary, but my efforts in the short term couldn't possibly demonstrate any competency on this assignment. I gave them what I could and turned my attention to the cumulative exam, at the end of the week. I hadn't studied one bit, so I contemplated not taking it. I knew the CMB program required these tests for competency in various subject areas, but I had difficulty remembering to prepare for them. I used my frustration to support "irrational beliefs" about the CMB program, UVM, and my life. I decided to take the exam anyway and knew, during that week, I made three fundamental errors and needed to shape up or I wouldn't last at UVM. I did my best but knew my efforts were again in vain.

By the weekend, I was down in spirit. I had squandered another exam and had to prepare myself for negative comments, from my mock grant application. Things had gone from bad to worse, but I kept my head up and hoped that the rest of the semester wouldn't be like the beginning. Snow was still on the ground, but the forecast for the next couple of weeks seemed to indicate an early spring. I kept a good pace in my classes but didn't give the effort I could have. As a result, my grades were an indication.

I spent the majority of my time complaining about Burlington, my workload, and a number of things that had nothing to do with my performance. The bottom line was that I was in an "uncomfortable" environment. My successes and failures fell completely on my shoulders. I wanted to blame someone, but who could I blame. This made me the most uneasy. I should have been enjoying my graduate school experience, but wasn't, and didn't know how to change my circumstances. I tried to talk with Josie about it and she listened, but I couldn't keep her words of wisdom and encouragement in my pocket. When I left her salon, the feelings of safety and security left as well.

I wanted to give up and quit, but I had to try to make it work. I still remembered why I came to Vermont in the first place, but my obstacles seemed to grow each day. A lack of motivation affected my studies, as I spent less time in the laboratory and spent more time reviewing materials for class. I felt I did well in all of my classes, but by the end of the semester, I earned another "C," a "B-," and an "A," in a specialty course.

The wheels of indecision were turning for me. I was just glad to get the semester over. My GPA was in shambles and I began to hear the term *"Academic Probation."* How could I possibly be on academic probation in graduate school? I pondered this question over and over in my mind, as my jovial days had come to an end. The harsh reality was that I started to believe I couldn't do it. Everything that came out of my mouth was negative. I guess my frustration stemmed a lot from low self-esteem. I had something to prove to myself and others, but didn't know how to do it. I needed to feel better, so I started writing again. Every word from every page seemed to give me a sense of purpose, but no one was grading me on how well I could write a book.

I talked with Barry about my feelings. He was forthright with me and mentioned that my *"background"* wasn't the best. I felt offended because *"I knew"* my background was pretty good, but in reality, I was paying for educational mistakes in the past. When the boomerang comes back around, it hurts a little more. Barry encouraged me to try to refocus over the summer and get busy in the laboratory. I thought he would give me the answer to all of my ills and was still looking for the "knowledge box." He had problems of his own and I didn't want to be one of them, so I tried to put a plan of action together over the next three months.

I called Dr. Reed from time to time, but we seemed to talk less. I was glad because it took a lot of energy to say with a straight face that I was on *"Academic Probation."* My standard answer to everyone in my family and friends was an emphasis on the fact that there were no Black people in Vermont. This was designed to divert from the fact that I was being challenged more in my life, than I had been before and was losing. When people asked me why I chose Vermont to go to school, I told them I wanted to see how the "other" side lives and why it's so different from what I was accustom to. All my hopes and dreams were wrapped up in this Ph.D., and maybe in a "green" way, I thought it would be easy.

I was encouraged that my problems were based more on stress, and thankful that I still could enroll in classes. I had an opportunity to do better. I worried the most about how I would look to my other classmates and the UVM scientific community. Every time I was absent from a class or meeting, everyone would know. I had to try to find a way to get back on track. For the rest of the summer, I worked hard in the laboratory and geared up for the fall semester. I traveled home once, but only stayed a week this time. If I was going to get this Ph.D., I had to believe that Burlington was a place I could live, breath, and grow in. Josie made it more comfortable for me, but she had a family of her own. I had to believe that I could do it.

Fall 1997

Before I started my second year at UVM, I did some research on the success and attrition rates of graduate students, in Ph.D. programs around the country. I found that the consensus in all arenas and disciplines was that the first two years were always the most difficult. I felt better about my rough start. To start the semester, I talked with Dr. Mossman and Barry about my course work. We all decided it was important to get back into *Biochemistry*. I knew it would be a challenge, but felt it was time for me to do what needed to be done.

I had other setbacks in my life and this was no different. I got some additional advice and decided to take *Biochemistry* and no other classes that semester. I figured if I focused totally on that class, I would be able to rebound and pass it. Barry and Dr. Mossman agreed that this was the best course of action. Barry told me not to worry about my laboratory work, but use my time to get *Biochemistry* behind me. I was glad he was supporting me, as I developed a new approach for studying. I was familiar with the course structure, but struggled most with the team-teaching method. By the time I understood the style and nuances of one lecturer, another lecturer took over the course.

I felt good about my chances. When classes started, I wasn't as "apprehensive" about *Biochemistry* and took the class with a new set of first year students. Meanwhile, I was still having difficulty paying my bills. My stipend was a blessing, but living in Vermont was getting more and more expensive. I probably was mismanaging my money. One heavy burden was my apartment, because the rent was so high.

I really missed those tax-free days in Dover and wondered where all my money went. I contemplated moving back on campus, but never followed through. I enjoyed living in my own place and felt that graduate students should live with some level of comfort. I started the semester strong and was ready to learn *Biochemistry*. The faculty organizing the course changed over the summer, so I didn't have an opportunity to hear similar lectures. It was cool, because I remembered what it felt like to have to withdraw last semester. I kept telling myself that this was a new day. I still felt isolated, within the class, and probably should have tried to engage more, but I didn't want to be social, even in the context of studying.

The first couple of weeks I studied day and night. The lectures were straightforward and now, I at least had some prior knowledge for the course. I wondered if anyone else in the class had as much difficulty as I did. I really respected Dr. Orr for trying to warn me about future dangers I would face. Expectations were high for my performance in the class. Barry and Dr. Mossman both knew that this was a new opportunity to get back on track. Each lecture I wrote furiously, then studied those notes right after class. There were some similarities between previous instructors, but I tried to keep everything in perspective, and took each class concept one day at a time.

By the time the first exam came, I was ready. I remembered panicking on the exam last year and felt more experienced this time. One of the other strategies I changed was sitting closer to the instructor. This year, I sat in the middle of the class, so I could see and hear more clearly and take better notes. The morning before the first exam I read my notes carefully, until class began. I sat in my usual place.

When I got my exam, I quickly opened the pages. I didn't panic this time, but did feel some anxiety because the first couple of questions were concepts I only studied briefly. I flipped through the rest of the exam. Other pages had questions I was familiar with, but I still worried. I sat there for about ten minutes to compose myself and then I started answering questions. When I looked up at the clock, there were only fifteen minutes left. I answered the questions, at the end of the exam first, and then struggled through the first couple of pages. By the time the instructor ended the exam, I barely had enough time to write my name on the front cover. I turned in my exam and thought about that day in class. I felt I did FINE, but was upbeat because I at least finished the test.

The next lecture was given by a new instructor. I wanted to concentrate on the new material, but my focus was the first exam. Many students inquired about the first exam, but the instructor hadn't finished grading them, until Wednesday of that week. That day, our first instructor came to the class and passed out the test. I waited patiently for my exam, as each name was read aloud. The instructor seemed to take forever to get to my name, but when he did I was nervous to see the results.

He gave me my exam; I opened up the front cover and was shocked to see a "D," based on the ratio of total points available and achieved. I felt a sickness in my stomach. I just knew this year would be different. I left the class frustrated and wanted to go to Josie's, but my appointment wasn't until Saturday morning. I couldn't understand what I was doing wrong. I studied hard, took good notes, but still wasn't scoring enough to pass the class.

I went home and studied that year's syllabus to determine how many points I needed to give myself a chance. I felt better because there were three more exams, worth more points, so all I had to do was study even harder to try to catch up. By the time Saturday came, I was more than ready to hear Josie's take on life. It was frustrating enough to be in a place where I felt like an outsider, but more disconcerting to know that my grades would help me make a quick exit. I tried not to think about it too much.

Josie was her usual self and she asked me if something was wrong. I told her about my experiences in graduate school and she sympathized with me, but reminded me that *"If it was easy, so many others would have done it!"* I understood what she was saying, but started to wonder if this was something I really wanted to do. I knew I was on a mission, but the tougher it got, the more I wondered if it would have been better for me to go to another HBCU, instead of UVM. At least, I would feel like there was a community for me. Here, I felt like every day was a challenge to try to "fit-in" and embrace northeastern culture.

Josie was supportive of my ramblings, but just consoled me, which helped me feel better. My haircut was done and I thanked her for her words of support and wisdom. When I left, I drove around Burlington for a while and then stopped on campus, at the **A**frican-American **L**atino **A**sian-American **N**ative **A**merican (ALANA) Student Center[61]. I read a brochure about the ALANA center, but never had an opportunity to visit. Tonight was different. The campus was quiet and I really wanted to do

---

61 ALANA Student Center- is a multicultural center for students who attend UVM. The center caters to students who are of African-American, Latina, Asian, and Native American descent and provides support to help maintain and increase student retention across cultures.

something other than go home and watch TV. The lights were low in the center, so I opened the door and to my surprise there were students, from all nationalities and races, studying and playing games. I introduced myself, sat down, and felt at home.

I was much older than many of the students there. It was still good to see other students who looked like me. I stayed there late because my house was only blocks away. At ALANA, I met and interacted with a population of undergraduate and graduate students I never knew existed. I met some great people at ALANA and tried to be more active within the UVM campus community.

The next couple of weeks went by fast. My next exam in *Biochemistry* was coming up. I kept Barry informed on my progress. Dr. Mossman wanted to know how I was doing. The last time we talked, she told me about a grant writing opportunity to apply for a *National Research Service Award* under the *Minority Pre-doctoral Fellowship Program*. I took the brochure and was immediately interested. I remembered how unprepared I was when writing my first mock grant, so this time would be different. When I read the parameters of the grant, I was excited about the stipend amount and the fact that it may open up more opportunities for me at UVM. I always wanted to write a successfully funded grant and had only seen it done.

Based on the brochure the deadline was approaching, so I wanted to get started as soon as possible. I talked with Barry about the grant and he agreed to help me write it. We planned a brainstorming session to layout the grant and fill in each section. I was motivated because my life was beginning to mean more than *Biochemistry*; I was actually learning how to get funding from the federal government.

Barry and I met on Monday of the next week. He asked me some simple questions to help me complete the grant application. His first question was *"What are your long-term goals?"* I answered like I had answered so many times before and said *"I would like to train and mentor 100 Ph.D. students and do groundbreaking research to be able to earn a Nobel Prize in science."* Barry paused, and then said I should be more realistic about my goals. I told him I was being realistic and felt "disrespected," when people discounted what I believed in my heart. He asked me again and I gave him the same answer. I could see he was frustrated. Then, he told me that my goals for this grant have to be more concise and clear, as well as relate to the work we were trying to do.

I guess I had been using that signature phrase so many years; it was

Four Tubas, a Guitar, and a Gallery of Cheerleaders

the only thing I knew to say in response to the "goal" question. Barry said he wanted me to reword my career goals to be more specific and he would help me choose language to compete for the grant. I was disappointed the shock value of my phrases were gone, but was happy to begin learning how to become a more focused and competitive graduate student. I studied for my next exam in *Biochemistry*.

In my spare time, I tried to come up with words and phrases that matched what I was doing and where I wanted to go. I had to table my grant writing for a week because of the test. My testing experiences were the same for the next exam. I still felt some anxiety, but did the best I could. As soon as I left the exam, I went back to the laboratory to work on the language of the grant. I only had to fill in five sections. Barry had to do the rest. I hoped his credentials would be strong enough to help me get the funding. I was already working on the training grant, but felt if I was funded again, this would improve my standing in the CMB program and at UVM.

Barry and I worked for the next two weeks on the language of the grant. Every time I wrote a paragraph, he would send it back to me with red marks and comments on both sides of the pages. It was frustrating, but I was learning. We went back and forth for another week and I got my scores from the last *Biochemistry* exam. I earned a low "C." I was very disappointed and knew that if I made below average on the next exam, I would surely fail the class.

Dropping or withdrawing wasn't an option. I had to stay in the class and pass it. I tried not to think about my academics too much, because my real motivation was to get the grant. I didn't care if it was a "minority" or "majority" grant, I just needed to be successful at something, and this was my best chance. During the revision process, Barry and I finally came to a consensus.

One day in his office, he helped me formulate my goals for the fellowship and the rest of my professional career. I modified my career goals over the years, but learned that day, how to be less "subjective" and more "objective" in my approach. Barry revised my career goals to say:

> "My career goals after earning the Ph.D. degree and postdoctoral training are to 1) become an independent, well-funded, hypothesis-based research scientist and professor, and 2) teach in academia and train students to become effective and successful researchers using the knowledge and skills that I have obtained. Working under the fellowship I hope to 1) gain valuable laboratory experience in mammalian genetics, human bio-monitoring, and genetic toxicology, 2) gain high quality experiences in basic science and research applications, 3) increase my knowledge of genetic mechanisms and consequences of somatic mutations in humans, specifically children, and 4) become an independent research scientist, who will be able to formulate hypothesis-driven clinically relevant research projects. Research training under this fellowship will contribute to my career goals by providing me an opportunity to do "cutting edge" research and obtain a Ph.D. specializing in the research areas of environmental pathology and molecular genetics."

This was very different from what I used over the years, but much more effective. I was more confident about the grant and began talking about my future in the laboratory. Barry was more pessimistic. He had been through a tough grant review process and wasn't funded, so he wasn't as upbeat as I was. I truly believed that we could get the grant, and felt Barry was really taking the time to teach me something. I really appreciated that. I had to fill out three more sections and verify with the graduate college, that I was in one of the underrepresented *Minority* categories.

I banked on the fact that being the only African-American, in the CMB program, would encourage reviewers to fund my research, to help establish more diversity at UVM. We finally got the entire application together. Barry reminded me to go back and check for typos and misspelled words. He told me *"If he reviews a grant and sees a misspelled word, he returns it because it meant that the sender didn't pay attention to the smallest detail."* The smallest details are always important. I learned how to meticulously going through the grant, word for word, and the importance of Barry's research.

Barry also helped me update my resume and showed me how to keep the most important experiences and get rid of the rest. Eventually, I understood what he meant by organizing the text that way and used his template to create my Research Training Plan. As I was going through the grant, I paid closer attention to section 35 *"Applicant's Qualifications and Potential for a Research Career,"* because it was an assessment of my abilities through the eyes of my mentor.

Barry wrote passionately about me as a person and talked about my commitment to doing cancer research. He also talked about my background and let the reviewers know that working in this environment was difficult for me. He praised me for my enthusiasm and said it was the reason why he decided to support my pre-doctoral training. Barry gave me a high recommendation for the award and wrote:

> "Sedrick's character as an individual, his persistent commitment to work hard and do what it takes to successfully complete a Ph.D. degree is truly outstanding and his strongest asset and the major reason why I am willing to accept the responsibility of being Sedrick's dissertation advisor and give him a high recommendation for this award. He is aware that his scientific background has been average and as a result challenges lay in front of him to succeed at this institution, but he remains extremely committed and is excited about taking full advantage of his academic situation here to aspire to his full potential as an independent research scientist. He is an extremely good listener and has demonstrated the ability to assimilate new information well. In addition, he is not afraid to ask questions, as well as probe for new ideas. He always demonstrates enormous enthusiasm for the laboratory and has been learning new techniques at the same rate and skill level of other pre-doctoral fellows. His proposed studies will allow him to develop sophisticated technical and laboratory expertise in the areas of genetic toxicology, genetic epidemiology, and somatic cell genetics in humans, especially children. It is my expectation that Sedrick's dissertation will result in two to three first author publications and place him in a competitive position to move ahead with his career goals. In conclusion, Sedrick is a unique individual who has outstanding perseverance, and self-reliance in pursuing career goals. *I feel he has an excellent chance in our environment to successfully complete a Ph.D. degree."*

It felt good to read a good report regarding my current and future skills, in the midst of my troubles with *Biochemistry*. I had to take another cumulative exam and hadn't studied for it like I should have, because of the grant and *Biochemistry*. I decided not to avoid any more exams and took them, whether I was ready to or not. I had seventeen more to go, in order to qualify for Ph.D. candidacy, so I would have other opportunities to get the averages I needed in each content area.

By the time I finished reviewing the entire grant, I found only one typo and quickly made the corrections. I asked Barry and Dr. Mossman for references. The most difficult thing was catching up with my reference writers, to get their signatures on the grant. I camped out and tried to be as cordial as I could, but needed the signatures, before it could be submitted. I finally got it done and reviewed the grant one more time to make sure everything was in place. Dr. Mossman's executive assistant helped me finish it and I thanked her for all of her help. We mailed the grant package by Fed-Ex on November 14, 1997 and hoped for the best. I was confident of its success because it kept me from thinking about *Biochemistry*, which was going to be a major issue very soon.

The next week was back to business. I wanted to hold onto thoughts of being funded for the next five years and everything I learned during the grant-writing process, but another exam was right around the corner. I had to refocus. I studied some, but was discouraged by my inability to test well. It just seemed like everything I studied wasn't on the exam. I knew it was my technique. I studied just as hard for this exam as before.

When I got my test scores, they were low. Out of three exams, I only scored enough to achieve a low "D," which meant that my grade would be an "F" for the course. I became very depressed and withdrawn. I had built myself up so much for this semester and now things had truly fallen apart. I didn't want to talk with Barry about it. I certainly didn't want to talk with Dr. Mossman, because she was the one that recommended I withdraw the first time and then re-enroll this semester. I don't remember if I studied at all for the last exam, but knew that my final grade would be an "F." I talked with Dr. Reed and he asked me how things were going. I said FINE, but the lack of enthusiasm in my voice was evident.

I felt like I was lying to him, like I did so many years ago to Dr. Orr, whose words were now burned into my brain. I kept thinking "Why didn't I listen?" "I should have listened!" Why didn't I listen?" until my days seemed endlessly long and my nights were filled with regret, doubt, and disbelief. I never shared what I was going through with anyone, not even Josie, because I was "embarrassed" and felt like I didn't measure up at UVM. It was the strangest feeling, because I knew I was a hard worker, but the one thing that stood in the way of my success was something I couldn't master.

Other times in my life, I could just make things go away or avoid them to prevent the pain or consequences. Now that wasn't the case. Each day was a constant reminder of those same low feelings. I took the last exam and did my best, but was despondent and knew what the final outcome would be. I took some time off and meditated in my apartment as a recluse, for three days. I didn't want to face Barry and let him know what happened and I didn't want to go home. The weather changed again and snow was falling everyday. The snow capped streets made me feel more alone and isolated. I thought to myself "What could I do to make things right?" then God sent me a message to stop avoiding the inevitable and discuss my problems with SOMEBODY, who could make the decision about my fate.

> Pride goeth before destruction and a haughty spirit before a fall.
>
> **Proverbs 16:18 (KJV)**

Meeting with the Dean of the Graduate School

Once I came out of my apartment, I decided to be more proactive. I scheduled a meeting with the Dean of the Graduate School. He met with me and asked how things were going. I thought about my response. This time I told an "absolute" truth and let him know that I wasn't doing well in my classes. I also told him I DID NOT want to leave UVM without my degree. He asked me about my biggest difficulty since coming to Vermont. I told him about *Biochemistry* and how I really struggle in this class. He thought I was a *Biochemistry* major at DSU, because of my thesis research. I told him I did take a specialty *Biochemistry* course, but it was geared for work in the field of Protein Chemistry. He then asked me about my undergraduate work and I told him I didn't take *Biochemistry* then. I will never forget that day, because I swallowed my "pride" and went into the dean's office and begged for another opportunity at UVM. I wanted to do that before they kicked me out.

He and I talked more, as he tried to understand why I wasn't doing well in classes. He knew the relationship DSU had with UVM because of DEVELOP, and then asked me if T.S.'s departure affected me in any way. I told him "No!" It never registered with me, but feeling alone did affect the way I approached living and working in Burlington. I wanted my message and plea to be clear. "I don't want to get kicked out of UVM." He made a few phone calls and before I left, I made a prophetic proclamation regarding my fate at UVM. I told him *"If I have to work at the grocery store to pay for my education, I will in order to finish what I started!"* I don't know why I said that, but it was "dramatic" and helped me let him know that I was totally committed to stay the course, regardless of what anyone thought.

When I left his office, I felt like I did the right thing. If the hammer came down for my dismissal, it wouldn't be a surprise for him or me. That same day, I stopped by Dr. Mossman's office and let her know I talked with the dean. I was encouraged by her calm nature and supportive attitude. I let her know that I wasn't making excuses, but wanted another chance to finish what I started. She told me not to worry about it, but I knew this was a big deal.

I saved Barry for last, to break the news to, and knew his response would be different from the others. I told him what my plan was and how this setback was affecting me. I tried to make the same bold proclamations I had made earlier in the day. I told Barry "If he supported me, he wouldn't be sorry." His response was *"I have heard that before!"* and he looked disappointed. I tried to fix it, but he was clearly questioning why he allowed me to join his laboratory. I knew at that moment that in order for me to be successful at UVM, I had to stop making <u>bold statements</u> and just get it done. I needed a spark, so I started writing again. I felt writing would at least take my mind off of what could be an abrupt departure from my doctoral studies. I also used the idea of publishing as a way to build my confidence.

Winter/Spring 1998

I returned to Burlington after Christmas, and wasn't as nostalgic for home as I had been in the past. The feelings that drove me to always go home for the holidays, to feel more connected, weren't as strong now. I was on a mission and realized I had to not only release some of my own stereotypes and feelings about UVM, but also try to focus "all" of my energy on academics. I knew I was in deep water and a "cat" like me only has nine lives. Most of mine were already gone. I just hoped a new approach would give me the chance to prove myself, instead of joining others who had tried to get the Ph.D., but failed along the way. I was so used to failing, that I devised strategies and reasons to try to support my stay at UVM, just in case it happened again. I was truly living and working by the Grace and Favor of God, manifested through the patience of the dean, Dr. Mossman, and Barry.

> And he said unto me, My grace is sufficient for thee: for my strength is made perfect in weakness. Most gladly therefore will I rather glory in my infirmities, that the power of Christ may rest upon me.
>
> **II Corinthians 12:9 (KJV)**

I should have been gone, but I believe my heartfelt speech to the dean and my true desire to make UVM home worked for me. I had never humbled myself like that before, but desperate times deserved desperate measures. I wanted to make the prophecy for my life, from Mr. Lowe, come true. Dr. Mossman was very supportive of my journey. This semester I decided to take the second part of *Biochemistry* and keep going through the curriculum.

I also enrolled in two pathology courses, to help boost my GPA, in case the unthinkable happened again. We knew it would be difficult because I didn't pass the first part of *Biochemistry*, but I convinced Dr. Mossman and Barry that this year would be my "breakthrough." I started to feel like a politician. Every semester started off with me making promises for the next six months.

I wasn't good at selling anything but myself, so I tried to make those skills flourish. I was only able to rest for a minute because of another cumulative exam. This time I was more prepared, and had studied over the Christmas holiday. I needed to start earning completion points, before I ran out of exams. When I wrote the exam, I felt more confident about my answers and the subject matter. There were always four areas tested.

I typically scored the best in Area IV. I believe it was because the questions were geared toward a broader understanding of the subjects, instead of regurgitating facts. I understood why they were important, because they helped me improve my research skills. Back then, there weren't as many online information search engines as there are today, so when I looked up information, most of it came from the National Institutes of Health Libraries or the UVM subject databases. When I was in Chicago, I was introduced to *comprehensive literature reviews* and now was finally able to use those skills. I wrote well during the cumulative exam, and scored in two out of four subject areas. It was a great boost and I needed everything I could get to help me pass *Biochemistry*.

I was back in *Biochemistry*, in the same room, in the same building, but with different instructors. This gave me some hope because I wasn't as confident with previous lecturers and their approach. This year I sat closer to the front of the class, but was still surrounded on both sides and in front by other students. I could hear better and see much clearer, the closer I was to the chalkboard. I really wanted to get this right this time. I still had test anxiety and wondered if I would ever pass this class. I also didn't have a study partner and was adamant to do it on my own. I don't know if it was shyness or just shear stubbornness that made me feel like isolation was the best way to improve my grades.

I learned in Delaware that graduate school can be a very selfish process, but for some reason that "selfishness" seemed counterproductive to my academic success in Vermont. I continued to believe that I could beat this thing on my own and shuffled things around in my life that could potentially influence my success. I was still writing and learning more about my alma mater.

Every night I tried to work on notes or organize facts in some way. The book was starting to take shape. I had written the names and musical names of all of my line brothers and as many of my line sisters as I could find. Some sections were incomplete, but I was confident I could fill in the rest. Writing made me feel good, so I kept doing it. I could sit down at 8 p.m. and not move until 3 a.m. Sometimes, I would have writer's block, which was quickly relieved when I thought about home and the idea of being published. I guess I was still trying to do something the fraternity or sorority had never seen before.

I talked with Josie about my book project and tried to get her to motivate me in her own special way. She gave great advice. When I came to get a haircut, she would always ask me about the project and how things were going at UVM. I really enjoyed being around her because she fed my good vibes and always had good things to say to and about me. Her conversation was what I really visited for.

As I became more comfortable, I would stop by unannounced just like most people in the community. Sometimes, I just wanted to say "Hello!" or find out what was happening over the weekend. She never turned me away. I tried to promote her business by letting everyone know how skilled and talented she was. Josie seemed to really care and that's what was most important to me.

I saw her as an older woman with wisdom and knowledge from multiple perspectives. Most of my mentoring had only come from men, who used logic, reasoning, and sometimes-brute force to deal with the challenges of life. Josie was different because she was strong, but delicate, and offered a new slant on almost everything I believed to be true. I always told her that she should get a Ph.D. in Psychology, because she was so good at listening to other people's problems and helping them find solutions.

She told me she was satisfied with her business. I didn't blame her, because her salon was servicing people from all races and nationalities. I never thought of Burlington or Vermont as a culturally rich place, but people from all walks of life would come into her salon. My eyes were opened because in Arkansas, people were designated as either black or white, with no other culturally specific title.

I found out she specialized in working with *Trans-Racially Adopted Children*. Josie often shared funny stories about parents, who needed help learning how to take care of their children's culturally different hairstyles. She was Afro-centric from head to toe, but also tolerant and understanding of the challenges bi-racial and trans-racially adopted children faced.

She encouraged me to spend more time at the ALANA Student Center, since Cleo had left UVM and was now teaching in Boston. Josie told me that it would give me an opportunity to meet others on campus I could connect with. She warned me that most of them would be younger, which I already knew. Our time together always seemed brief, but re-energized my spirit. When I went home, I studied as usual and then wrote until the early hours of the morning. My first exam was next week and my additional courses made me more paranoid about *Biochemistry*. I liked the other classes, but *Biochemistry* was the only thing that could prevent me from completing my studies at UVM.

NEBHE and BSCP

Things were really moving this semester. I lived my life without distractions, until a couple of organizations got wind of my studies at UVM. The New England Board of Higher Education (NEBHE) and the Biomedical Sciences Careers Program (BSCP), both based in Boston, Massachusetts were actively recruiting minority students, from graduate programs throughout the New England area. Dr. Reed tried to collaborate with NEBHE and BSCP, while T.S. and I were studying at DSU. These organizations waited until my enrollment in UVM and then relentlessly tried to get in contact with me. Their goal was for me to attend one of their annual student enrichment meetings. I was skeptical of NEBHE and BSCP and didn't want any additional responsibilities. I spent the majority of my time trying to avoid them. NEBHE and BSCP would call me at home, at work, and even contacted Dr. Mossman and Barry.

I had no intention of joining or participating in their student enrichment programs. Dr. Mossman told me I had to deal with them on my own. I was hoping she would let them know why I had to be so focused on my studies, but she deferred and made me directly responsible for their calls and contacts.

When I finally talked to NEBHE and BSCP, I let them know what was going on with me. They told me they could help me improve my academic situation. I thought it was another sales pitch to increase their minority participation and membership. They were sincere and really used their resources to try to help other students like me, complete their doctoral programs. My mind was focused on *Biochemistry*. They could have been writing and distributing blank checks to students and I would have missed out, because nothing was more important to me than that class.

I got my scores back from my first exam and they were low. I was studying new material and excited about learning, but couldn't achieve more points on the tests. I talked with the lecturer, who knew me from the class last year. He told me I did better, but was still missing the big picture. I was so frustrated that I began second-guessing my whole life up until that point. What else could I do to make this work for me? I thought repetition would do the trick. I thought studying longer would make me smarter. I thought sitting closer to the lecturer would somehow infuse wisdom into my brain, but all these things in tandem didn't equate to better scores.

I talked to Barry about my progress. He was skeptical and wanted to see my grades at the end of the semester. I tried to focus on the grant we submitted, to try to give me a boost in his eyes, but he wasn't moved about potential possibilities, when I could be kicked out of UVM any day. He was more concerned with my current progress. Barry did support me, but his background was a mystery to me. One day we were talking and I found out he wasn't White or Caucasian, like I always thought. Barry was actually Jewish. I never separated religion and race in that context before.

I told him that where I was from, you were either Black or White. Barry told me about some of his experiences as child in Kansas City, Missouri, growing up in New York City, and training in Dallas, Texas. I don't know why I was so amazed he was Jewish. I didn't know what being Jewish meant, but the fact that my perception of him changed all of a sudden was interesting. I must have been maturing. I think living in Burlington started to open my eyes to other cultures in society and changed the ways I used to label people.

I was born (African-American) Black and had a Black view of the world. Now I started to see individual differences in people, who were once grouped the same. I was loyal to HBCUs and give them the honor and credit for my greatest successes in education, but I really wanted to know how education, at predominantly white college and universities differed from my own. I got a good dose of reality in Burlington, from various points of view. My whole world changed from "All Black" to "All White," and I was stuck in the middle trying to make sense of it all.

Maybe that's why I was so uncomfortable in my classes and why I shied away from studying with other students. I guess I was afraid of my own black identity and what that looked like in a majority white environment. Stereotypically, I was supposed to be able to dance, speak the latest slang, be hip and cool, and of course be an expert on all of Black America. I could dance because of my experiences in band all those years; I did know some slang, but it was never relevant where I was living.

I was never considered hip and cool. I always tried to find a common place where I could belong. This mindset created an interesting dynamic with me and my peers. I developed a mentality that I must not fail or falter, because that would mean I somehow let my race down. Of course this was probably one of the most ridiculous assumptions I had made up until that point, but it motivated me to keep pushing toward completing my degree, in the midst of *Biochemistry*.

The next exam I took yielded the same score. I was running out of ways to keep my spirits high. I had already been depressed last year and now was falling back into that same mode. To keep my mind off the almost inevitable, I worked more hours in the laboratory and spent more time at the ALANA center. ALANA was a good place to relax. Being there, helped me remember my days in band and ΚΚΨ.

I wanted to be more involved at ALANA, so I talked with Mr. Leon Lawrence, who was the director. Mr. Lawrence told me that I was one of a few graduate students, who frequented the center, and if I was interested I could advise some of the groups. I did feel older and wiser and looked forward to mentoring others, who would have to face similar obstacles in their academic journeys.

I hoped my experiences would somehow help them and then I could feel connected with a larger community, which could help me. I told Mr. Lawrence I was interested and needed to get to know some of the student leaders. He recommended I attend a meeting of the New Black Leaders (NBL) next weekend. I told him I would be there. The opportunity to interact with students, at ALANA, helped me feel I just wasn't just going there to watch TV and see people of color. Now, I would really be involved with student organizations. I went home that night and thought about my experiences at UAPB and all the ideas I wanted to try there.

The next week Barry called me into his office and told me he received the funding score for our grant review. Our magic number was **236**, which wasn't good, but it also wasn't bad. This was the first time anything I was apart of was critique by outside professionals. Barry explained that the lower the score, the better our chances were for getting funding.

In his eyes, we were right on the borderline. He wasn't optimistic at all. The critiques from each reviewer were positive. They felt Barry was highly qualified to receive the award and I was in a good environment to achieve a Ph.D. One reviewer noticed that I was struggling academically, which I tried to gloss over, but it was evident after submitting my transcripts.

The upside was that I was commended for my prior research at UAPB and experiences at Northwestern University. UVM ranked high as a place that did good research. Every line I read made me feel more confident I made the right decision about my education. The other reviewer was more general in their comments, but praised Barry's laboratory structure and said *"It is necessary to assure that the applicant will adapt effectively to the research environment."* When the sponsor (Barry) was critiqued, the same reviewer stated that *"He (Barry) has been successful in obtaining research funding, and it is likely that he (Barry) will be able to provide both guidance and the appropriate laboratory environment, which are necessary."* I was upbeat and shared the scores with Dr. Mossman.

She was confident in the score, told me not to worry about it, and to keep her posted. This was some good news and I still believed we would be funded. I needed a break. My daily thoughts were on that grant. I just had to get something to give me some leverage to protect my future at UVM. There grant would be a good incentive to keep me there. Around the same time, I received another letter in the mail related to my application to the American Association for Cancer Research (AACR).

Early in the spring semester, I applied for a minority scholarship to attend their annual meeting in New Orleans, LA and hoped I would get funding to go. I used the same template Barry taught me, when asked about my current and future cancer research goals. This was another venture for me to try to prove to Barry and the graduate school, that I did have some major academic bumps and bruises, but if given a chance, I could get things together.

The letter informed me that I was chosen as one of the *1998 AACR Minority Scholars in Cancer Research* and would be funded to attend the annual meeting at the end of March. I was so excited to get the news that I rushed to let Barry and the laboratory know. I was also blessed because I didn't have a poster to present, which is normally required to get travel funds to major research meetings. I was accepted nonetheless. I felt like my momentum was building and all I needed to do was pass *Biochemistry*.

I had an interesting time in New Orleans and learned a lot more about cancer research. I was in a selected group of very competitive students. I envied many of them, because they had achieved more than I had, within their first two years of graduate work. I wondered if they had difficulties in their classes, or were they more prepared to meet the challenges than I was. Many were doing top-notch research already, while I was still struggling with courses.

During the meetings, my mind would wonder about my future at

UVM, and I lost focus to the real reason I was there. One thing that was depressing was the fact that I missed another scheduled cumulative exam, which didn't help my score totals or path toward candidacy. This made the trip more difficult. I was second-guessing my decision to travel.

When I got back to Burlington, I focused more on the *Biochemistry* lectures and did more reading to try to remember and comprehend as much information as possible. I was calmer during my exams, but my scores were still too low. I averaged a "C" on the next three exams and knew based on my point totals, anything less than a perfect score on the next test would mean another "F."

I talked with the instructor and he told me that going to that meeting probably wasn't a good idea, in the middle of the semester, but it was the only glimmer of hope I had at the time. Going was always an option for me. The other two courses were in subjects I enjoyed and I did enough work in them to get two "A's". I did my best that semester, but when the *Biochemistry* final came, I panicked again because I couldn't answer the first question.

When all was said and done, I had failed again. I was very depressed and tried to avoid as many people as possible, especially Barry. What could my excuse this time possibly be? I was out of answers and didn't want to try to explain. I wondered if I had a learning block or if *Biochemistry* was something I just couldn't do. I pondered why something so basic was so critical to my next steps in life.

> Therefore I say unto you, Take no thought for your life, what ye shall eat, or what ye shall drink; nor yet for your body, what ye shall put on. Is not the life more than meat, and the body than raiment? Behold the fowls of the air: for they sow not, neither do they reap, nor gather into barns; yet your heavenly Father feedeth them. Are ye not much better than they? Which of you by taking thought can add one cubit unto his stature? And why take ye thought for raiment? Consider the lilies of the field, how they grow; they toil not, neither do they spin: And yet I say unto you, That even Solomon in all his glory was not arrayed like one of these. Wherefore, if God so clothe the grass of the field, which to day is, and to morrow is cast into the oven, shall he not much more clothe you, O ye of little faith? Therefore take no thought, saying, What shall we eat? or, What shall we drink? or, Wherewithal shall we be clothed? (For after all these things do the Gentiles seek:) for your heavenly Father knoweth that ye have need of all these things. But seek ye first the kingdom of God, and his righteousness; and all these things shall be added unto you. Take therefore no thought for the morrow: for the morrow shall take thought for the things of itself. Sufficient unto the day is the evil thereof.
>
> **Matthew 6:25-34 (KJV)**

I just wished I could start all over again, but time stops or goes back for anyone. My only hope was that the pre-doctoral grant would be funded. I prayed for its success. All I had left was my dream to publish a book. Writing seemed like a frivolous venture, but was the only thing that held my mental anguish in check. I believed I could write a book about a subject that was near and dear to my heart; the marching band and my fraternity, using research skills I obtained at UVM.

I tried to disconnect from the pain associated with my grades, but eventually the verdict was in and I had to deal with Barry and Dr. Mossman. They met separately with me. One suggestion was for me to take summer courses to try to catch up. Barry was opposed to this strategy and advocated for me. He wanted me to work full-time in the laboratory and wait until the fall to take any more classes. He was adamant about that. It was the first time I saw him defend me against justifiable persecution. Barry went to bat for me and told me that I should be studying *"old tests"* and reviewing with the instructor. I asked him about *"old tests"* because I wasn't familiar with that learning concept.

Studying Old Tests

Barry explained that courses like *Biochemistry* stored old exams, in the reference section of the library. Current students can use those to predict questions for each test. I was blown away. I never thought to use old exams, because I didn't know they existed. During my academic career at UAPB and DSU, the professors prepared their exams "fresh," so there were never any old tests. They didn't want students to be able to predict their questions and have an advantage. Apparently, I was the only person in the class that didn't know this. After following up after the course, I learned that groups of students would get together and study old exams throughout the semester. This "revelation" helped me feel a little better about my performance in *Biochemistry*.

I tried to read, comprehend, and remember the material, while most students used *"old tests"* and looked for patterns and similarities of questions. Now, I didn't feel so inept and knew that if given another opportunity, my first goal would be to master the *"old exam"* questions and their answers. I appreciated Barry's words of wisdom and was relieved that he didn't ask me to leave the laboratory. Barry had a big heart for students and used his influence to open up doors that others would have probably closed. I followed his words of wisdom. His continued support motivated me to study harder for my next cumulative exam. I was just grateful he still believed in me enough to allow me to see the summer in his laboratory, when my life finally changed for the better.

> For by grace are you saved by faith; and that not of yourselves: it is the gift of God.
>
> **Ephesians 2:8 (KJV)**

Summer 1998

Soon after classes ended, God still granted me "amazing favor," because I had failed the same course again and was still a student at UVM. It must have been my destiny to be there and God obviously wanted me to learn something in the process. I had another issue brewing, which was my monthly rent that was consistently late. I also got a ticket because my vehicle registration was expired. Vermont's strict environmental laws required yearly emission maintenance on vehicles, which I couldn't afford. I wanted to get my car inspected, but my exhaust pipe was corroded beyond repair, because of the salt used to de-ice the highways and streets during the winter. I tried on numerous occasions, but didn't have $800.00 for a new exhaust and catalytic converter. When the officer gave me the ticket, he recommended I stop driving the car and that is exactly what I did. Now, my dilemma was that I had a car I couldn't drive, but still needed to pay the car insurance just in case another miracle occurred in my life. I was out of money and even though my stipend supported me, it just wasn't enough.

Working at the Grocery Store

My goal was to get another part-time job during the summer. I always wanted to work at the grocery store and remembered the bold prophetic statement to the Dean of the Graduate School. I submitted an application to *Price Chopper*[62] in South Burlington, and was hired as a produce clerk making $5.25/hour. I was excited to get a job at the grocery store because it meant more income to pay my car insurance. I didn't know that workers in grocery stores were paid every week, which meant I would always have some cash. This was one of those situations I kept to myself. Barry wanted

---

62 Price Chopper- is a supermarket chain based in upstate New York that services the New England, New York, and Pennsylvania areas.

me to work full-time in the laboratory, which I did, but I also had to work at the store, after 5 p.m., during the week, and all day on weekends.

The store was about two miles from my house, so I pondered how I would get there every day. I couldn't drive and risk getting another ticket, so my plan was to briskly walk there every afternoon. The first time I walked to work, I had fun going because it was all downhill, but when I tried to get back, it was more difficult. I learned the job fast.

After they trained and quizzed me on the different types of fruits and vegetables, I was ready to make my debut on the showroom floor. I never knew how hard working in the different departments of the grocery store were, until I worked my first nine hour weekend shift. I shadowed a more experienced clerk and learned to move boxes with speed and don't remember slowing down. It was hard work stocking and restocking all the fruits and vegetables on sale and making specialty orders for customers, but I did it.

I was tired the first couple of nights because I had to walk home, after standing for seven hours. My bones ached when I reached my apartment, but I was slowly getting into shape. I never missed a beat during the daytime. Barry was out from time to time, due to clinical rounds, so I planned my workdays carefully. I did what I had to do to get my car insurance money and earned every penny. I liked this type of work because the goals were always clear and it was a good change from scientific research, which offered no promises or guarantees. It took me about three weeks to get going and in top shape. I worked as hard at the grocery store, as I did in the laboratory.

Meanwhile, I was waiting to hear back from the grant selection committee and anxious for the results. Their first letter stated that decisions would be made in the summer and that their last council meeting was at the end of May. Every day I frantically went to my mailbox and every day nothing but campus mail was there. I wondered if this was a sign I didn't get the grant. I talked with Barry about it. He didn't want to hope for something that didn't come, so he encouraged me to focus on my research, but I still believed.

Now faith is the substance of things hoped for, the evidence of things not seen.

Hebrews 11:1 (KJV)

Four Tubas, a Guitar, and a Gallery of Cheerleaders

No news can sometimes be good news and I prayed and hoped for the best. I watched for a response for the entire month of June and called the Grants Division of NIH for support. They told me a decision hadn't been made, so be patient. By the beginning of July, I stopped looking and concentrated on my experiments and my job as a produce clerk. I developed a good relationship with the workers at the grocery store, and was recommended for service awards by customers. When I told Josie I was working at the grocery store, she laughed but understood that I had to do what I had to do to make ends meet. The only thing I couldn't do was keep people from eating the produce in the store, which ultimately led to more work for me.

One of the favorite snack items for people, who shopped at the Price Chopper, was *Bing Cherries*. I could never catch them putting them in their mouths, but knew many people ate them in the store. At the end of the night, there were hundreds of stems and seeds scattered in the produce section. It always intrigued me why people would brazenly eat produce off the shelf.

I worked in the back of the store where shipments came, and sometimes boxes would break and fruits and vegetables would be mishandled ending up on a very dirty floor. We always told customers to please wash their fruits and vegetables before consumption, but it never stopped people that were used to sampling.

The produce job was working out. I was grossing about $80.00/week after taxes, which allowed me to pay my car insurance, but I couldn't drive the car. I never thought to ask anyone for the money because I still would have to make the vehicle environmentally compliant, so it was best it stayed where it was. I got tired of walking to work everyday and wanted to get there faster, without using the bus. I had to do something different because my walking routine, from 5 p.m. until 12 a.m., was wearing me out.

I used my Sony walkman to help me keep up the pace. My daily musical companions were *DMX* and *Big Pun*. DMX's music was angry and sometimes violent, but it hyped me up to work a long shift. I listened to Big Pun on the way home because it was mellow and helped me unwind. The music was great and the walk was energizing, but I needed a faster mode of transportation. I wanted to buy a bicycle, but didn't have any money to get a good one.

I knew I needed a mountain bike to hold my large frame, but they ranged from $300-$3000.00. My funds were low and my *American*

Express™ card payment was late, so I thought I couldn't use it. I went by the local bike store to browse and I took my American Express™ card with me, just in case I saw something I liked. I never expected to be able to buy anything, but one bike stood out for me.

It was green, had twelve speeds, and cost $300.00 with taxes. Something told me (God), to try to buy it, but I was nervous because I didn't want to be embarrassed in the store, if the card was declined. I thought about it, took the bike off the display rack, and rolled it to the cashier. I hoped beyond hope that the charge would go through. When I heard the tape processing and the clerk asked for my signature, I was saved again by another credit card. I thanked God I could buy that bike. The first time I rode it to the grocery store I got there in ten minutes instead of thirty. From that point on, that bike became my sole mode of transportation.

I hadn't forgotten about what was most important to me and still hoped for the best regarding our grant application. I was also resolved to work another year on the training grant, if I was still at UVM. Before the Fourth of July, I checked one last time for a decision about the grant and promised myself it would be the last time. There was still no word.

I worked the holiday at the grocery store, which was fun, because I got overtime pay and met some very interesting people. It was like an indoor bizarre. Customers bought all the charcoal, meat, fruit, and vegetables they could find. We almost ran out of product to sell. While I was working that weekend, I saw the Dean of the Graduate School browsing through the apples and peaches. I know he saw me, but we never made eye contact. I wasn't ashamed to be there, because I predicted and demonstrated my goal to finish at UVM.

> Whatsoever thy hand findeth to do, do it with thy might; for there is no work, nor device, nor knowledge, nor wisdom, in the grave, whither thou goest.
>
> **Ecclesiastes 9:10 (KJV)**

The next week, I returned to the laboratory sore and tired, but happy to be successfully working two jobs. I went to the mailbox and the only letter in there was from the Department of Health and Human Services. I knew that today would be the day I would know if my prayers and hopes were answered. I walked back to my desk and opened the letter. All I saw was *"Mr. Rice, It is a pleasure...."* and I knew we were funded. I hastily read the rest of the letter. It said *"An individual National Research Service Award had been recommended for approval and if you intend to accept, please send us an approximate beginning date."* I walked into Barry's office and pretended as if it was bad news. I had a somber look on my face and let him know that I received a response from that National Institutes for Environmental Health Sciences (NIEHS).

He took the letter and was already upset about his other grant experiences, but smiled when he saw our score was accepted for approval. It was a good feeling to show him that letter and I appreciated his help. My self-esteem grew. I emailed Dr. Mossman and let her know our scores were funded. She congratulated me as well. I probably told as many people as I knew and wanted to share a personal victory with the world.

I was more than blessed that day and felt that God was looking down on me and my plight. Now, I had some leverage and it was important for me to finally take care of *Biochemistry*. I joked with Barry when he asked me who would be the principal investigator on the grant, which is also the person who controls the money. I told him "me," and he said "Yeah Right!" It was another bold statement, but all bets were off that day because my **P**rayers, **H**ard work, and **D**edication paid off. I was extremely happy. My new enthusiasm helped me score more points on my final cumulative exam of the summer and things seemed to be turning around. I worked the rest of the summer at the grocery store, but quit before the fall semester began.

Fall 1998

I was renewed when the semester began and more motivated than ever to succeed. I was still on academic probation, but felt the grant would help me leverage my time in Vermont. I was proud of that accomplishment and felt Barry was more supportive of my efforts. All I thought about was the grant and how I could use the resources. I was also excited that every year, for the next five years, I would have funding for the laboratory, indirect costs for the school, and a yearly stipend that increased at the end of each quarter. I decided to talk with Dr. Mossman more formally a week after I got the news. We made plans for me to transition from the training grant, to the NIEHS grant. She was excited and would now be in a position to have me be involved with the training grant, but use my open slot to recruit other students. I felt different now. My mood was better than it had been in a number of years.

Tutoring for Biochemistry

The next step was to pass *Biochemistry*. This year I got a brand new strategy. Dr. Mossman was directly involved in the process and offered to sponsor a tutor for me. I never had a tutor in my former college days and was a little skeptical, but excited to be able to finally study with someone, who knew the subject matter of the course. Dr. Mossman recommended a graduate student from the *Biochemistry* department, who did well in the class, and was looking to make some extra money. She never told me where the money came from and I never asked. I just followed her instructions because I was "desperate" to pass this class. We set up a meeting schedule and when I finally introduced myself to the tutor, I was ready to get to it. The tutor was a little nervous at first because she didn't know what to expect, so we both took about three days to develop some expectations. By our third meeting, we both were in tune to each other's personality and expectations. I appreciated having a skilled, non-biased person, to analyze my work and study habits.

The first thing we changed was how I took notes. I seemed to have a problem studying and grasping the most important concepts. Because I lacked a background in *Biochemistry*, I tried to know everything, which is impossible and may be the reason why I had so much anxiety during the exams. I over studied but never learned the basics because I spent so much time trying to catch up. Over the previous summer, I had an idea to try condensing my notes on one sheet of paper, so I could study the most important points.

I still loved football and had a passion to play, but also had a passion to coach, when I watched the games. I noticed the head coach had all of his plays on one sheet of paper labeled and organized, from front to back. I wanted to adopt this style because it would mean that the most important concepts from *Biochemistry* were condensed onto one sheet of paper and I could study them at will.

This technique helped me in two ways. First, it made me only consider

Four Tubas, a Guitar, and a Gallery of Cheerleaders

and write the most important points in the class and condense the way I organize and think. Secondly, these *"Prep Sheets"* would eventually become my guide for translating class notes and were the only things I studied before the exam. I eventually laminated my *"Prep Sheets,"* so I could take them anywhere on campus and not worry about my notes getting messed up because of weather. I also did this because it usually took me hours to decipher my notes from a class lecture, onto sheets of college ruled lined paper. Whatever I wrote, I wanted to save.

Laminating became my favorite thing to do, before I studied for an exam. I knew once my notes were sealed in permanent form, they were the best hope I had for passing the class. I could always refer to them, while I studied. I showed my tutor the idea and she believed that it would help me grasp more information. She agreed to view my notes, before they were sealed in their final form. This helped me understand what was most important about *Biochemistry*.

Now, the class didn't seem so daunting to pass. The approach I developed to studying and note taking, during my graduate school years, is the same approach I use today to organize and preserve important facts. I didn't realize it at the time, but from 1998 until 2003, I spent over $3,000.00 at the local *Kinko's*, now *FedEx Office*, preparing and preserving my notes in this fashion. It was worth every penny.

My tutor and I met after each class, and analyzed what I missed by not taking *Biochemistry,* as an undergraduate student. The concepts of *Biochemistry* weren't as foreign to me now. I credit God, my developing patience, and the skill of my tutor. It was fun going over a study strategy and for the first time at UVM, I felt like I belonged there. My constant need to be in Arkansas diminished. I knew to be successful I had to learn to love Vermont and its people and that's what I planned to do.

This was a good semester. I became more involved at the ALANA student center. Mr. Lawrence was helpful in supporting undergraduate and graduate students. I also didn't feel as alone in Vermont, because the DEVELOP program sent two more students I knew. I was glad they came because it was nice to be able to talk with people from DSU. My goal was to immediately share with them what my experiences were like in Burlington.

I tried to be positive and not scare them off, but felt I had some tenure in a place that could be very isolated. Things seemed to be turning around in the city and on campus, as departments and groups became more diverse. Mr. Lawrence was instrumental in recruiting a number of students to change the dynamics of the institution. His job was to support their endeavors.

The new graduate students from DSU were getting the royal treatment and when they first arrived, it was my job to show them around. Before that time, I hadn't ventured out beyond the borders of the downtown area, but one Saturday, the new students and I decided to visit a former UVM faculty member and scholar, who spent a lot of time working on diversity issues in the city and state. We heard a lot about Dr. Jackson Clemmons[63] and I remember hoping he was African-American (Black), as we drove through the countryside to a place called Charlotte[64]. I vaguely remembered Charlotte from the drive from Delaware, but never wanted to travel past the Burlington city limits.

I was still starved for culture and camaraderie, but eager to try new things, even though the anxiety of living in Burlington for a few years shaded my view. I believed that no people of color lived outside the city limits. I wanted to visit and talk with people, who could understand my journey, as I sped around the winding curves and approached Dr. Clemmon's home. I couldn't help but feel strange because I didn't know what to expect. When we arrived, he was standing outside and my thoughts and anxieties diminished because he was an African-American (Black) man. This broke all of my stereotypical views about people who lived in Vermont. For the first time since moving there, I wasn't the self proclaimed expert on African-American culture.

I approached Dr. Clemmons and shook his hand. He was an older gentleman with a graying beard and spoke with a light direct voice. I'm sure he wondered why I smiled so brightly to see him, but I couldn't believe that another Black man was living in Vermont on purpose. I had a lot to learn. Today was one of those "green" moments, because it showed how out of touch with reality my assumptions and perceptions could be. I also met his wife, who operated an African goods and supply store in Charlotte.

We spent most of the day talking and fellowshipping. Dr. Clemmons

---

63 Dr. Jackson Clemmons- was one of two Black faculty members at the University of Vermont's College of Medicine in 1966. The other faculty member was Dr. Lawrence McCrorey. During that time, there were six minority students on the entire campus.

64 Charlotte, Vermont- is a town in Chittenden County Vermont located on the outskirts of Burlington and known for its rich and fertile land that supports sugar bushes, orchards, dairies, berry farms, wineries, and market gardens.

asked me about my studies and I told him the difficulties I was having in *Biochemistry*. He told me to make sure to study the *Metabolic Pathways* and take a more structured approach to the course. He didn't talk much about his time at UVM. I already knew he was the first, and one of two African-American faculty members. He had a wealth of knowledge to share regarding the university and the changes it had made over the years. I was like a kid working at my grandfather's shop. I wanted to stay there all day and learn from an elder. Dr. Clemmons was very friendly and I found out in 2003, that his first post-doctoral student was *Dr. Clifton Orr*, my mentor from UAPB.

This was one of the most amazing things that happened to me in Vermont. I never knew it was such a small world among seemingly unrelated people. Dr. Clemmons talked fondly about Dr. Orr and told me he tried his very best to get him to come to Vermont to study with him. In previous conversations, Dr. Orr told me he wanted to come to Vermont, but didn't because of his family. Dr. Orr also talked about how much his wife enjoyed visiting the area and always reminisced on how beautiful the mountains and leaves were. Dr. Clemmons said he tried to pressure Dr. Orr to come to Vermont, but he still declined and mailed him a letter stating why. Dr. Clemmons said he saved that letter and still cherishes it today.

By the end of the day, we were all tired and ready to leave. I thanked Dr. Clemmons and his wife for their hospitality. I learned a lot that day. The most important thing was to stop *"Judging a book by its cover!"* and to be more open to the culture Vermont has to offer. It was motivating to feel like I was trailblazing in the state, but I realized my experiences as a Black man were only possible because of people like Dr. Jackson Clemmons and Dr. Lawrence McCrorey, who opened doors for me. I was inspired by meeting an African-American trailblazer and appreciated his timely wisdom and advice. I thought about that interaction for many days afterwards and every time I felt like quitting or felt like Vermont wasn't the place for me, I thought about Dr. Clemmons and Dr. McCrorey.

The next week was back to business. *Biochemistry* was my only concern. It was the only class I enrolled into that semester and was focused, as I could be. I knew I had to make *Biochemistry* my passion and get over the fact that I missed some opportunities in the past. Now was the time to do what I needed to do to pass this class. I tried not to relax because I was still on *Academic Probation*.

The CMB program director (Dr. Anne Huot) was watching my

progress very closely. I have to admit she intimidated me, because she held my life in her hands. It was up to me to try to reclaim my stake at UVM. I noticed that a lot of the bitterness I brought with me from Arkansas and Delaware was leaving and I embraced Burlington and Vermont as my home.

The laboratory was more social and I tried to interact, as frequently as I could, with other CMB students. I felt like I "belonged" now. I owe my newfound confidence to the Grace of God, receiving the pre-doctoral grant, and the support from Josie, Dr. Mossman, and Barry. I felt like one hurdle was passed. Some success was enough to make me believe it was possible. My energy was high. I was still writing and determined to publish a book.

The success from the grant was addictive and I wanted to succeed in every aspect of my life. I was in a good rhythm. I didn't worry too much about my research, as long I had enough information to present once a year at the CMB seminars. I tried to improve my oratory skills. Barry grilled me on the details of the research, and what our short and long term goals were. My project focus was still in its early stages, which bought me some time to try to finish my course work.

I was still getting calls from NEBHE and BSCP, until I finally decided to talk with them and see what they wanted. It must not have been my time to interact with them before now, but as soon as I learned about their bigger role in undergraduate and graduate student education in the northeast, my avoidance turned to anticipation. NEBHE and BSCP would eventually be one of the most valuable assets, during my time at UVM. One of their biggest selling points was the fact that they wanted me to attend their annual meeting and symposiums in Boston. I didn't mind going to Boston, but my car was still down and I was riding my bicycle everywhere in the city. I was excited about NEBHE and BSCP, but couldn't get to their meetings.

Meanwhile, I was spending more time at the ALANA Student Center and worked with New Black Leaders, which was a group of African-American students, who formed a club to create an atmosphere to support their studies. I attended their first meeting and really wanted to help them grow and do more on campus and in the community. Once I remembered I was still in Vermont and here to do graduate work, I stepped back. Surprisingly, they wanted me to continue advising their group. I was honored to receive their vote of confidence. Once I learned about their history and their annual celebration called "Ebony Fest[65]," I was happy to participate. Most of the students liked me, but there were a few who didn't like anyone giving them unwarranted advice.

I still wondered about NEBHE and BSCP, but didn't have a way to get to Boston. Amazingly (God), Mr. Lawrence approached me about chaperoning a group of students to a meeting in Boston. I asked him what I had to do. He told me that I would drive to Boston with fifteen students and make sure they attended the meeting. My other responsibility was to bring them back safely.

This was just what I needed. This opportunity could help achieve two goals and I could finally understand what these organizations had to offer. I was happy to accept the job, and we planned our first trip to Boston in the early spring. Mr. Lawrence asked me how much I would charge him. I said "nothing" because it was an opportunity to get to Boston. Mr. Lawrence asked me again. I gave him the same answer, until he offered me $150.00 for the weekend. I said "O.K."

I had been so busy over the summer and during the early days of the semester, with my new tutor and the ALANA Student Center, I hadn't seen or talked with Josie. I missed her and knew if I went to her salon, she would brighten my spirit. One day I called her to schedule an appointment. She answered the phone and said "Well, Hello Stranger!" I knew she was playing, but felt bad I hadn't been in contact with her. I told her *"I needed to get my counseling, from the most famous hair stylist in Vermont and on the East Coast, and if she could please pencil me in at her exclusive Winooski, Vermont salon."* She laughed and said sure. The day of my appointment, I arrived early.

Josie was in her usual bright and cheery mood. Today was different because I was her only client, so we had time to talk and chat. She told me how business was going and then let me know that her husband was still thinking about going back to school at UVM. I was excited for him and her. I really believed in education and thought it would be good to have another student I knew in the graduate school. As soon as we finished that conversation, he walked in the door. He seemed like a cool guy and reminded me of someone I had seen before in Arkansas. He asked me about my experiences at UVM and I told him of the difficulties I had in *Biochemistry*. He shared his experiences in Florida and told me how

---

65 Ebony Fest- was a yearly multicultural celebration organized and scheduled by NBL to highlight the best in African-American cultures, as well as other cultures on the campus.

he passed a very difficult *Biochemistry* course. I was all ears. He had the experience I needed and seemed willing to share it with me.

I don't know if Josie planned for us to meet again that day, but I was glad we did. It was another example of how her salon was not only the site for culture in the city, but she served as the coordinator of one of the most important meet-and-greet networking centers in the area. Josie seemed to know everyone in the state of Vermont. If she didn't know someone you were looking for, she knew people who did. I learned that whatever I needed to do or whoever I needed to talk to in Vermont, she was the "doorkeeper."

Josie's husband left and she finished cutting my hair, while updating me on what I started calling the *"Life and Times of People of Color in Vermont."* We had a great conversation. I still got my scalp massage and wash before I left, which was her trademark. I thanked her for introducing her husband to me and then jumped on my bicycle and rode back to my apartment. When I got back home, I reviewed my *Biochemistry* notes and prepared to pay my rent for that month. I was still having financial problems and needed more money, in lieu of my new stipend from the grant.

I had more stability and a little more money, but the rent was still more than I could pay. My car was parked, which helped with gasoline costs. Meanwhile, I learned to use the College Street Shuttle[66] and the CATS Off-Campus bus to get around Burlington. My bicycle made transportation faster because I didn't have to use normal travel routes. The stronger I got, the faster I could peddle and get to my destinations. I still wondered why I wasn't making enough money and thought about another job, but decided to focus primarily on my studies. *Biochemistry* was still my first priority and since Dr. Mossman hired a tutor, I would have no reason not to pass the class.

Every week, the tutor and I would meet after each class. Her help was a major boost to my understanding of *Biochemistry*. At first, we seemed to differ in strategy, because I really wanted to learn and embrace the concepts, but her role was to help me learn the key points and pass the class. It took about three sessions for me to understand the "big picture," which quickly changed my expectations. I reconciled that if I pass the class now, I would be able to learn and use the concepts in the future. This

---

66 College Street Shuttle- is a historic bus line that transports people from UVM to the waterfront adjacent to Lake Champlain.

approach was difficult, because knowledge of the subject was so important to me, which may have been my problem during testing.

I just didn't want to regurgitate what I had been studying, but be able to engage and speak about the major concepts. My aspirations were misplaced, considering the fact that I was still inches away from having my graduate school admission revoked. I had to change, so I bought into what Dr. Mossman and the tutor were trying to get done. I carried the *Biochemistry* book everywhere I went. I stepped into the laboratory after each class, and used that time to try to polish up on the points I struggled with the most.

I was building for the first exam and had seen the structure so many times I knew how important it was to get a good start. Every point was crucial and there was no room for mistakes. Every week I made *Prep Sheets* and reviewed them with my tutor. I was more engaged in the classroom discussion, but didn't spend time trying to remember a concept. I asked specific questions. Some students in the class tried to take up a large part of lecture time, by asking questions with obvious answers, to try to help the class end sooner. All that did was annoy the instructor and waste time. I needed a complete lecture and was upset when class time was spent discussing a concept that wasn't going to be on the exam. I wasn't in the mood for SOMEBODY to "discover the scientist within." The lecturers began to recognize a pattern of irrelevant questions and asked that questions be tabled until the end of class.

My goal was clear and that was to get this class done. I was under the mentorship of Dr. Mossman, who also taught a *Special Topics* class that semester. The interplay between *Biochemistry* and *Special Topics* helped me balance my thought processes and made me believe that I could be successful. The build-up was near for the first exam and I was ready. More focused now with the tutor's help, I matched concepts with test questions. Barry wanted to know where my head was and I told him I felt good and desired to do much better this semester. He told me" *The time was now to achieve and that I should invest as much of my life as possible to getting this done, because he couldn't take me to the next level, unless I passed this great hurdle."*

I appreciated his words of encouragement and was compelled to do my best. I talked with Dr. Huot about my goals and progress in the program. She agreed with Barry and Dr. Mossman that if I didn't pass this class, there would be no future for me at UVM. This affirmation wasn't new to me, because I had been on the brink of expulsion for the last two years.

Through the Grace of God and resilience, I managed to hang around. What her words did was be a constant reminder of what needed to be done and I was willing to do whatever it took.

The day of my first exam, I was nervous and anxious and tried to remember not to panic if I couldn't answer the first question. I looked to my left and another student brought a small piece of fabric that read "Don't Panic!" This made me feel good because I realized I wasn't the only person in the class, who suffered from testing anxiety. The room became quiet, as the instructor walked in with the exams and response books. I closed my eyes and told myself that this was it. I reminded myself of my experiences up until that point and then went back in time and saw Dr. Orr and Dr. Reed encouraging me to get it done.

When I opened my eyes, the exam was in front of me. I opened the first page and went to work. I expected anxiety, but there was none. I expected not to be able to answer the first question, but I was able to. I expected to fall back into that rut as usual, but my confidence "superseded" those feelings. I kept my head down the entire exam. When time was called, I had finished the exam early and was able to go back and check my answers. I was more confident than ever, satisfied with my efforts, but cautious about the results. I left the room wanting to "Holler," because the pieces of my life seemed to be coming together.

Later in the week, I met with my tutor and we talked about the exam. When I reviewed my notes, there were some mistakes, but not as many as before. I bought into what Dr. Mossman had done for me. When I told Barry about my classroom experience, he was upbeat and told me to focus on the laboratory work, when I had a chance. I almost forgot about the research goals we established, when I first got to Vermont, but now felt I could manage the laboratory and my studies. The week went by fast and it was almost time for me to get my scores. I was patient and calm, but wanted to know what I made.

When I finally got my exam, I was pleased with the score because it was the first time I wasn't starting behind in the class. I still made some silly mistakes and was concerned why I would discount the obvious, and try to calculate the impossible, but it was an improvement. I talked with my tutor about my irrational feelings during the exam and she told me not to over study. "*Overanalyzing the materials and questions is just as bad as not studying at all, because the concepts tested for are often missed.*" She also told me that "*No one cares how much you know or think you know*

Four Tubas, a Guitar, and a Gallery of Cheerleaders

if the questions aren't asked." "In this class, there was no room for creative thinking." "Just answer the questions as written and things will be O.K."

I thought about what she said and tried to apply it to the rest of my time in the class. I wondered how my thought processes evolved to the point that would prompt me to know the answers verbatim, but write responses to the questions opposite of what I knew to be true. Then, I remembered growing up and always having difficulty with reading and comprehension assignments. It wasn't that I couldn't read, but when I read something and had to answer a question about what I read, I would always inject my personal views, which caused my answers to be wrong.

For example, I read a story about a boy, eating apples under a tree and singing a song. When the teacher asked me what the boy was doing under the tree, I would go into a long story about why the boy was eating the apple, what kind of tree it was, and describe the song he was singing. None of my creativity was relevant or even correct, which is why my answers were always wrong. My imagination was so vivid and clear, that growing up teachers thought I had a learning disability and couldn't read well enough to go to the next grade. Their reason was that none of my answers matched the questions they asked, so they felt I had problems reading and comprehending. When I tried to explain my position, they would commend me for my effort and then grade it wrong.

This was going through my mind, as I talked with my tutor. Now, my goal was to try to limit my imagination, which seemed to be my best trait. *Biochemistry* was no place to be creative and if I didn't understand that "facts were facts," I would have a very difficult time. I processed what she said and thought how I could stop doing what was obviously costing me points. I was still writing a book about my experiences in Arkansas and those creative skills were critical for me to finish that project. I was happy, but indecisive.

Either I needed to stop writing my book, or keep scoring low in *Biochemistry*. I made a hard decision to stop writing and focus all of my energy into *Biochemistry*. It was kind of a shock for me, because writing was my love, and one of the motivating factors of my life. Once I decided to put the book project down, it was final in my mind. I felt a void and really wanted to catch up on my writing this semester, since I didn't have to take any cumulative exams until the summer. I already knew the best course of action.

The rest of the semester went by fast, as I transitioned off the training grant and began using my own research funding. It was cool and an honor to be in a position to be supported for the next five years. I had no intention of staying in Vermont that long, but the grant provided tremendous support. My next *Biochemistry* exam was coming up and this time I was mindful of my tendency to go beyond the question. I studied old tests and started modeling my "*Prep Sheets*" from previous exams. The problem was that the teaching rotation changed and the same materials were taught, but the instructors were different. I did my best work calculating what would be on upcoming exams. Tutoring helped me, when I wanted to stray from important concepts.

The second exam was more difficult and required me to explain the answer to the question, which was my biggest challenge. Exams that were once "fill-in-the-blank" and short answer now became "extended essay." When I approached questions that were more difficult than I was prepared for, I fell back into the same mode and began extrapolating facts that were interesting, but not relevant for the answer.

I knew I was doing it, but vowed to always answer the questions on the exams fully, even it meant making up something to fill in the spaces. I turned my exam in and knew that it probably wasn't my best work, but hoped that the major concepts were stated. I went back to tutoring the next day and she asked how the exam went. I told her FINE, but decided to discuss some of the questions and determine how she would have been answered them. I knew she could hear my anticipation and she told me to "*keep studying the notes as they were written.*"

I was somewhat disappointed and wanted to go home and write, but decided to wait until the semester ended. I was back in a funk and decided to spend more time at ALANA with New Black Leaders. This was my release, along with going to Josie's. Both experiences made me feel connected and "whole." I was down for a couple of days. My work in the laboratory was lethargic. I knew what was wrong, but tried to blame Vermont, UVM, and the absence of African-American people, which was a very old and irrational excuse.

As soon as I started making excuses, I envisioned Dr. Orr and Dr. Reed scolding me, for a lack of attention to detail, and telling me to get it together and do what I needed to do. I wanted to reach out to someone who knew me and knew what I was capable of, so I called Dr. Reed for some of his inspirational words. Dr. Reed was glad to hear from me and asked me how things were going. I told him FINE as usual and discussed my funding from the National Science Foundation (NSF) and NIEHS. I wanted to go into more details about my experiences, but when we talked

I recognized that complaining or seeking sympathy wasn't something Dr. Reed ever bought into.

I was his protégé and had to be an example of his mentoring and teaching efforts. His conversation did inspire me to push harder and I wanted to show him I could earn a Ph.D. in Vermont. I kind of felt he knew my conversation was trying to get him to "soothe my wounds," but I was too scared to go there with him and then have to listen to him telling me what I already knew.

In his words, *"Be a man and fight for what you want!"* It was funny because I was trying to be cavalier on the phone, but he didn't support my assumptions of possible failure. This taught me something about Dr. Reed and let me know that in order for me to achieve what he achieved; I had to do what he had to do. If that meant sacrificing everything I had, then that is what I had to do. We ended our conversation on a good note and before I hung up the phone, I hoped he would buy into my self-defeating attitude. But, as one of the smartest, disciplined, and principled men I had ever met, that wasn't going to happen.

The next couple of weeks, I spent my evenings in the ALANA center and studied. The next exam in *Biochemistry* came much quicker. I was ready and did my best, but was still having problems answering the essay questions. My point totals from all previous exams, were in line not to fail the class again, but I needed to make a "B" to stay at UVM. My tutor and I were on the same page, with one more exam before the end of the semester. I had to get as many points as possible. I worked diligently to get my notes organized. My *"Prep Sheets"* were crisp and concise. I went over every aspect of the last exam and then asked the lecturer questions after each class. I was determined to make this semester be my best semester and couldn't get another "F."

Everything was on hold, including social interactions. People saw me on campus with a *Biochemistry* book in one hand and laminated notes in the other. For the next twelve days, I slept and ate *Biochemistry*. My tutor reminded me not to over study, but *Biochemistry* was my conversation and every day life. I studied so much that one of the ways I practiced for the exam was drawing and labeling the chemical intermediates of major biological pathways, as suggested by Dr. Clemmons. I memorized all the structures and could draw them on blank pieces of paper in their reaction order.

One day I was drawing the *Citric Acid Pathway,* on the board in the classroom. The instructor walked in and commented that my sketches reminded him of a college professor's work. I was glad he saw me writing and learning the materials and hoped if I missed this point on the exam, he would remember I could do it. By the time the exam came, I was ready to do what I needed to do. My heart was racing and my pulse was pounding. I didn't care about anything but the exam. As soon as I opened my test, I went to work. The pressure was on me, because I was close. My anxiety level peaked at the beginning of the exam, but subsided halfway through.

I answered the questions to the best of my ability and before I knew it, I was at the end of the exam. I took the remaining time to recheck my short answer points and review the content in the essay section. I was satisfied with my answers, but not as confident as I should have been. The instructor called "time", the exams were retrieved, and he let us know that the scores would be ready next week. I met with my tutor after class and she asked me how it went. I told her it was difficult, but I answered to the best of my ability.

I wanted to go into more detail, but really wanted a break from thinking about *Biochemistry*. I went to the laboratory to calm down. It took me three days to relax. As soon as I got back to my apartment, I turned my attention to writing. I wanted to publish more than ever and was willing to put the work and time into this endeavor.

The next week couldn't come fast enough and when I picked up my exam and saw the score, I knew I did my best, but the highest grade I could get would be a "C." I was distraught but upbeat and when I reviewed the exam with my tutor, I saw the obvious mistakes I had always made since I was a young boy. I added more than what was necessary, but it didn't answer the question. I thought I had addressed this issue.

I was happy my grade wasn't an "F," so at least I was going in the right direction. I thought my graduate career was over. The only thing that saved me was the grant, and the fact that I earned an "A" in the *Special Topics* class taught by Dr. Mossman. The "A" balanced the grade, which remained a "C," from a GPA standpoint, but I still had to deal with Dr. Huot. I knew she would be tough on me because my progress seemed to stall.

> But God hath chosen the foolish things of the world to confound the wise; and God hath chosen the weak things of the world to confound the things which are mighty.
>
> **I Corinthians 1:27 (KJV)**

Four Tubas, a Guitar, and a Gallery of Cheerleaders

I asked Dr. Mossman to advocate for me and she agreed to do so. This really showed me how much character she had. I told Barry what my final grade was. He was curious about the next step and then recommended that if I was still at UVM, I shouldn't take any more *Biochemistry* this school year. Dr. Mossman agreed with his assessment. Barry felt I was burnt out on *Biochemistry*. He wanted me to start focusing more on the laboratory work and finishing the cumulative exams. I was happy to get their support and thanked my tutor, who was a big Jimmy Buffett fan, by buying her a collection of her favorite Jimmy Buffett CDs.

She was surprised by my generosity, but thankful. She let me know that whenever I took the second part of *Biochemistry*, I would need a personal tutor and she was interested. By the end of the semester, I was exhausted and wanted to go back to Arkansas and rest. I escaped another challenge in my life, but was still "walking on eggshells" and couldn't relax one moment. I learned what Dr. Reed tried to teach me. *"In order to get a Ph.D., it takes more than effort, it will take unflinching will!"*

Winter/Spring 1999

This semester was a new beginning for me. I built some momentum to fix my academic problems. I talked with Dr. Huot about my progress and she recommended, along with Dr. Mossman and Barry, for me to take another *Special Topics* class to try to improve my GPA. I was happy to comply because it would allow me to gain some valuable skills and rest from *Biochemistry*. I was grateful for the support Dr. Huot and Dr. Mossman were giving me. I tried to let them know that, as often as I could. Barry asked me why I always thanked people in the department and around the campus for advocating for me. He felt it was their job to aid and assist students, but my feeling was that "no one had to do anything for me." This was the reason why I wanted those who helped me to know that their support was pivotal in my success.

I had some breathing room, so I used my research skills and time to finish compiling a book. At first, I just wanted to talk about the musical fraternity and sorority, but then I became more interested in the history of UAPB. This presented a problem because I had enough information to finish the project, but the story would be incomplete. There were so many gaps I couldn't fill in. I became frustrated and almost stopped writing, but decided to travel home for a weekend and do some additional research.

Sederick C. Rice

My template was done, but the "meat" of the book was still lacking. When I flew home, I decided to spend some time on the UAPB campus, to try to interview as many people as possible. The project had grown from just writing about music. I felt God was directing me to talk more about the history of an HBCU, which I had never seen in print.

While I was in the Bluff, I stopped by to talk to *Hud,* to get more information about the history of the UAPB Music Department. We talked about KKΨ and he mentioned *U.G. Dalton, III,* as one of the pioneering members of our chapter. I never heard his name before and was dumbfounded, when *Hud* mentioned some of his accomplishments. He told me that Dr. Dalton was a faculty member at UAPB for many years and in line to become the chair of the music department.

As he talked about him, he could see the look of confusion on my face, which caused him to pause and ask why I didn't know more about what he was saying. I felt like I did when "Chico" was quizzing me about the pledge lines of KKΨ, but this time I focused on the fact that Dr. Dalton may hold the key to helping me finish my book. *Hud* talked at length about him as a person and I took notes. I realized at that moment that I needed to try to honor people within this book, who made significant impacts in my fraternity and in the UAPB Music Department.

I wanted to know more about U.G. Dalton, III so my book could be unique in every aspect. During our chat, I wanted to find out where he was, so I could interview and talk with him. *Hud* told me that he had passed away. I was stunned and disheartened because I felt I was close to a breakthrough. As I left his office, *Hud* asked me to finish the project because it was important. I felt inspired but wanted to know more about Dr. Dalton. I walked across the campus to the library to do more research, and decided to talk with Mr. Fontenez, the Director of the Library, a long-time faculty member, and former neighbor. I grew up with his daughter.

When I played football or basketball with Mrs. Glover's children, she was there and joined in. I talked briefly with Mr. Fontenez and he recommended I talk to *Trenton Cooper,* who knew Dr. Dalton very well. I walked back across the campus to Mr. Cooper's office and was lucky to catch him, before he left for the day.

I waited about ten minutes to speak with him and let him know what I was doing and why. I tried to sell my project as best I could, so I could get as much information as possible. My time was running out to be in the Bluff, and this was the last day I would be in the state. Mr. Cooper was glad to talk to me. He gave me more information about Dr. Dalton and then said the words that changed the way I looked at the project.

We were having a general conversation and I asked him about Dr. Dalton's personality to try to accurately represent him in the book, along with other influential musical faculty members at UAPB. Mr. Cooper said, "Have you read U.G.'s dissertation?" I paused and said "What dissertation?" Mr. Cooper then talked in depth about Dr. Dalton's dissertation assignment at the University of Michigan, which spoke a great deal about the history of the AM&N/UAPB music department.

I felt like God was moving me to finish this project because I never knew someone had already written so much about the subject I was interested in. My eyes brightened as Mr. Cooper talked about Dr. Dalton's vision and approach to music. I was ready to leave to try to find and review his work. I knew God was helping me because if I didn't have the conversation with *Hud,* then I wouldn't have talked with Mr. Fontenez. If I didn't talk with Mr. Fontenez, then I would have never known to talk to Mr. Cooper, who could tell me about the prolific work Dr. Dalton did.

I left Mr. Cooper's office excited and anxious. I was ready to get back to Vermont to use their library resources to try to find Dr. Dalton's dissertation. My mind was set on how I would do the book. My historical piece would be highlighting those, who had come before me, to try to honor their legacies for future generations. As soon as I got back to Vermont, I went to the library and used several search engines to find Dr. Dalton's dissertation. UVM had great resources. I used their Interlibrary Loan program[67], to get rare articles and books to help me finish the project. I searched and couldn't find the dissertation, until I used Dr. Dalton's full name and chose the university he attended.

This change allowed me to retrieve the dissertation. I slowly read the bibliographic abstract, which gave me a rush. The entire synopsis of Dr. Dalton's work was exactly what I needed. Each line seemed to be a prophetic guide for me. I really felt like Dr. Dalton's spirit was encouraging me. I got a sense of peace that day because for the first time, since envisioning this project in Arkansas, I knew I could do it.

I ordered the dissertation through Interlibrary Loan and used that information and resources, to retrieve other books and dissertations that supported my goals. It was cool because the research skills I learned to try

---

67 Interlibrary Loan Program- was a database listing of books, dissertations, and materials that could be shared between libraries for a nominal fee. This program was also used to promote discovery during research.

to publish a book were the same skills I would need years later to finish my dissertation. I was so happy to feel like I was "called" to do this work and it became more than work, it became my passion.

When I read the dissertation from cover to cover, I was blown away by the detail. I was compelled to honor Dr. Dalton. Without his work, I would have never been able to finish the project. If he were alive, I would have liked for him to be my co-author and been able to interview him about his experiences at UAPB and at the University of Michigan. I did have those moments of doubt and disbelief, but as soon as I thought about what it would feel like to compile a book, *"on a subject often overlooked in American society*, I was motivated to push forward. My life was changing. Even though I lived in Vermont and had academic troubles, I knew if I could publish a book, it would help solidify my existence at UVM. The thought of publishing overwhelmed me. Now that all of the pieces were in place, I had to figure out who would publish me.

The first thought that came to mind was "control." I wanted to guide the project from the beginning to the end and do it my way. I knew that publishing was difficult and time consuming, but felt that if I could get a company to do it for me, it would be worthwhile. I searched the internet day and night and compared and contrasted small presses with major publishing conglomerates, but was frustrated by their timelines. Most major book companies were backlogged. If they accepted a manuscript, it would take more than a year to publish the work. I kept searching. The more research I did, the more I wanted more control of the project, than what traditional publishing companies would give me. I then looked at "self-publishing" companies and did a significant amount of research on the "pros" and "cons" of their publishing process.

One of the biggest issues with publishing is reaching a targeted audience. My book would be published in Vermont, but talked about the life and times of an HBCU and used music as a primary theme. I finally made a decision to self-publish. I found a company called *Morris Publishing*, out of Nebraska, that had a publishing package I could work with. They also gave me ultimate control over the destiny of the book. I called them and they sent me a publishing guide. Morris Publishing had a reputation of helping first time authors develop and publish their works.

I felt my purpose in Vermont was changing. I knew I was there to get a Ph.D., but my circumstances evolved to try to publish a book. Meanwhile, I was still working in the laboratory but wasn't as concerned about the research, because my dissertation project was still in its early stages. Barry was busy doing rotations in the hospital and I used that time to try to pursue other interests.

I kept up appearances in the laboratory and did the minimum, but my focus was publishing. I talked about publishing all the time, as a way to help motivate me to complete self-imposed deadlines. My research skills were improving and it took less time to find specific articles and reviews of interest. The scope of book project changed. After reading Dr. Dalton's dissertation, I wanted to include as much historical information as possible, to make the project meaningful and worthwhile.

I tried not to write it like a textbook, but decided to use the same format, so it could be used as a reading and reference piece. I knew that a difficult topic to discuss would be the role of education at HBCUs, and how that related to music and music education. Dr. Dalton's dissertation helped me put all the pieces together.

I was having fun in Vermont, while doing something that was really important to me. My mood changed. I truly felt a sense of happiness. Josie was still my cheerleader and we fed off each other's ideas. We both didn't know what the future held, but believed that all things were possible through a strong belief in God and hard work. Josie and I could dialogue for hours about writing and she shared with me her passion to write books as well. I would motivate her and she would motivate me. She never let me down in spirit and regardless of how she was feeling; she always had wisdom and kindness to share. I thought she would get tired of me talking about the book, but she never did and eventually became an important contributor.

I was still doing hours of research everyday and using the library more than ever to try to fill in the gaps of my historical story, but a major piece was missing. I wanted to talk more about the birth and development of HBCUs and focus more on education, but didn't know how to find that information. Dr. Dalton's dissertation was thorough, but didn't go into detail about the real purpose and impact of HBCUs.

I tried to make my searches more targeted. One day I used the keyword "Education and HBCU" and the name *Morrill* came up. I did the search again and the name Justin Morrill[68] appeared in the reference box. I didn't think anything of it, but somehow that name was familiar to me. I couldn't remember where I saw it. I kept the name and did more research on Justin Morrill and found that he was the senator that introduced a

---

68 Justin Morrill- was a United States Senator from Vermont whose legislation established public colleges and universities.

bill in 1857, to establish state funded land-grant institutions. When I thought about his influence, I put together the ideas and realized he was responsible for establishing HBCUs. This was so exciting to me because I felt like God was helping me put the final parts of the story together. I still couldn't remember where I saw his name.

> Ask and it shall be given to you; seek and ye shall find; knock, and it shall be opened unto you. For every one that asketh receiveth; and he that seeketh findeth; and to him that knocketh it shall be opened.
>
> **Matthew 7:7-8 (KJV)**

One day I was walking toward the Bailey-Howe Library and for some reason (God) my attention wasn't focused on getting to the library to do work. For the first time, I was interested in the landscape of the UVM Green. This was an area that included buildings and architecture in the main part of campus. As I walked up the sidewalk toward the library, I saw a building adjacent to my path. For some reason (God), I turned my head and on the top of it read "Morrill." I stopped and my mind started churning.

I almost began hyperventilating because I just knew that I wasn't in the vicinity of everything I needed to finish the book and didn't know it. I closed my eyes and remembered the facts about Senator Justin Morrill and his role in land-grant institutions. I had never been in the building and slowly walked up the path to verify my initial assumption. As I walked toward the entrance to find out the first name on the dedicated building, I thought to myself that if it was Senator Justin Morrill, how in the world could all of these pieces fall together for me, at the right time, after my rocky experiences in Vermont? No other explanation than by the Grace of God!

When I got to the entrance, I never went inside the building. The cornerstone was inscribed *"Dedicated to Justin S. Morrill"* and the building housed to agricultural sciences. I closed my eyes and knew that whatever it took, I was publishing this book. I felt it was one of the reasons

I was in Vermont. I was speechless and walked away feeling destined for authorship.

It wasn't all joy, because I felt a heavy burden, but for the first time I was ready to embrace it. When I got to the library, I searched and researched everything I could about Senator Justin Morrill. It was so convenient. UVM had everything I needed stored in their archives. It was such a great feeling to know that a "seed" planted so many years ago would actually happen.

> And Jesus said unto them, Because of your unbelief: for verily I say unto you, If ye have faith as a grain of mustard seed, ye shall say unto this mountain, Remove hence to yonder place; and it shall remove; and nothing shall be impossible unto you.
>
> **Matthew 17:20 (KJV)**

I called Josie after I left the library and told her the "epiphany" I had that day. She was excited and inspired me even more because she truly believed in me. I didn't tell many people I was compiling and writing, because I wanted to surprise them when it was published. I'm so glad I told Josie because she was able to help me stay focused. I felt on a roll and turned my attention back to the self-publishing process and wanted to finalize the deal with Morris Publishing. I still hadn't decided on a title for the book. I wrote down as many phrases as I could, to incorporate the concept of the book. Music was always a central theme and after going through over seventy-five titles, I still didn't feel like they would accurately describe the book.

I had titles such as *"Must Be The Sound," "The Power of Music,"* and *"Music On My Mind."* After about two weeks, I changed and revised the titles by merging words from each phrase and tried to use different combinations to get a more creative affect. I was so excited to be fifty percent sure of a title, that I wanted to tell Josie. I scheduled a haircut to update her on the project.

When I got to her salon I had to wait, because she had a client in her chair. We discussed the book, while I waited. I read her my titles, but wanted her advice because I didn't know how interesting they were. Josie was a businesswoman and familiar with "guerilla marketing," so I knew she would be the right person to ask. She thought about the book and theme.

Then all of a sudden, she started humming a song. I listened intently and watched her multi-task. She had to check on her young children, and process hair, but she kept humming and singing. When she stopped singing she said, "What about Must Be The Music!" I asked her where she got the title from. She told me that when she was in her "Partying and Disco" days, she used to listen to a song called *Must Be The Music* by *Secret Weapon*[69]. She smiled and then sang the chorus.

> "Must Be The Music, *That's Turning Me On*, Must Be The Music!; Must Be The Music!, *I Cannot Go Wrong*." "My Voice is On, so Let Me Em Cee." I Spin My Records Get You Closer To Me." "The Way You Dance is Blowing My Mind." I'm in the Mood Watching You All the Time, Must Be The Music." "Must Be The Music, *That's Turning Me On*, Must Be The Music!; Must Be The Music!, *I Cannot Go Wrong*."

When she finished singing, I knew "*Must Be The Music*," would be my title because it fit so perfectly with the writing concept. I told Josie she was a genius. For the rest of the time, we talked about the best ways to market the book. I told her I would definitely give her credit in the book, for her creativity and help.

I rode my bicycle back home and thought about the title, but was concerned that it had already been used for a song. I wanted that title, so I researched and found that *Must Be The Music* was used multiple times for songs, and albums, but never for a title of a book. I added a subtitle to make it unique. The title became *Must Be The Music, Vol. I. Memoirs of a Musical Dynasty*. It was catchy, cool, and final. I was in a good mood because my title was done. I also didn't have to take *Biochemistry* this

---

69 Must Be The Music- is a song originally released by Unidisc Records in 1983 and sang by the group *Secret Weapon*.

semester and was doing well in my *Special Topics* class. I never told Barry I was writing a book.

Once everything was in place, I wrote every day and night and added any subject or concept that was related to music, or music education to its pages. The book turned into a textbook of sorts, because I told a story but would stop to discuss a subject I felt was important for readers. I wanted people to read the book and be inspired to go research and read the historical impact of people, places, and things in their lives. I also learned more about the self-publishing process and knew that all I had to do was write the book, format it, and it would be published.

I was so busy writing that I forgot about the three cumulative exams scheduled for this semester. I needed to score more points and should have been researching my exam topics, but my desire to publish overshadowed the requirements of the CMB program. I stopped writing for a month to study for my exams, which were scheduled for February and April. I scored in two areas in February, which raised my cumulative average and one area in April. My extracurricular research helped me prepare. Unfortunately, I was running out of time and needed to increase my cumulative average, in order to reach candidacy. I didn't feel too bad because there were four more exams left. I felt if I really concentrated and focused, I could get the scores I needed.

I was in a good space because my book was shaping up and my life in Vermont seemed to have purpose. Mr. Lawrence sent me an email and reminded me that I promised to chaperone students to the BSCP conference in Boston. I had almost forgotten about my promise, but remembered this would be an opportunity to get to Boston and finally understand why BSCP called and hounded me so much. I talked with Mr. Lawrence about the trip and he gave me everything I needed. I carefully drove twelve students, in a 15-passenger van, to the meeting. This was the first time I had been to Boston, so I was especially careful with directions, but still got lost on the way into the city. Fortunately for me, one of the students was from the area and directed us where we needed to go.

When we finally got there and registered, I got a chance to see Cleo. The conference was great. I interacted and networked with high school, undergraduate, and graduate students around the region. I was glad I came and Cleo was glad to see me. I was happy to learn more about BSCP and promised them that I would be an active participant in the future.

All of the students were pleased with the BSCP experience and more inspired to pursue careers in science. After the conference, I said my goodbyes to Cleo and brought the students back to UVM. Mr. Lawrence kept his word and paid me $150.00 for the weekend. I was just glad to go and be able to get the students back safely. I learned just as much as they did and asked Mr. Lawrence to always consider me to be a chaperone for those kinds of events. It was easy money and I enjoyed traveling to Boston.

When I returned, I prepared to take my final cumulative exam of the semester and continued to write Must Be The Music. I made good progress and felt I would be published by the summer. I tried to create a buzz with Josie's help. I talked daily to Morris Publishing and reviewed examples of newly published books at local bookstores, to make sure my book would be up to standard. I needed my book to be professional. It needed to be edited. I wasn't an editor and from research learned that editing was one of the most expensive processes during book publishing.

Even if the text was good and the layout was unique, the words and sentences had to make sense. I talked with Josie about it. She recommended one of her clients, who owned an editorial business. I was glad to get the contact and called her immediately to see if she could help get this project together. Josie's salon was network central and I finally had a chance to use one of her clients' services. The editor's name was Clara Cavitt, owner of Blue Pen Editorial Services, based in Jericho, Vermont.

When we talked, she was excited about what I was doing and wanted to know more about the project. I asked her about editing. She told me what she could provide. I let her know that I was still writing and would like her to edit the book, once the manuscript was complete. Clara agreed and now I had an editor for Must Be The Music.

Everything was in place, but my major concern was money. To get published would cost money, to get the manuscript edited would cost money, and to buy the books I needed would cost money. I was able to pay my rent but didn't have extra money to spend. I thought about getting another job, but didn't want to work anywhere, so I developed a plan to save the money I needed. I knew it would cost me about $2000.00 to get published.

I only had $500.00 saved up. In order for the publishing process to start, I had to give Morris Publishing a down payment of $1,000.00. I delayed getting another job because I still had responsibilities in the laboratory. I didn't want my time being spent delivering pizzas, or working long hours in a grocery store. I needed to make lots of money in a short period of time, while following a schedule that wouldn't interfere with my writing or daily activities. I let the idea go and decided to delay the project because the money wasn't there. I got some bad news from home and it threw all of my plans out the window.

Close to the end of the semester, my mother called me and let me know that she was downsized from her job and wouldn't be working for Georgia-Pacific anymore. I was glad she finally retired, but worried because she would lose her health benefits and prescription drug coverage. While she was working, the company subsidized about $300.00/month in prescription drug costs that now had to be paid, as out of pocket expenses. I knew my mother needed medicine for a variety of things and when she began to worry, my perspective changed. The option of not getting an additional job wasn't logical anymore and my goal to be published changed.

My first goal was to find work that would help me accumulate $300.00/month to help buy my mother's medicine. My older brother decided to help too, but because I was still single, I wanted to contribute the most. The next day I searched the want ads and used a calculator to figure out how many hours I needed to work, in order to come up with the money.

My graduate stipend was helping but wasn't enough for my rent and an additional $300.00 bill every month. I had a few prospects then I saw a flyer on the medical school bulletin board, for a high-paying part-time position working with adults in the community. I was interested. By coincidence (God), when I got to the laboratory, I overheard one of the post-doctoral fellows talking about a job he worked only in the evenings and on weekends. He was talking about the same position I just read about. I wanted to know more information.

He told me he worked for *Howard Health and Human Services* as a residential treatment counselor and was responsible for helping adults live more independently in their community. I asked him if they were hiring. He answered in the affirmative and told me he could pass my name off to his supervisors. I thanked him because this was the break I needed. From the way he described his job, he could work in the evenings and on weekends, was paid to sleep, and helped people along the way. This was the job for me. I needed to make money fast so my mother wouldn't be without her medication.

Chapter 7.
Must Be The Music

> Know ye not that they which run in a race run all, but one receiveth the prize? So run, that ye may obtain.
>
> **I Corinthians 9:24 (KJV)**

Summer 1999

The time had come for me to achieve one of my life's greatest goals, but things seemed to be in a constant state of chaos. My mother lost her job and benefits, I was still on rocky ground academically, and my bills were pilling up. All these things I processed daily, but was still focused on publishing a book. The first step was to find additional income, which now needed to be allocated to buy medication. After talking more about the post-doc's part-time job, I called Howard Health and Human Services to schedule an interview. My hope was that his recommendation and my desire to work unusual hours would help me land the job.

When I arrived at Howard Health, I waited about ten minutes for my interview to start, and then was ushered into the director's office. I walked in as she was busy signing papers and making phone calls. She paused and asked me to give her a moment. I nervously looked around her office and saw awards, plaques, and pictures. When she hung up the phone, she introduced herself and we shook hands. She told me she got a recommendation from a medical student and wanted to know why I wanted to work for Howard Health and Human Services. I told her I liked what the organization did in the community and wanted an opportunity to make some extra money. She paused and asked "What do you think mental illness is?"

The question caught me off-guard. I quickly came up with a general definition, while remembering all the interviews I blew, because of my desire to try to "impress" the facilitator. My answer was short and sweet. She agreed with my definition and we had a light conversation about Howard Health and their programs. After about fifteen minutes of dialogue, she asked me if I had any more questions. I said "No!" I was waiting for an indication of my employment, but she only talked about the programs and how they worked.

I thought a decision would be made later, but she left the office for a moment and came back with a tablet full of paperwork. She told me to fill out all the forms and asked if I would agree to a background check. I was willing to comply with all of her requests. By the time I finished all the paperwork, she told me that someone would be in touch with me. Then, she welcomed me to Howard Health and Human Services.

I stood up, shook her hand, and tried to hold on to that feeling of accomplishment, as I left the office and walked down the hall. I was "ecstatic" and began calculating how much I needed to work to make the money my mother needed and to get published. That was one of the best days of my life in Vermont. I felt God was influencing people in my life, and opening doors for me with favor. When I got back home, I called Morris Publishing to talk more about the publishing guidelines. It was the end of May and my goal was to be published before the end of the summer.

I still needed to get the book edited and was glad Josie connected me with an editor, so I could save money and be able to control every aspect of the project. By June, the book had come together nicely. The hardest part was determining where to stop the story. I had another "epiphany" to end the book like I started it, by focusing on my fraternity brothers and sisters. Once that was done; the work of writing was over.

The idea to add and highlight musical icons at AM&N/UAPB made the project unique. I was so proud to be able to give readers a glimpse of people they may or may not meet. I tried to complete the fraternity and sorority rosters, but some names were irretrievable. I included all the information I could find. Finally, the writing was done and thanks to Josie, *"Must Be The Music , Vol. I. Memoirs of a Musical Dynasty"* was formatted and ready for publication.

The next week was busy because the laboratory moved to a new location. Barry was excited about getting new space for his staff and students. We didn't move very far, but our environment improved considerably and was more open. The move wasn't on my mind because my focus was the book. I tried to contribute as much as I could, so that my presence wasn't missed. When we finally completed the move, Barry bought new equipment and collected research relics from other non-functional laboratories. My desk was in the back and by the time we organized all of our laboratory supplies, I could tell our laboratory group was growing.

Barry hired another laboratory technician. I decided to try to spruce up the laboratory some, by bringing in a fish tank. I always wanted to have a pet, after growing up without ever owning a dog or cat. My first intention was to set up the tank in my apartment, but was afraid the drastic changes in temperature would kill the fish. I knew the laboratory's temperature would be stable enough to sustain small life. I don't remember asking Barry if it was okay to bring in some fish, but his philosophy was *"Do your work and everything else will work out!"* I was proud of the fish tank. Everyone in the laboratory contributed, by buying fish and helping clean the tank. I really wanted to be more involved in the laboratory work, but my main concern was financing the book.

I was worried about my mother and her situation, but relieved that I had an opportunity to make some additional money to help her. I didn't believe she needed to take any pills, but she was a firm believer in following doctor's orders, so I tried to support her any way I could. We worked out an agreement that I would send her $300.00/month and my brother would send her the remaining balance. Getting the money was no easy task. My schedule at Howard Health was so open, I could volunteer to work everyday and night.

Fortunately for me, the job was flexible enough that I could work in the afternoons and overnight. I never told Barry what I was doing in the evenings, and was mindful of the policy that graduate students weren't allowed to work outside jobs. I had no choice. Bills had to be paid. So much was going on that summer. I almost forgot about my next cumulative exam. The goal was to work and write. Everyday I tried to focus in the laboratory, but instead focused more on the book. I was in constant contact with Morris Publishing. It was almost time to submit my completed manuscript.

I talked with Josie about my timeline and plan. She reminded Clara to review and make all the corrections I needed. Self-publishing was no joke, but I did it this way to save time and be in complete control of the project. After formatting, the book was 204 pages. I set the price at $15.95, because I knew I had to mail it to market it. My goal was to charge a price that people could live with and be cost effective to ship. One thing I always disliked about ordering anything from a company was the six to eight week wait for orders. It was important for people reading my book to tell others.

At that time, the United States Postal Service (USPS) offered priority (1-3 day) shipping for a little over $3.00. This was perfect, because at $15.95/book and $3.45 to ship, my customers could receive their books for $20.00. Twenty dollars has always been a magic number for me, so my plan was working out. The best part was that I could control the ship date and guarantee delivery in three or four days.

As soon as I finished my final draft and made the correction from Clara, I mailed the manuscript to Morris Publishing. I was glad to get it off my plate. Now, I could concentrate on raising the rest of the money for the finished product. I called my supervisor at Howard Health and asked about working overtime shifts, at night and on the weekend, to try to get as many hours as possible. Howard Health was willing to give me more hours because it gave their regular employees needed relief. I was so excited about the possibility of publishing that I worked every night and weekend. The money was good, but I had to make a decision because it didn't come fast enough for my goals. Every paycheck I sent money home.

My mother was stressing, which wasn't good for her medical condition. I was so blessed to be able to help her. I set a plan to work everyday and night for the next three months, but I totally forgot about my monthly rent. All my resources were stretched as thin as they could be. I was paying for an apartment I couldn't live in most of the time, because of work. I did manage to make the rent payments, but there was little left for anything else. My car was still down and the most cost effective way for me to travel was by bicycle.

I remember how people would laugh at me, when I rode past them going up and down the hills of Burlington, but I didn't care. I guess they thought I should be driving a car, but economically it wasn't possible. I adored my bicycle because the maintenance was minimal; I never had to gas it up, and could take it anywhere. By the middle of June, I was exhausted but happy because my mother had her medication and the rent was paid. Unfortunately, the money to make the final payment to Morris Publishing to finish the process was nowhere to be found.

I was too far into publishing to stop now. I tried everything to get the money I needed, including applying for a personal bank loan, which was denied. I also volunteered to work more hours at Howard Health. I never wanted to borrow the money. I had come this far without doing that and wanted to finance the project from the beginning to the end myself. I got to the point that no more money was available and I had to get some help. I didn't want to ask my parents or other family members, who I already knew were low on cash like me.

I got frustrated and decided to ask Cleo, since he was working as a school teacher in Boston. I knew Cleo had the money. He was the only person I ever met who graduated from college and graduate school with no debt. Cleo was smart and used scholarships and worked his whole career at the University of Toledo, so he could graduate debt free.

He had a cost-effective personality. I respected him because he didn't owe anyone. I thought about our friendship and how I would ask him for the money. I decided to make it a business proposition. I wanted to sweeten the deal and remembered how my grandmother (Big Momma) would give all the grand children *"Turpentine and Sugar"* to combat intestinal problems. The goal was to get the small dose of turpentine in our systems and the sugar was the vehicle to help us take it. I used the same approach with Cleo, because he was my last hope. I knew I would have the money at the beginning of next semester to pay him back. I decided to get a graduate student loan and use the refund to replace what I borrowed from him. My plan was to also use part of the refund for living expenses.

I decided to go ahead and make my plea to my friend. I called him up and he answered the phone as he always does "What's Up Black Man!" Then, I started my pitch. Cleo and I had talked about the book before. He was one of my biggest supporters. I began the conversation like this. *"Cleo, I need to ask you a favor! I need to borrow some money to publish my book*, and…" Before I could finish what I was saying, he said *"The check is in the mail, how much do you need."* I was stunned and grateful that before I went into all of the details of how I would pay him back, he agreed to give me the money.

I told him I only needed $1000.00 and would pay him $1,200.00, once my loan check came through. He jokingly said, *"I was only going to charge you 10% on the dollar, but your terms are good enough for me!"* Cleo told me to stop stressing about money, because the check was really in the mail. A week after our conversation, I received a check for $1000.00. I knew Cleo was a loyal friend and a great example of what happens, when you make good financial decisions early in life and can now help others. I talked with Dr. Reed about the book. He was concerned that my focus had become this book and not my graduate work. He also wondered if the project would be professional. I really wanted to show him I had grown and matured during my time in Vermont.

Now that the book was almost ready for publication, I began to think about marketing. Josie was a master at promoting her business and I asked her questions about her marketing technique. She always talked about using "guerrilla marketing" to sell or promote products, but this time she went into more details and outlined specific steps. As I listened to her stories of entrepreneurship, I developed a unique promotion technique. *I also learned that "It isn't what you say, but how you say something that can make the difference."* My research into publishing taught me that the back cover is the most important selling point for a book. I thought about the words for the back cover for a while. Now was the time to try to put together something that would be interesting for readers, and help promote the book.

I already made a decision about the front cover and used a historic picture of one of the early AM&N marching bands. I thought about marketing and wanted to show that the book was worthy for purchase.

I felt I needed someone to endorse it. God sent me that idea, because as soon as I thought about it, I couldn't let it go. I brainstormed for two weeks to try to think of SOMEBODY to endorse the book. I wanted someone involved in music, who could relate to the project, and who would be comfortable enough to allow me to use his or her name.

I thought and thought and then decided to call Wash, but I didn't know his number in Washington, D.C. I did know he was still at Howard University, so I found and called the main number. The university switchboard transferred me to his office, but I was only able to leave messages. I called *Hud* to see if he knew how to contact him, but he only knew the number for Howard University. I tried to reach Wash for about a week. Then, I decided to write the back cover description and have him endorse it. I really didn't know what to include, because the project entailed so many things. I knew I needed to let the audience know why this book should be purchased.

The next morning, I came into the laboratory and sat at my desk and thought about the project and my potential audience. God took over my mind and words. What happened next was "supernatural." I opened up a blank Word document and literally typed for twenty minutes non-stop without back spacing or misspelling any words. As I typed each sentence, I felt like someone else was typing for me. I experienced this before, when I was trying to finish the original manuscript, but this was the first time the words in my mind flowed so freely. I just sat there and let God take control of my thoughts, emotions, and creativity.

> Trust in the Lord with all thine heart; and lean not unto thine own understanding. In all thy way acknowledge him and he shall direct thy paths.
> **Proverbs 3:5-6 (KJV)**

When my hands stopped moving, I was done and had summed up the book in three fact-filled paragraphs. When I looked up, I felt mentally exhausted and stood up to get some air. Every time I looked at those words and saw how perfectly they were written and organized, I knew the hand of God was with me that faithful day. I never re-wrote the back cover and it was done. The next day, I tried Wash again and he answered.

Four Tubas, a Guitar, and a Gallery of Cheerleaders

The Back Cover

Must Be The Music is a small glimpse at an often-overlooked segment of American education, the Historically Black Colleges & Universities (HBCUs), and contains three principle themes including: The growth and development of an HBCU-the *University of Arkansas at Pine Bluff*, and the impact music played in that development. A historical perspective of the struggle and triumphs experienced by Black Americans, after Emancipation, to attain an education in Arkansas and throughout the United States, and highlights two national music organizations, Kappa Kappa Psi, National Professional Honorary Band Fraternity, Inc. and Tau Beta Sigma, National Professional Honorary Band Sorority, Inc. Prominent members include *Earth, Wind, and Fire, Lawrence Welk, John Philip Sousa, Claude T. Smith, Karl L. King, Frank L. Simon, Branford and Wynton Marsalis, O'Neill Sanford, Quincy Hilliard, Count Basie, "Dizzy" Gillespie, Stevie Wonder, Ray Charles, Lionel Richie, William (Bill) Jefferson Clinton*, the author and several other musical icons. Sederick C. Rice attended the University of Arkansas at Pine Bluff from 1990-1994, earning a B.S. degree in Biology, and marched with the *Marching Musical Machine of the Mid-South*. He then pursued a M.S. degree in Biology, from Delaware State University, in Dover, Delaware, from 1994-1996, and marched with the *Approaching Storm*. Presently he is a third year graduate student at the University of Vermont, in Burlington, pursuing a Ph.D. in Cell & Molecular Biology, with special emphasis in pediatric oncology and environmental toxicology. At age 26, Sederick has experienced and continues to experience life struggles and triumphs created by pursuing higher education, but has never lost his love, respect, and admiration for his Alma Mater, and its significant impact on his life. He lives for music and understands that it *Must Be The Music* that has made it all possible and worthwhile.

Wash and I talked for about five minutes and then I told him what I wanted to do. I asked for his current title and he gave it to me. He asked me to read the write up and I did. He agreed to allow me to use his name and position at Howard University. That experience, taught me so much about the way goods and services are sold to consumers. I had my endorsement and did a great deal of self-promotion, with very descriptive terms, by letting my audience know how old I was, and my career path.

I was relieved that this phase of the process was done. My anticipation for seeing the finished project was high. There were so many things going on that summer. I tried to put things in perspective and not be overwhelmed. My primary focus was the book. I tried not to forget about my graduate work, in the midst of the excitement, and remembered that there was still much more to do. I needed to make my final payment for the book. The loan from Cleo helped, but I knew if I wanted to market and push the book on my own, more money was needed.

My work at Howard Health, at night and in the evenings, was the only way I saved the rest. There were many opportunities to get additional hours as a residential treatment counselor. I always made myself available. My flexible schedule and willingness to work the shifts no one else wanted made me a hot commodity within the organization. I also gambled a lot with my apartment, by not paying my rent for three months, which in most circumstances would have meant immediate eviction.

The apartment complex was connected to UVM, so I negotiated with the property manager to pay the balance in full, once I got a refund from my student loan. I knew every dime I made had to go to the book project. Tuna fish became my favorite meal because it was quick and cheap. My car was still down, so paying for transportation wasn't an issue. Most of my responsibilities were close enough to use the bus system and my bike.

In the laboratory, the new staff settled in and I worked on projects with limited results. Barry was busy managing his staff and less concerned about my academic status, because I made some progress in *Biochemistry* and on my cumulative exams. On the writing front, I received a proof for *Must Be The Music*, from Morris Publishing. The proof looked like a small book and I slowly reviewed each page. I had to be extra careful because whatever was submitted, after reviewing the proof, would go to press. I was confident it was a good read because Clara did an excellent job reviewing and editing the words and passages. I kept thanking Josie for connecting me with her. It was so exciting to see the actual book nearly complete and I knew I would soon be a self-published author. All my revisions were simple. I express mailed the proof back to Morris Publishing and waited. The next couple of weeks were grueling because all I could think about was the book and how it would look, when I finally got it. Each week was more stressful than the next.

I called the company every Friday to check on the status of the order and they told me not to expect my books for another three to five weeks. I don't know what I was the most nervous about. I think it was the fact that I had completed a major project that had nothing to do with my graduate work. I know I was unsure if Morris Publishing would print the book as I envisioned.

I was tired of waiting for my books and decided to take a break from badgering the company. The time was well spent organizing and preparing for the big day. I went to Josie's to get my culture and conversation. She was just as excited about the finished product as I was. Now when we talked, it was all about the best marketing strategy. She encouraged me to approach book sales with an aggressive, but professional mindset.

I had some ideas and shared them with her. Instead of totally dismissing my approach, she listened attentively and then offered several alternatives. I felt like I was learning basic and intermediate business strategies every time I got a haircut. Josie and I would always mix business with the social aspects of Burlington and Vermont.

Josie noticed that I was more anxious because of the long delay in receiving the books. She calmly told me to be "patient" and things would eventually work out. The next week, I relaxed and looked forward to celebrating the Fourth of July. During the middle of the week, I got a call from Morris Publishing. They told me the books had been shipped via UPS and I wrote down several tracking numbers for the packages. I was so excited to get the call, I quickly checked the registry online knowing that the representative just told me the books had been shipped and would arrive in five to seven business days.

It wasn't easy waiting the rest of the week, but I made it to Saturday and expected the books to arrive before the Monday holiday. I sat in my apartment all day, but the books didn't come. The next week I checked the registry again, which indicated that the books had arrived at the UPS depot in Winooski, Vermont and were scheduled for delivery on *July 12, 1999*. All I could think about was those books, but my work schedule was full during the day at UVM and at night with Howard Health. I checked the registry one more time and it said the same thing, so when Monday came I stayed home and waited. I acted like a child at Christmas.

Every noise and knock at the door, I ran downstairs to see if the packages had arrived. After several false alarms, I fell into a light sleep so I wouldn't miss the delivery. At 11:30 a.m., I heard a firm knock at the door and ran downstairs because I knew it had to be the books. I opened the door and the UPS driver brought six boxes to my front step.

I smiled as my heart raced before signing the receipt slip. The boxes were heavy, so I only took one upstairs and quickly tore the top off and grabbed the first book I felt. When I saw the cover and binding, I screamed out "Yes!" as loud as I could. Then I grabbed all the books in that box, until books were laying all over my living room. I was ecstatic and jumped on my bicycle because I wanted to show Barry the finished product.

Before I rode to UVM, I stopped by the rental office and talked with the property manager about my late rent. She was concerned and disappointed, so to console her and buy more time, I asked her if she wanted an autographed book. She said "Yes!" She actually received the first copy of *Must Be The Music*. This was my way of letting her know that her patience was appreciated and not in vain. I darted out of the office and jumped on my bicycle and raced toward campus, using the sidewalks and bike paths. Three books were in one hand and I used the other hand to hold the handlebars.

I never peddled that fast before and it seemed like I arrived on campus mere minutes after I left. Once there, I ran upstairs to Barry's office, but it was lunch so he was dining with other medical school faculty in the cafeteria. I walked into the dining area, but didn't see him, but I did see the Dean of the Graduate School. I walked over to him because I wanted to show him my greatest accomplishment, up until that point.

This was so important to me because it was the dean I begged not to kick me out of UVM. He looked at the book and was impressed and asked if he could have a copy. I was willing to give him one, because one of the strategies I learned from Josie was to market my product by giving it to influential people on campus, so they could advertise for me. I pulled out my pin and signed the book, as I had practiced many months back. I was so excited that I forgot it was his lunch and just sat there gleaming with joy. I really wanted to give Barry a book, but he was still missing in action. I thanked the dean for giving me an opportunity to continue at UVM and he gave me praises for a wonderful project and promised to read it.

I left the cafeteria and headed back upstairs to Barry's office. This time he was there, but on the phone. I paced back and forth with anticipation as he saw me through the reflection in his office window. His conversation couldn't have ended fast enough. As soon as I heard the receiver hit the base, I knocked on the door. Barry greeted me like he always did, as I smiled from ear to ear.

He asked me what I wanted and I told him that I finally did what I said I was going to do. Then, I revealed the book and gave it to him. He grabbed the book and said something incoherent, but I knew he was expressing his utmost support. He shook my hand and stared at the cover for about three minutes without saying a word. I sat down and will never forget the words he spoke as he turned the pages. He said, "*I am so proud of you!*" This was really what I wanted to hear, because Barry had done so much for me at UVM.

My success was because of his support. We chatted about ten minutes and he congratulated me again and told me he was going to show his family and the other members of the laboratory. My next stop was Dr. Mossman's office. I went there to give her a book, but she insisted on buying one. She pulled out her checkbook and said, "When did you have time to do this?" with a look of excitement and intrigue on her face.

I relished that day for a long time and knew that the best was still yet to come. My confidence was as high as it had been since leaving Arkansas. The experiences with Barry and Dr. Mossman really set the stage for my future studies at UVM and my attitude changed. I felt like I "belonged," and had proof. This made me more determined to get the Ph.D.

MUST BE THE MUSIC

VOL. I
MEMOIRS OF
A MUSICAL DYNASTY

SEDERICK C. RICE

"Momma"
Shirley Ann Rice

Sunrise April 27, 1946- Sunset October 25, 2009

To Be Continued............

Four Tubas, a Guitar, and a Gallery of Cheerleaders

"When Fear Meets Faith"

Transition in the Life of a Black Ph.D.

Part II.

Sederick C. Rice

About the Author

Dr. Sederick Charles Rice was born and raised in Pine Bluff, Arkansas and graduated from Pine Bluff High School in 1990. He was always interested in science and music so after high school he attended the University of Arkansas at Pine Bluff. From 1990-1994, he earned a B.S. degree in Biology and performed with the Marching Musical Machine of the Mid-South. Dr. Rice then pursued an M.S. degree in Biology from Delaware State University (DSU), from 1994-1996, and performed with the DSU Approaching Storm band. From 1996-2003, he furthered his studies at the University of Vermont and achieved a Ph.D. in Cellular and Molecular Biology, with special emphasis in Pediatric Oncology and Environmental Toxicology. Dr. Rice was selected as an American Association for Cancer Research (AACR) Minority Scholar in 1998/2002 and did foundational research on the genotoxic effects of chemotherapy in children with acute lymphocytic leukemia. In 2003, Dr. Rice was selected as one of Ebony magazine's *"Young Leaders of the Future,"* and featured in the magazine's February 2003 issue, which highlighted 30 individuals aged 30 and younger who have "excelled in sports, the arts, religion, medicine, business, and education."

Following his doctoral studies, Dr. Rice accepted a post-doctoral appointment with the National Center for Environmental Assessment (NCEA) in Washington, D.C., as a Research Biologist/Toxicologist in the Effects Identification Characterization Group (EICG). There he received specialized training in Genetic Toxicology and Chemical Risk Management and worked on several chemical risk assessment projects including Bromobenzene, 1,2-dichloroethane (1,2-DCE), and Antimony. In 2006, Dr. Rice became a public school teacher, at Bowie High School, in Prince George's County Public Schools (PGCPS) and now teaches *Integrating the Sciences, Biology, Microbiology*, and *Anatomy and Physiology*. His work with non-traditional students has given him an opportunity to teach the "whole" student and mentor science related subjects with "real world" applications.

Dr. Rice believes in effective mentoring and sound teaching strategies on every level. He has worked extensively with the New England Board of Higher Education (NEBHE) and the Biomedical Sciences Careers

Programs (BSCP), associated with the Harvard University Medical School, to promote opportunities for students interested in biomedical science fields and careers. He now teaches at the University of Arkansas at Pine Bluff, his alma mater, as an Assistant Professor in the Department of Biology. Dr. Rice loves learning and teaching. His goal is to share his experiences to help students at UAPB develop a "Sense of Urgency" and achieve their greatest accomplishments. His keys to success are a strong relationship with God, powerful mentor relationships, and a close network of family and friends.

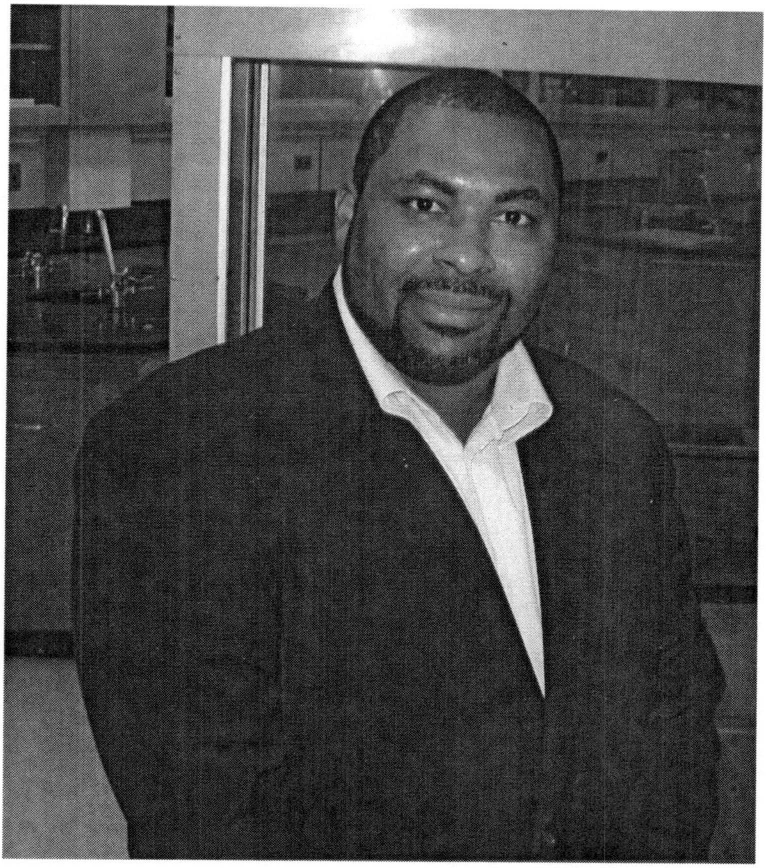

APPENDIX

Reference Scriptures (KJV)

I. Corinthians 13:9-11
Psalm 19:14
Galatians 6:3-10
Ecclesiastes 3:1-8
Proverbs 3:13-15
Psalm 18:1-3
Ecclesiastes 7:12-14
Ecclesiastes 7:5-8
Malachi 3:10
Malachi 3:8
Psalm 1:1-6
Ecclesiastes 11:9
Ecclesiastes 12:1; 12-14
Hebrews 11:8-10
Proverbs 18:24
Philippians 4:6-7
James 3:1-6
James 1:3-4
James 1:19-20
Proverbs 16:18
II Corinthians 12:9
Matthew 6:25-34
Ephesians 2:8
Hebrews 11:1
Ecclesiastes 9:10
I. Corinthians 1:27
Matthew 7:7-8
Matthew 17:20
I. Corinthians 9:24
Proverbs 3:5-6

World Impact Christian Center

Building a Strong Church, With Great Faith for Challenging Times

World Impact Christian Center
9601 Ardwick Ardmore Road
Springdale, MD 20774
http://worldimpactcc.org/
Email: info@worldimpactcc.org

We are a multicultural church that is dedicated to developing champions for God! Every person has a God given purpose that can only be fulfilled through a personal encounter with Jesus Christ, instruction in the Word of God and faith. We are building strong individuals and families that will excel beyond their own limitations and circumstances and accomplish extraordinary things for God. We invite you to come and join us and let World Impact Christian Center help you fulfill your destiny.

Pastors Marc and Nanette Buntin

Excerpt from WORLDIMPACTCC.ORG© 2006.

Marc and Nanette Buntin have been extremely active in the ministry of two large churches in Texas (Abundant Life Christian Center, LaMarque, TX) and New Jersey (Faith Fellowship Ministries World Outreach Center, Sayreville, NJ). They have served as Directors of Evangelism and World Missions Outreach Leaders until 1986. In addition, they have been very active in prison, nursing home, and music ministry. Marc served as a bible school teacher at PowerHouse Christian Center in Katy, TX. Thousands have been saved; hundreds filled with the Holy Spirit and healed from various diseases and other forms of bondage. In addition, they have trained hundreds in the Body of Christ to win souls supernaturally. Marc and Nanette have a unique testimony and ministry. Just before Marc became a Christian, he was, academically, a poor student in high school and went into the United States Air Force. During his time in the service, a close friend told him about Jesus Christ and His wonderful plan of salvation! Although, Marc did not receive Jesus as Lord right away, his friend kept showing him the love of Jesus.

Soon after getting out of the service, Marc received Jesus as Lord! Marc then went to college and after several years of study, he achieved what he and others thought impossible. He received a Bachelor of Science degree in electrical engineering; a master's degree in biomedical engineering; and a doctorate degree in biomedical engineering. In addition, he went on to pursue and accomplish his dream of becoming a pilot. After college he went to work for the National Aeronautics and Space Administration (NASA) where he was twice selected as an astronaut candidate interviewee. Marc has inspired many, in both the secular and Christian world with his testimony.

Nanette was a chemist for AT&T Bell Laboratories and Senior Coordinator of Graduate and Corporate Student Recruitment for University of Houston-Clear Lake. Nanette was born again at a crusade conducted by Dr. Frederick K.C. Price in New Jersey. She currently serves as Church Administrator and Women's Ministry Director. Pastor Nanette is specially anointed as a teacher and exhorter. Her practical, down to earth and thought-provoking message is a blessing to the body of Christ.

After 13 years of marriage, standing on God's word, Marc and

Nanette became parents of a son, Jonathan. Jonathan is their miracle baby. Jonathan, now an elementary school student, is a testimony of the faithfulness of God. The Buntin's, joyfully tell others who are waiting for the manifestation of God's glory, "Just keep on standing on God's word, and you will see the impossible become possible!" With a heart for people and a vision to build a multicultural church that is dedicated to developing champions for God, the Buntin's invite you to join World Impact, grow in faith, and fulfill your destiny in Jesus Christ!

> Pastors Marc and Nanette have a vision to build a multicultural church that is dedicated to developing champions for God! Every person has a God given purpose that can only be fulfilled through a personal encounter with Jesus Christ, instruction in the Word of God and fait. Marc and Nanette are dedicated to building strong individuals and families that will excel beyond their own limitations and circumstances and accomplish extraordinary things for God. We invite you to come and join us and let World Impact Christian Center help you fulfill your destiny.
>
> **Dr. Marc and Nanette Buntin, Pastors**

National Institutes for General Medical Sciences (NIGMS)

Minority Biomedical Research Sciences (MBRS) Program

Minority Biomedical Research Support (MBRS) programs are aimed at increasing the number of faculty, students, and investigators who are members of groups that are underrepresented in the biomedical sciences. MBRS grants are awarded to 2-or 4-year colleges, universities, and health professional schools with 50 percent or more student enrollment from underrepresented minority groups to support research by faculty members, strengthen the institutions' biomedical research capabilities, and provide opportunities for students to work as part of a research team. Historically, individuals who have been found to be underrepresented in biomedical or behavioral research include, but are not limited to, African Americans, Hispanic Americans, Native Americans (including Alaska Natives), and natives of the U.S. Pacific .

Robert Wood Johnson Foundation (RWJF)

The Robert Wood Johnson Foundation seeks to improve the health and health care of all Americans. To achieve the most impact with our funds, we prioritize our grants into four goal areas:

To assure that all Americans have access to quality health care at reasonable cost. Nearly 45 million Americans, over 8 million of them children, go without health insurance. This is the single greatest barrier to obtaining timely, appropriate health care services.

To improve the quality of care and support for people with chronic health conditions. One hundred million Americans suffer from chronic health conditions, and that number is almost certain to increase as the population ages.

To promote healthy communities and lifestyles. Our health behaviors, level of social interaction, and other factors outside medical care are important influences on overall health.

To reduce the personal, social and economic harm caused by substance abuse—tobacco, alcohol and illicit drugs. Tobacco, alcohol and illicit drugs inflict an enormous toll on Americans, especially among our youth.

Summer Medical and Dental Education Program

An ongoing national program of the Robert Wood Johnson Foundation (RWJF) is a free, six-week intensive academic enrichment summer program to help qualified undergraduate students from minority and disadvantaged groups compete successfully for medical and dental school admission. They live in dormitories, where medical and dental school students serve as residential advisers and teaching assistants and offer academic and other support. In addition to housing, meals and the educational curriculum, the host university provides participants with a stipend, access to campus recreational facilities and opportunities for social activities. The university introduces the students to physicians from a variety of backgrounds and takes other steps to solidify the students' interest in the medical profession and increase their confidence that they themselves can become part of it. At the University of Virginia, for example, each participant receives a medical school identification pass and a white coat to wear daily to class, making them indistinguishable from regular medical school students.© RWJF 2006 P.O. Box 2316 College Road East and Route 1, Princeton, NJ 08543.

Environmental Pathology Training Grant

University of Vermont College of Medicine

Since the inception of the training program in 1982, 39 predoctoral students have received their PhD degrees while in the program and 25 postdoctoral fellows (MDs, DVMs, and PhDs) have finished training. These trainees have been recruited to academia, government and industry. A total of 23 highly interactive faculty members from 7 different departments participate in the program. All have funded research programs and are nationally recognized in disciplines related to environmental pathology.

Our program emphasizes concepts of basic pathology and "state-of-the-art" approaches such as computer-assisted teaching (CATs) in environmental pathology, cell imaging, and molecular and cellular approaches for studying mechanisms of environmental disease. Strongly interactive programs exist in mechanisms of DNA damage and repair, cell signaling and control of mitogenesis and cell death. A Howard Hughes Medical Institute (HHMI) research award to the Medical College for establishment of a program in Structural Biology, long-standing NSF, EPSCoR and HHMI Helix grants with mentoring programs for high school teachers, junior faculty members, undergraduate women and minorities, an NCI-funded comprehensive Cancer Center grant, a Center of Biomedical Research Excellence (COBRE) in Translational Research in Lung Biology and Disease, complementary training programs in Cancer Biology/ Cardiovascular Disease, and an NIH-funded DEVELOP (Delaware-Vermont Linkage to Open the Pipeline) grant to encourage minority students to enter our training program, are strengths at UVM.

Other strong aspects of our program include its multi departmental participation, its Environmental Pathology and Cell Signaling Seminar series, a Microscopy Imaging Center, and a new program project grant on "Signaling in Epithelial Injury, Proliferation, and Fibrosis" in models of asbestosis and asthma. Both pre-doctoral and postdoctoral (MD, PhD, and DVM) traineeships are presently available.

Contact: Dr. Brooke T. Mossman, Department of Pathology, University of Vermont

American Association for Cancer Research

Minority Scholars in Cancer Research Awards

AACR Minority Scholar Awards in Cancer Research are offered to eligible minority scientists wishing to participate in Annual Meetings and Special Conferences of the American Association for Cancer Research (AACR).

Financial Support
Financial support (up to $1,800 per Scholar) will be provided to awardees wishing to attend AACR Annual Meetings. Annual Meeting registration and travel will be processed by AACR staff for all awardees. These costs will be deducted from the award total of $1,800. The remaining funds will be distributed to awardees for expenses incurred in conjunction with attendance at the meeting or conference, i.e. hotel, meals, taxis, etc. According to IRS regulations, this award is subject to federal income tax. Thus, all awardees will be issued a 1099 misc tax form at year-end for the amount of the award. If an awardee is unable to attend the meeting for which the award is given, the award must be forfeited.

Eligibility
Candidates must be full-time graduate students, medical students, residents, clinical or postdoctoral fellows, or junior faculty members. Only minority groups that have been defined by the National Cancer Institute as being traditionally underrepresented in cancer and biomedical research are eligible for this award: African Americans, Alaskan Natives, Hispanics, Native Americans, and Native Pacific Islanders. Candidates must be citizens or permanent residents of the United States or Canada.

Contact
AACR Minority Scholar Awards in Cancer Research Program
American Association for Cancer Research
615 Chestnut Street, 17th Floor
Philadelphia, PA 19106-4404
Telephone: (215) 440-9300
Fax: (215) 440-9412
E-mail: micr@aacr.org

New England Board of Higher Education (NEBHE)

Six States, Countless Opportunities, One Address

NEBHE was founded in 1955, when six visionary New England governors – realizing that the future prosperity of New England rested on higher education – committed their states to the shared pursuit of academic excellence. Soon thereafter, NEBHE was approved by New England's six state legislatures and authorized by the U.S. Congress. Much has changed since our founding: New technologies have transformed our workplaces, schools, and homes – and a college education has become a prerequisite to economic prosperity, social mobility, and civic engagement. Yet the importance of higher education to the regional economy remains as critical as ever. New England's economy and quality of life depend on the quality and diversity of our region's extraordinary higher education resources. The New England Board of Higher Education (NEBHE) promotes greater educational opportunities and services for the residents of New England. In pursuit of this mission, we work across the six New England states to:

Engage and assist leaders in the assessment, development, and implementation of sound education practices and policies of regional significance.

Promote policies, programs, and best practices to assist the states in implementing important regional higher education policies.

Promote regional cooperation and programs that encourage the efficient use and sharing of educational resources.

Provide leadership to strengthen the relationship between higher education and the economic well-being of New England.

CONTACT
45 Temple Place
Boston, MA 02111
www.nebhe.org

Biomedical Sciences Careers Program (BSCP)

The Biomedical Science Careers Program, Inc. was founded in 1991 and incorporated as a not-for-profit organization in 1994. The first BSCP student conference was held in March 1992 and was attended by 300 high school, college, and medical and graduate minority students. Since its inception, more than 5,000 minority students and 500 post-doctoral trainees and junior faculty have participated in BSCP programs. The Biomedical Science Careers Program, Inc. (BSCP) provides students of every race, ethnic background, gender, and financial status with encouragement, support, and guidance needed for the successful pursuit of careers in biomedical science. BSCP that the individual potential of each student should not be lost or ignored believes.

OBJECTIVES

Identify, inform, support, and provide mentoring for academically outstanding students, particularly African-American, Hispanic American, and American Indian/Alaska Native students. Disseminate information on programs in biomedical science available to students, particularly minority students.

Provide a forum for the exchange of information among individuals at various stages in their academic development. Highlight the need for and use of mentors/advisors in making career decisions. Improve communication among physicians/scientists and students at varying stages in their career development.

Scholarships: Through annual corporate sponsorships, BSCP awards $7,500 scholarships to BSCP high school, community college, college, medical, and graduate students who are active in BSCP programs.

CONTACT
Lise D. Kaye -Executive Director Biomedical Science Careers Program
Web Site: http://www.bscp.org

Wikipedia, The Free Encyclopedia

Excerpt taken with permission from www.wikipedia.org

Wikipedia is a multilingual, web-based, free-content encyclopedia project based on an openly-editable model. The name "Wikipedia" is a portmanteau of the words *wiki* (a technology for creating collaborative websites, from the Hawaiian word *wiki*, meaning "quick") and *encyclopedia*. Wikipedia's articles provide links to guide the user to related pages with additional information. Information from Wikipedia.org was used for all footnotes within the text pages of Four Tubas, a Guitar, and a Gallery of Cheerleaders, Transition in the Life of a Black Ph.D. Part I.

> November 15, 1970
> **40 Years**
> November 15, 2010

Congratulations to the Epsilon Chi Chapter of Kappa Kappa Psi and the Delta Pi Chapter of Tau Beta Sigma for celebrating their 40-year chapter anniversary.

Music will always be the key. We will miss Brother Dexter Baggett, Brother Cornelius Pickens "Tank," Sister Jackie Johnson, and Dr. Joseph "Doc" Miller. May we all continue to "Strive for the Highest!"

LaVergne, TN USA
27 October 2010
202376LV00002B/3/P